Nkosi's Story

Nkosi's Story

by
Jane Fox

With a foreword by
Danny Glover

A Life Story Project

THE
LIFE STORY
PROJECT

First published 2002
Text © The Life Story Project
Published work © The Life Story Project & Spearhead

Published in South Africa by The Life Story Project & Spearhead

The Life Story Project (Pty) Ltd, PO Box 72069, Parkview 2122, South Africa
& PO Box 3056, Bellevue Hill, NSW 2023, Australia
(www.lifestoryproject.com)

Spearhead is an imprint of New Africa Books (Pty) Ltd,
PO Box 23408, Claremont 7735, South Africa

ISBN: 0-86486-533-3

Editing by David Medalie & Graeme Friedman
Proofreading by Sean Fraser
Typesetting by Peter Stuckey
Cover photograph by Juda Ngwenya (Reuters)
Cover design by Peter Stuckey
Origination by House of Colours

Printed and bound in the Republic of South Africa by ABC Press, Epping

Printed on Sappi Laser Pre Print 80 g/m²

The word for fine paper

THIS BOOK IS DEDICATED TO
NONHLANHLA DAPHNE NKOSI
AND
GAIL JOHNSON
WITHOUT WHOM THERE WOULD HAVE BEEN NO
XOLANI NKOSI JOHNSON

Author's Note

I HAVE SOMETIMES put two conversations together, which probably took place at different times. I have also taken the liberty of recounting conversations that in the context of the story were likely, but which did not necessarily take place.

Acknowledgements

I WISH TO thank the following very warmly for their help while I was writing this book:

Nkosi's foster family: Gail and Nicci Johnson, Alan Johnson and Colleen Roberts.

Nkosi's biological family: Billy Mlambo, Fika Mlambo, Mavis Khubeka, Busisiwe Thiba, Dudu Khumalo, Pat Mashaba, Ruth Khumalo and Zanele Khulu.

Melpark Primary School: headmaster 'Badie' Badenhorst; teachers Megan Hastings, Maria Serrao and Glynnis Pitchers; school counsellor Jan Grobbelaar; pupils Eric Nicholls, Aubrey Dube, Paul Rossouw and Emmanuel Tshielo.

Nkosi's Haven: directors Laurette Scheffer and Gary Roscoe; administrative manager Oscar Martin; residents Grace, Feroza, Eunice and Sibongile.

Nkosi Johnson Foundation: public relations officer Gary Scallan; board member Dolores Fredericks.

Experts and individuals in various fields: The AIDS Consortium (particularly Valerie Fichardt and Sharon Ekambaram), Warwick Allan, Ruth Bhengu MP, Judge Edwin Cameron, Dr Ashraf Coovadia, Dr Hoosen Coovadia, Morné Cornell, Dr Liz Floyd, Dr Costa Gazi, Inigo Gilmore, Dr Glenda Gray, Peter Hawthorne of *Time* Magazine, Hilda Khoza, Very Revd Peter Lenkoe, Father

Stephen Mbande, Kevin McKenna of Boehringer Ingelheim, Rev. Gift Moerane, Saint Molakeng, Credo Mutwa, Rev. Brian Oosthuizen, Shaun O'Shea, Tony Poco, Dr Ruth Rabinowitz MP, Charlene Smith, Dr Nono Simelela, Father Gary Thompson, Herman van der Watt.

Friends of Nkosi's families: Anso Thom, Gerda Kruger, Sharon Black, Ross Jamieson, Nombeko Magagla, Paulina Zwane, Rob Black, Jane Stapylton and Rev. Annelize van der Ryst.

For allowing us to use their photographs without charge: *Femina* (and Carol Abrahams for her research), the *Sowetan* (particularly Poggy Tau), Juda Ngwenya of Reuters, Themba Hadebe of Associated Press, Giselle Wulfsohn.

I would also like to thank Doreen Levin, Nicky Ferguson, Siyabonga Nkosi and Lionel Abrahams for their practical help, and finally my colleagues and editors at *The Life Story Project* for their meticulous work, patience and understanding: Graeme Friedman, Tracey Segel, Sandy Tasman, Paula Soggot, Michelle Aarons and David Medalie.

J. F.

The Life Story Project specialises in the writing and publishing of biographical works for individuals, families and organisations, for public distribution or private publication. *www.lifestoryproject.com*

The major share of the royalties from the sale of copies of *Nkosi's Story* is to be donated to the Nkosi Johnson Foundation.

Many individuals, businesses and organisations have, over time, offered their generous assistance to Nkosi's Haven and The Nkosi Johnson Foundation. They have done this in a wonderful spirit, without seeking publicity for their good deeds. Some of these donors have been mentioned in the course of this book. It would have belaboured the story, however, to have attempted to mention them all.

Foreword
by Danny Glover

I FIRST MET Nkosi and his remarkable foster mother, Gail Johnson, at the 13th World AIDS Conference in Durban, South Africa, in 2000. I was attending in my capacity as Goodwill Ambassador for the United Nations Development Programme (UNDP). Nkosi and I were both participating in a press conference on AIDS orphans. By then, Nkosi was already a seasoned campaigner in the fight against the disease.

He stood on the stage in front of the audience and television cameras in his white sneakers, his emaciated body hidden by his jacket and trousers. Frail as he was, he delivered a speech that had far greater impact than all those of the dignitaries and scientists put together. I was so impressed by him and the tremendous amount of courage that it took for him to stand before the world and tell his story with such confidence, I asked him for his autograph. In fact, we exchanged autographs.

After the conference, I travelled to Johannesburg where I visited Nkosi's Haven, the home for HIV-positive women and their children established by Gail and Nkosi. At the time, the home was in desperate need of funds in order to continue its work. Along with a group of other people, I participated in facilitating the purchase of the building so that the incredible work that was being done there could continue. While in Johannesburg, I participated in a press conference renaming Nkosi's Haven to Nkosi's Haven and Friends. Over the following year I was fortunate enough to see Nkosi on at least two other occasions in both Johannesburg and New York. He was, on the one hand, a normal young boy, inquisitive about the films I had acted in, keen to talk about his heroes. On the other hand, our conversation would turn to the workings of Nkosi's Haven and the terrible toll that HIV/AIDs was taking – subjects that, in a better world, should not have been troubling an eleven-year-old child.

But trouble him they did. Nkosi was thrust into the spotlight when Gail tried to do what millions of parents do all the time: enrol their child at school. A group of ill-informed parents attempted to bar Nkosi from the school. There was no established policy for the educators to follow. Gail, nevertheless, pressed the authorities for a ruling. This was a test case for the rights of HIV-infected children. Gail and her supporters won the case, and Nkosi was allowed to attend the school. It was this event, more than any other, that turned mother and child into HIV/AIDS activists. In time, through their example of a loving family getting on with life, they were able to win over even the most prejudiced of the parents at Nkosi's school.

Like any child, Nkosi's character was influenced by the members of his family: in his case, this meant by members of both his black and white families. He straddled the divide between suburb and township and, in my opinion, represented the best of both these worlds. This was especially evident in his sense of justice and desire to help others. However, his public life would not have been possible but for the energy and care of Gail. Nkosi must have felt swept up by that energy – exhausted by it on occasion, elevated by it on others. But it imbued his life with meaning, and packed a great deal of action into a pitifully small number of years.

Nkosi's brave battle against HIV/AIDS, and his ability to talk about it with a wisdom way beyond his years, touched the lives of millions of people across the globe. For this role he was posthumously made the co-recipient of the World's Children's Prize for the Rights of the Child – the 'Children's Nobel'. I wish he could have been alive to receive it himself. He slipped into a coma in December 2000 and died in June 2001, having accomplished his goal to reach 12 years old.

In this book, Jane Fox has given us a beautifully drawn, intimate portrait of Nkosi's life, and that of his country. These pages are filled with irony, not least of which concerns a little black boy who is brought up in a white home both pre- and post-apartheid. As such, they speak movingly of South Africa's struggle to transform itself, of the angry divisions left by apartheid. They tell us of the disadvantages of Nkosi's biological family and the millions of other impoverished families of AIDS sufferers throughout the world – many of whom do not have the resources to help their loved ones. Most of all, this book shows us the immense goodwill of South Africa's people, a sense of community that somehow, miraculously, survived the country's racist past. And despite the tragedy of Nkosi's illness, this is not a tragic story; it is at times funny, alive and above all, hopeful. It shows us what determined individuals can do.

Maya Angelou wrote: 'Children's talent to endure stems from their ignorance of alternatives.' Nkosi never really knew an alternative, a healthy life. But he knew that others had it and that he didn't. He was at times sad and very troubled about being sick, but he was never bitter, as far as I could tell. On the contrary, he showed great generosity of spirit, an ability to give to others when so much was being taken from him. Part of the meaning of Nkosi's life for me is that children will lead us, if only we will follow.

HIV/AIDS continues to infect and kill millions of people, and leave millions of children orphaned. With the application of the right resources, education and care, this situation can be improved. Nkosi's voice was clear: the adults, the decision-makers in society, must do more to eradicate this scourge. I miss Nkosi greatly and continue to be inspired by him.

Prologue

'ALL RIGHT, LET'S talk about Nkosi,' says the Rev. Brian. 'I just remember him as the little boy with the falling-down pants who stood up in my church and talked to us about sick children.'

'Look, he used to zoom in on you,' says Gail. 'He was very perceptive. He used to say "Mommy, let me rub your back, you look tired".'

'He love the pizza,' says Mary.

'He love the pizza too much!' says Gail. 'Naughty little shit.'

'He was my baby,' says Grace. 'But at Nkosi's Haven, he was the father.'

It is Tuesday, 12 June 2001. In a small, slightly shabby house in Melville, Johannesburg, five people are sitting in the living room: Gail, Elizabeth, Grace, Mary and the Rev. Brian.

The room has a spare, waiting look, as though people pass through it often but don't have time to sit there. On every surface there are bowls and vases of flowers. The walls are a deep rose pink, the sofas and chairs are covered in worn black leather. There is an open fireplace and beside it a dark hole shows where the floorboard is broken.

On the wall is a poster with the photograph of a child. He is wearing a baseball cap and a cheerful smile. But if you look closely at his eyes you see that beneath the cheerfulness they are sad.

Nearby is an oil painting of the same child. He sits, surrounded by darkness, looking out at the viewer with those same deeply sad, deeply wise eyes. His body dissolves into the gathering shadows; his face, dark-skinned, seems nevertheless to be a source of light in itself.

His name is Nkosi Johnson, and until twelve days ago he has lived in this house with four of these people. He has grown up here and gone to school every day from here, and fed the cats and done his homework and watched television. He has ridden his plastic scooter bike round and round the pool and played with his model racing track.

Last week they held a memorial service for him in the city, attended by nearly two thousand people, a vigil with hundreds more people in the township, and his funeral and burial service in Hero's Acre in West Park Cemetery. There have been television crews, dignitaries and representatives of the press from all parts of the world pouring through this small house for months.

Now the people who live and work in the house are sitting quietly together with the minister who has come to give comfort. Mary has provided coffee, Gail's cigarettes are at hand, Duke the German Shepherd lies flaked out on the floor beside them and the cats are making brief, unobtrusive appearances. They are sitting together, now that the uproar is over, and talking about their child. Just sitting and talking, laughing more often than not about the little daily events that happened in the life of Nkosi Johnson.

Chapter
One

XOLANI NKOSI (Nkosi Johnson's legal name) was the second child born to Nonhlanhla Daphne Nkosi. Daphne came from a rural Zulu family living on their farm not far from the town of Newcastle, in northern KwaZulu-Natal. She was born in 1968, and had spent her childhood there, along with her mother, grandmother, and an extended clan of brothers and sisters, cousins and second cousins. According to her contemporaries, cousins Busisiwe and Mavis who grew up with her, it was a happy, peaceful childhood, tending goats and the younger children, going to a nearby school, playing jokes on each other, doing household chores.

Daphne was famous in the family for her stories and jokes. Busisiwe remembers that they could spend the whole day talking and laughing and listening to Daphne telling stories, and then get into trouble with the grown-ups because the work wasn't done.

As soon as they had woken up and washed themselves in the mornings, it was their job to go out into the surrounding veld to collect kindling for the cooking fire. Then they would go down to the river to fetch water. This was a quick run down and a much longer trudge back balancing big tins of water on their heads.

When they were older, Daphne went to school further away in Annieville, but during the holidays she would be with Busi and Mavis again. She was the eldest of nine children, and had to work hard, cooking, helping in the house, looking after her little brother Fika and the smaller ones who came after him.

When she was still at school in 1986 she fell pregnant and gave birth to a daughter, Mbali. She went back to school after the baby's birth, but failed Standard Nine at the end of 1987 and decided that now was the time to leave school and earn a little money. She got a job at a small supermarket in Madadeni Section 3, near to Newcastle. She had a sense of responsibility as well as a sense of humour and she wanted to help her mother pay for shoes and school uniforms for her younger brothers and sisters.

In 1988 she moved up to Johannesburg. She had Mbali, two years old by then, and now she was pregnant for the second time. Her mother, Ruth Khumalo, was angry with her for falling pregnant again: 'Your first child – it's a mistake because you are still innocent. But with the second one you have no excuses. You know what's what!'

So little Mbali stayed with her Granny Ruth in Newcastle, while Daphne went to stay with her maternal grandmother, Sibongile Khumalo, who lived in Daveyton, a township to the east of the city. There Xolani – a boy – was born on 4 February 1989.

The South Africa into which he was born was in turmoil. PW Botha's government was still in power, apartheid was still in place but being fast eroded by the push for change. The Johannesburg City Council, for instance, voted to open municipal facilities to all races that year. But violence was on the increase. So-called 'collaborators' in the townships were murdered by being 'necklaced' with burning tyres. Detachments of the South African Defence Force rolled into the black areas daily to suppress rioting, and many innocent people were killed in the resulting crossfire. Would there be a full-scale uprising? It was hardly surprising that nobody, at that stage, was giving much thought to the creeping threat of HIV/AIDS.

As yet, the incidence in South Africa was still relatively small: probably fewer than 100,000 infections.[1] In 1990, only three out of every hundred pregnant women tested were HIV-positive. Opinions among the people were varied and sometimes wild.

There was this new disease called AIDS, which you could get, it was rumoured, by sleeping around. Some said it was a rumour started by whites so that there would be fewer black children. Some said it was a germ introduced into the black community by whites so that blacks would die. Some said that if you had sex with a virgin you wouldn't catch it or you would be cured if you had it. Some said you would be all right if you wore a condom. Many people thought it was insulting to be asked by your partner to wear a condom. Many people thought that if you wore a condom it meant that you had the disease. Some had never even heard of condoms.

Sibongile Khumalo was an *inyanga* – a spiritual and herbal healer – and people would come to her house for help and advice. Daphne's younger brother Fika Mlambo, in an article he wrote for his departmental magazine, described how their grandmother would often treat her patients with a mixture of traditional herbs, holy water, razor blades and the 'prickle' known in isiZulu as *inshobo. Inshobo* is made from a hedgehog, and is used to give someone strength. Sibongile used it on Daphne when she was pregnant with her child Xolani, according to Fika. Since the blade was never sterilised, this may have been the cause of her becoming infected with the HI-virus. The other, more likely, possibility was that she was infected by sleeping with Xolani's father.

There were no complications with Xolani's birth, but the baby was often sick, crying and coughing. One week he would be fine, the next not well at all, not wanting to drink, his chest bubbling and his nose running. Daphne took him to the local clinic where he was diagnosed as having TB.

She had found employment with a hairdresser – 'Hair Lovers' Cut and Blow' – in the nearby town of Benoni. It was in Cranbourne Avenue in the centre of town, and was for white clients. Daphne was kept busy, washing hair, holding curlers for the assistant doing the perms, sweeping up hair clippings. Her friend Paulina who also worked there had got her the job, and she quickly became a very popular assistant.

Jane Stapylton, the part-owner and manager of the salon, was an immigrant from England. There the subject of HIV/AIDS had been in the forefront of the news throughout the 1980s, and when her popular employee Daphne started exhibiting certain symptoms – bumps on her neck, pains in her hands and feet – she suspected at once that it might be AIDS.

When she asked Daphne what was the matter, Daphne told her that she didn't know, but she had been to an *inyanga* who had advised her to go back to her birthplace and carry out some ritual involving the blood of a goat being poured into the river. Jane did not think that this would do her much good.

'Go to the clinic,' she advised on several occasions, 'get yourself checked out.'

Jane remembers that she had a very happy bunch of employees. 'We were in it to work,' she was to say later, 'but we were in it to have fun, too. We had Christmas parties, birthday parties, Halloween parties – even driver's licence parties in the salon.'

Coming from overseas as she did, Jane's approach was that there was no reason why a black hairdresser could not become as successful with white clients as a white hairdresser. And Paulina and Daphne were both excellent at their job. When the salon was not busy, and sometimes after hours, they played with 'dolls' – polystyrene heads fitted with wigs on which they practised cutting and perming and colouring. In pre-1994 Benoni, however, where the customs of apartheid were still firmly entrenched, her ideas did not take off, and her black assistants had to remain washers and tidiers. Daphne took the failure of Jane's revolutionary ideas philosophically, shrugging her shoulders with her usual impish smile. 'One day...' she said.

Meanwhile, her health was not improving. Paulina remembers sometimes having to half-carry her friend to the bus, and then into her grandmother's house at the end of the day.

There was something else to worry about. Neighbours had come to Daphne and told her that baby Xolani was screaming a lot when he was left with Sibongile. They were sure that he wasn't being properly cared for. Another friend, Nombeko, suggested that he should go to the crèche where her children and Paulina's were during the day. Daphne could drop him off at Paulina's mother's place, she would take all the children to the crèche, and fetch them at the end of the day, and Daphne could pick him up from there. This seemed like a really good plan, and Paulina's home became a second home to Daphne.

She would walk in at the door and say to Paulina's mother: 'Hello, Mummy! Here I am again. Don't worry, I'll cook the supper today!'

When Xolani became acutely ill, Daphne took him to the township clinic. The clinic in turn sent him on to Glynnwood Hospital, since through her work, Daphne belonged to a medical-aid scheme. After he had been there a few days, they sent for her.

She and Paulina go there as soon as work is over. The doctor in charge calls her into his office and sits her down.

'Daphne, your baby is very sick. I understand you've been taking him to the township clinic since he was born. He is now – how old? Two. Tell me, Daphne, do you know what the HI-virus is?'

'It's like an infection?'

'Yes. It's like this, Daphne. We've all got an army inside that protects us – keeps us healthy. And when sicknesses like TB, pneumonia and so on attack us, this army fights back and helps us recover. Medicine helps, but it's really the immune system that wins the battle. Now the HI-virus is a very cunning virus. It attacks our immune system army from the inside, like a spy or a guerilla fighter, and stops it from fighting all the other diseases like pneumonia and TB and so on. And so far, we haven't found anything that kills it. And we think that's what's happening to Xolani. He's getting sick all the time because his immune system isn't working properly. I want you to let us test him for HIV.'

Daphne can feel her eyes pricking. 'How do you test?'

'We take some blood – just a little – and we find out how many

T4 cells there are in it. Those are the soldiers in the immune system army. We count them. It's called a CD4 count. Healthy people have a CD4 count of between 1500 and 500. HIV kills them off so that the count drops. When it gets to below 200, we say that the person has got full-blown AIDS. That stands for Acquired Immuno-deficiency Syndrome.'

AIDS! The thing nobody talks about: everyone is scared. If you have AIDS, you are a bad person.

'But Xolani is only a baby. How could he get it?'

'Daphne, there are three ways that people can get infected. Firstly, by having sex with a person who is infected, secondly by coming into contact with an infected person's blood through an open wound – like, for instance, using the same needle for an injection, and thirdly by being infected at birth by your mother.'

Daphne is quiet, taking in the implications of this.

'I want you to let us test both of you, Daphne.'

She would rather not know. This doctor must be thinking it's AIDS otherwise he would not be saying this. If it's AIDS, she's going to die and Xolani too. If she doesn't know, they can carry on as usual. What will Paulina and Nombeko and Jane say? They will turn away from her. They won't want her to be their friend. What will Grandmother Sibongile say? She will tell the family. They will be angry. She can't tell them. She can't tell anyone.

The doctor leans forward. 'Daphne, if we test, then at least we know where we are. We can give you medication that will help. You are on a medical-aid scheme, aren't you?'

She nods.

'Well, then, shall we go ahead?'

She nods again. If she refuses, the doctor will maybe not help her any more.

On the way home, she doesn't talk. Paulina, understanding that maybe she heard something bad at the hospital, doesn't push for her confidence. She knows that when Daphne wants to talk to her, she will.

What the two girls did not know was that the Sister at Glynnwood was cousin to Paulina's new boyfriend.

In a couple of weeks, the boyfriend comes running to Paulina.

'Paulina, do you know your friend Daphne is sick?'

'From what?'

'From AIDS! You must leave her!'

Paulina is frightened. 'How do you know?'

'My cousin works at the hospital. She told me. You mustn't see her any more, Paulina. You might get it.'

Paulina thinks of Daphne. Of their friendship. Of how warm and loving and funny she is. Of how she came and bathed her baby for her when she was weak after childbirth. Of how she cooks and cleans for her mother – like any sister.

'You know what? I'd rather leave you than my friend.'

'Why?' says the boyfriend, greatly surprised.

'Why? Because she's my friend. She's like my sister. She's my friend for a long time. I can't leave her when she's struggling.'

Next time Daphne sees Paulina she says: 'I have something to tell you.'

'What's that, Daphne?'

'I have AIDS.'

Paulina puts her arm around her. 'Don't worry, Daphne. You are still my friend.'

The two women hug, and then Daphne breaks away, wipes her eyes and blows her nose.

'Xolani, he has it too. The doctor said he got it from me.'

'How, Daphne?'

'Maybe from my blood when he was still inside, or when he was getting born, or from breastfeeding. You know, my Granny, she knew something was wrong and she made me tell her. She doesn't want me to stay with her any more. Me and Xolani. Sometimes I think it would be better if I take Xolani and go to the golf course and sit down, and I give him poison and then take some myself.'

'Daphne! You can't do that! That's terrible!'

'He's very sick. He's supposed to die before me. But if I die first, who will look after him? I think it's better we die together.'

'Daphne, everything we do is in the sight of God and when He

wants to take us He takes us in His time, not when we want. Listen.
Me and Nombeko, we are your friends, and Jane is your friend. I
will speak to her that she mustn't fire you, you will see – it will be
all right.'

'Don't worry, Paulina,' says Jane. 'I know what's the matter. I'm not
going to fire her. We're all much too fond of her, and besides, you
don't turn your back on someone who has AIDS.'

But Daphne herself did not feel it was right to continue in the job
if she was going to be off sick so often. In 1992 she resigned. To
earn money, she started selling plastic buckets and dishes and
Tupperware to the women living in the township.

Xolani was having ever-increasing bouts of acute illness. She
took him to the AIDS Clinic at the Hillbrow Hospital, and there she
was told about a care centre for people with AIDS that might help.
So far, apparently, it was mostly for adult white male patients, but
they might be willing to take Xolani, if she explained the
circumstances. They would telephone for her, and make enquiries.
They telephoned, and the reply was favourable.

She herself, she knew, would not be able to stay there; it was
miles away from the township where she could earn money, but
maybe this was the solution to her biggest problem – how to care
for Xolani.

So, feeling that this might be her last hope, she left the toddler
with neighbours for the day, and went to visit The Guest House in
Houghton.

Chapter
Two

IN 1990 THE Guest House Project was started in the comparatively old and wealthy suburb of Lower Houghton, Johannesburg. It was intended as a refuge for people living with HIV/AIDS who either didn't have families or whose families were not prepared, or were unable, to help them in the final stages of their illness. It quickly became a hospice. Nearly all those who came there turned out to be terminal. There was a nursing staff, and the aim was to keep people comfortable and as pain-free as possible until they died. It also offered an outpatients' facility, a counselling facility, and later on a home-based care facility for people who weren't coping and needed practical guidelines at home.

Mostly, the residents were white males – Houghton in those days was a 'white' suburb and the referrals came from 'white' clinics and hospitals, but towards the end of 1991 the outpatients section started seeing more and more black South Africans with HIV. It had never been the intention of The Guest House to be for whites only. On its Board of Trustees were Edwin Cameron, Philip Marcus, Steven Miller, Laurel Prast, David Stone and Gail Johnson.

Gail had been instrumental in founding The Guest House. Her great friend Carol's brother had had AIDS, and had lain alone very ill most of the day when Carol had to be at work. Carol and Gail eventually persuaded him to agree to be admitted to a hospice, where he finally died. It was his death and Carol's trauma that spurred Gail into helping to found The Guest House.

Towards the middle of 1991 David Stone, then Operations Director of the project, told the other board members that a woman named Daphne Nkosi had approached him via the AIDS Clinic to ask whether they could take her child at The Guest House. He was sick and HIV-positive, she was not well herself and had to go out to work to support him and another child. Her immediate family in Daveyton were apparently unable to take responsibility for him. There were no other babies at the project, but the other trustees agreed to take him on.

The matter was urgent – the child had to be fetched that very evening. If Warwick Allan would go, Daphne would accompany him and they would bring the baby back to The Guest House. Warwick, a young psychologist then in the process of applying for admission to a Master's programme, was the Operations Manager of the project. He agreed, so the two of them climbed into his ancient Volkswagen Beetle and set off for Daveyton. It was quite a lengthy journey, and it was already late afternoon.

From Houghton, they take a winding route through the inner suburbs, up over Sylvia Pass into Observatory, where they can see the whole of the southeast part of the city laid out in front of them, down through Cyrildene and Bruma onto the main highway leading east out of Jo'burg. It's a straight road now, past the airport and through the satellite towns of Germiston, Boksburg and Benoni.

As they chug along, Daphne tells Warwick about her daughter Mbali and the little boy they are going to fetch. He's sick with TB, she says, and he's tested positive for HIV. He's got this snotty nose and all the time a bad cough. She isn't there in the day to see he takes his medicine because she has to go out to work. She doesn't have family who are willing to look after him and the crèche is getting too expensive. In any case, he can't go there now that he is so sick.

They run through the old empty Van Ryn Gold Mining area and into Daveyton. All the street names here are African – Venda,

Lobedu, Kheswa. In the big shopping mall on their right, lights are beginning to come on. They pass a sports ground where a few kids are still kicking a football around, and then they are in an area where there are no shops, where the houses are looking a bit run down and a few of them are just shacks made of corrugated iron.

The road runs along the side of a cemetery for a while, then through a big stretch of waste ground, and finally they get into a maze of smaller, muddy roads where the car has to negotiate deep ruts filled with water. They are in the squatter camp known as Zenzele.

Warwick is feeling anxious. The East Rand townships are very volatile – almost every week there's some kind of a riot, with burning tyres and stone throwing. He wants to fetch the child and get out as quickly as possible. More run-down houses, more shacks, many people in the road, staring at this car driven by a young white man.

'Here! Here!' says Daphne at last. He stops the car outside one of the larger dwellings. Out she gets and disappears into the house.

Now he has to wait in the gathering dusk. Should he keep the engine running or is that silly, just a waste of petrol? He switches off. Everyone who passes slows down and peers into the car. It is almost dark.

The small figure of Daphne reappears, carrying a child and a hold-all. He leans across and opens the passenger door, then starts the engine. Daphne slings the luggage onto the back seat and settles the toddler on her lap.

'How old is he?' Warwick asks, as they reverse up the track.

'Two. He is three next year, February.'

'Hello,' says Warwick to the child. 'What's your name?'

The little boy stares at him, but doesn't say anything.

'Say "Xolani",' says Daphne to her son. 'Say "My name is Xolani Nkosi".'

Nkosi, as he came to be called – probably because few people at The Guest House could manage the Zulu click in Xolani – and his mother stayed at The Guest House for a little while, but as soon as she was sure he had settled down and knew everybody, Daphne left him and returned to Daveyton. She visited him every weekend at first, and then every other weekend, and then perhaps once a month. She never took him to live with her again.

It may seem that Daphne let her son go too easily. Warwick Allan, however, has a different view.

'Nkosi would probably have had very little chance if she had tried to keep him with her. At The Guest House and subsequently with Gail, he really was being properly cared for, and Daphne could see that. In acknowledging that, she could let him go. There is also a cultural difference to be considered – a socio-economic product of apartheid. Black mothers have had to become accustomed to being parted from their children. They have a resignation and a stoicism about it that may seem unusual to the rest of the world. Daphne would have realised that this was something she had to do, and with the realisation would have come acceptance. By the time Nkosi came to live with Gail, Daphne would have understood that she had no need to fight for him any more; Gail was doing that better than she could.'

And Daphne's cousin Billy Mlambo says: 'Maybe it was a question of common sense and of trust. She was no longer physically strong, she needed someone else to take care. She was the eldest and was providing for all the rest of the family as well, since Ruth Khumalo, her mother, was divorced and had no regular employment.'

One morning, he wakes. Something is different. His blanket is the same, his cot is the same, but something is different. He lies looking through the bars. The doorway is in a new place. Now he can see through it.

Somebody passes, too quickly for him to see who. His mother? No. And she's not there in the room with him as usual. Her bed isn't even there.

Nkosi stands up in his cot. He can hear people talking nearby.

'Mama?' he calls, but it is Warwick who comes, lifts him out and says: 'Good morning, Nkosi, and how are you today?' And he puts his jersey on over his pyjamas and says: 'Let's go and get some porridge.'

All through that day Nkosi waits for his mother to come back. Wendy is there, Brett is there, Elsa and Evelyn are there and the people in the beds are still there, but not his mother. He has his breakfast and his lunch in the dining room upstairs. Afterwards Warwick gives him his *muti*.[2] He'd like to shut his mouth tight against it, but somehow the way Warwick comes with the spoon, quite sure he's going to take it – well, his mouth seems to open of its own accord. In spite of the terrible taste he manages to swallow it, and since it's followed by a hug and a swing around he can soon forget about it.

When Elsa and Evelyn go round the house with the big roaring machine that sucks up all the bits from the carpet, he follows them and they shout and laugh and he joins in. Sometimes he goes to see the people lying down. They don't talk much. They say 'Hello, Nkosi,' but they seem very sleepy so he doesn't stay long. Sometimes there's a bad smell around, like when his nappy has to be changed. There's one big man who lets him climb on his lap when he's sitting in the garden.

Sometimes he rides through the passages and into the kitchen on his yellow bike, and Brett is in there fixing taps. He often says: 'Come on, Nkosi, let's go and walk around the garden.' Brett is the tallest person Nkosi has ever seen. When he puts Nkosi on his shoulders the ground looks very far away.

Wendy is downstairs in the office and she's the one who says what all the visitors must do. A lot of them come and sit and read books until she says they can go and talk to David in his room.

One day he is eating lunch and suddenly his mother is there. She runs to him and she picks him up and hugs him, and he cries and cries. Not for long though, and now she's the one who gives him his *muti* and changes his pants. And that night she sleeps with him too. But soon she has to go again. Then he cries, but it doesn't make any difference, still she goes. He just has to get used to it.

Nkosi's days at The Guest House were routine. There were certain times when he had to eat, to be bathed, to take his medicine and to go to bed. It was a kibbutz style of life: he had multiple parental figures. Because of the staff shortage, everyone there had to be able to prepare food, clean, train volunteers, care for the residents. And that included caring for Nkosi. Whoever was on duty would see to it that he was looked after. He seemed to bond well with everybody. In retrospect, Warwick is not surprised that Nkosi became such a charismatic figure. 'Even as a very small child he had a remarkable ability to interact with other people. At The Guest House everyone was very drawn to him. He was very warm, very good, very sweet. He would go to strangers and start talking to them at once.'

In November an article by journalist Lyn Smerczak appeared in the magazine *Femina*. She visited The Guest House and talked to the staff and to Nkosi, aged two.

'*David Stone... met me at the door and set before me the face of AIDS I didn't believe existed or would ever see,*' she wrote. '*Smiling shyly, and with some reserve, probably because his mouth was still infected with thrush, was a tiny, frail child. I asked him his name and he lisped, 'Nkosi.' How old was he? He proudly held up two diminutive fingers. I asked if he would like to sit beside me. He spread his arms wide, looked up at me with complete trust... and launched himself at my lap... Nkosi is two years old but weighs no more than a nine-month-old baby... According to the staff, Nkosi is a delight, so good and quiet. He never cries. Sometimes he likes to show off, like any two-year-old. Three months ago he couldn't walk, but his development occurred very quickly (said David Stone)... "He was starving to death because he couldn't eat... We admitted him to the Lady Dudley Nursing Home, where we debated on the quality of his life if we decided to fight his illnesses. It was very difficult, not knowing what would be kind. But we decided to go for it, and although for a few days it was touch and go, Nkosi fought back and has improved so much since then that it's hard to believe. Here at*

The Guest House alone, forty-two people have died since the beginning of the year. I think that we've seen... a spate of deaths of gay, male AIDS sufferers. Next will be the women – the mothers of today's AIDS babies. Our next big wave will be these children. After this will come the deaths of the greater public. And then we'll be talking about thousands, not the hundreds we speak of today".'

Sometimes Gail comes. The first time he is sitting on the stairs with his back to the front door talking to Laurel and David, and he hears this husky voice saying 'Hello, everybody,' and when he turns round this tall lady is coming across the hall, *click, clack.* She crouches down beside him and says: 'Hello, sweetheart, I'm here.' She has long hair and big round glasses. She gathers him up and squeezes him tight, like his mother does.

He sees her often after that, and one day she takes him with her to visit at her house. On the way she tells him that Brett lives there too, because he is her child (how can such a big man be her child?) and she's got another child called Nicolette, only everybody calls her Nicci, and there's a Daddy called Alan.

When they arrive there's a lot of noise and excitement and a big dog that jumps around, but Alan the Daddy picks him up so he's safe and they all go inside. Nicci sits on the couch with him and they watch TV. And they all have supper sitting on the couch. And then he gets put to bed in Nicci's room. Nicci is big. She is eleven and goes to school. He likes her because she hugs him a lot and lets him play with her woolly animals.

One day he gets taken there, and there's a tree in the lounge with a lot of coloured lights on it going on and off. And a pile of parcels. And they are all saying: 'Happy Christmas, 'Kosi!' and some of the parcels are for him. He doesn't know what to do at first and then Brett shows him how to take the paper off and underneath there are toy cars. Brett says: 'Come on, 'Kosi, let's play! Zoom! Zoom!' and they drive the cars all round the carpet.

Money was always very tight and The Guest House ran on a skeleton staff. Then David Stone the Operations Director left, and

Warwick moved into the house so as to be on call day and night. In the end they were not able to go on paying the nursing sisters, and Warwick found himself running the place with the help of one or two volunteers.

Eventually, lack of money forced the Board of Trustees of The Guest House into the decision to close it down. For some time they had not been able to take on new residents, and now they began trying to find alternative accommodation for those who were still there. There remained the problem of what to do with Nkosi. Maybe, Warwick thought, he could stay with Gail until a more permanent solution could be found; at least while he himself got on with the miserable tasks of explaining to 'the boys' why they had to leave, telephoning homes such as St Francis House on the East Rand to see if they could go there, and trying to scrape up enough money to pay some of the outstanding bills.

'Yes,' said Gail, when applied to. 'He can stay with me. Of course he can stay with me. How can we let a little boy like that go to Sacred Heart or St Francis? They are hospices. He'd be going through yet another trauma. You can't do that to children.'

And this arrangement was minuted at the final board meeting at the end of January.

Nkosi had spent several weekends with the Johnsons as well as Christmas while he was at The Guest House, but at the end of January Daphne had fetched him to spend his third birthday with his family. As soon as she brought him back from his visit to the township, Warwick explained to her what had happened. 'Don't worry,' he said, 'we're not abandoning Nkosi. He's going to stay with Gail. Just until we can sort out something permanent.'

As soon as he had a free moment, he bundled the little boy into his car with his luggage and drove him across town to Gail's house in Melville.

In the Johnson house, the family were sitting around in the dining room after a heavy day of shifting furniture. They were hot and tired – it was a warm night in the first week of February and the renovations to the house were almost finished. The dining-room light had just failed so they were in semi-darkness. The telephone rang. Gail got up to answer it.

'My God! Of course – I'm on my way.'

Steve Kealy, motoring editor of *The Star*, was test-driving a Lada which she, as Public Relations Consultant for the Lada account, had given him, but which she had forgotten to fill up with petrol. He was stuck somewhere near the Teachers' Training College.

'Now you're in shit,' observed Alan, taking another swallow of his whisky.

'Absolutely. I'll have to go right now. By the way, Nkosi's coming to stay.'

As usual, the family were not fazed. Nkosi wasn't a stranger – he had spent several weekends with them while he was at The Guest House. Nicci thought – well, cool, he can sleep in my room like before.

Not long afterwards came a knock at the door, and there stood Warwick Allan with Nkosi on one arm and his little yellow bicycle under the other. Nkosi looked like a chipmunk, Nicci thought, with his fat cheeks and his round eyes. She jumped up to take him.

'Hello 'Kosi! Hello, big boy!' And Nkosi, who had begun to look tearful, cheered up at the feel of her familiar arms and voice.

'Sorry – I'm not staying,' said Warwick, 'I'm still trying to clear up everything at The Guest House. Here's his bag of stuff.' And he was gone.

Alan lit another cigarette. 'So we've got another stray,' he said. 'He looks rather brown, doesn't he? Never mind, your Mom burns everything – toast, porridge, whatever.'

'Dad!'

'Just joking.'

Suddenly, there were nappies to be thought of, as he wasn't potty trained. There was *muti* to be remembered three times every single day; there was crying at night. But then Nicci was there for him, a little girl who like her mother loved babies and knew how to comfort. Poor Nkosi had had so many changes in his three years:

Daveyton, hospital, Guest House, the other hospital – and where, now, was his mother?

At first he cried a lot, and eleven-year-old Nicci, needing sleep herself, would roll out of bed, gather him up and take him into her own bed for the rest of the night, but as he felt more at home he would whimper for a bit and it would be enough to chuck one of his fluffy toys at him and he would soon quieten down.

He was just the latest of several babies who had come to stay with the Johnsons. Shortly after Nicci was born in 1980, Gail had volunteered as a Lifeline counsellor. She decided to do this because – well, she'd always had help at the eleventh hour and she understood that the isolation and loneliness that come with a crisis are always alleviated if someone is there. She wanted to be there for people if they were in need. Then she moved on to the 702 Crisis Centre.

The Centre, staffed by mental-health professionals and trained volunteer counsellors, offered telephonic and face-to-face intervention for those in psychological crisis. Gail's idea of help, however, did not always chime with the therapeutic framework of the Crisis Centre.

One evening a young woman burst into the Centre when Gail was on duty. She was pushing a pram in front of her. Bang! Crash! She pushed it right against the stairs. She appeared to be drunk. In the pram was a very small baby, who Gail thought was newborn, but which, the mother said, was already a month old. He had been premature and needed feeding every two hours. She was a single mother, she told Gail, and unemployed. She was staying in a hostel for people down on their luck. The walls were paper-thin and the baby kept screaming and the other residents banged on the walls and threatened to throw her out and she could never get any sleep.

'You don't need counselling,' said Gail, 'your problem is you can't cope at the moment. How about I take the baby to stay with me over the weekend and you can get a bit of peace?'

Jenny, the mother, was very grateful for this, and the upshot was that baby Donovan spent many weekends with the Johnsons, sleeping in his carrycot beside Gail's bed, having to be fed every two hours. Alan did not enjoy the experience.

When the management of the 702 Crisis Centre found out about this, they were concerned. Gail's action, helpful as it might have been, fell outside the therapeutic boundaries that existed for the counselling centre and its staff.

'It's not the policy of the Centre to intervene physically, Gail. We need to refer this client to an appropriate service.'

'But that baby was in danger, and who is going to help? When you are exhausted and a baby won't stop crying, it needs a superhuman being not to throw it out of the window. What that woman needed was not talk but a rest.'

She decided to find another way of giving help, and that was when, prompted by the death of her friend Carol's brother, she co-founded The Guest House in Houghton.

Chapter
Three

IT IS WINTER 1959. A loaded car is travelling northward along the main road from Beaufort West in the Cape Province to Potchefstroom in the Transvaal. Dad is driving, Ma sits next to him and an eleven-year-old and her grandmother are in the back, the child slouched into her corner, frowning at the distant line of mountains.

When they drove out of their gate that morning Dad had said: 'They're waving, Gail. Come on, wave back.'

Gail had remained slumped, facing forward. What was the point? What was another minute of looking at him when she was never going to see him again? He won't remember her, so what's it matter?

The car pulls them further and further away from their life in Beaufort West, from Anneline sitting at her desk beside Gail's. She'll be best friends with someone else, now. And who's going to pull Tony along in his cart? Rattle, rattle, bounce behind her bicycle, and he loved it so much, his fat hands gripping the sides, his round black face shrieking with delight.

The car stops at a picnic place near Noupoort. There's a concrete table and two benches and a rubbish bin at the side of the road, and four skinny bluegums for shade. Ma is unpacking the picnic basket.

'Can we let the cats out to pee?'

'Of course not, Gail, they'd run off and we'd never catch them.'

She knows that, really. Dusty and Prince are quite all right in the box Dad built for them with a pitched roof. They've got raw mince and milk to keep them happy. Ma gives them raw mince with cod-liver oil for their fur every morning. It must taste like *kak*³, fish and meat together. But now they keep howling. Shame, they must be scared, whizzing along like that on top of the car, tied down with string.

'Who'd like a boiled egg?' asks Ma.

'I'll have one, thank you,' says Granny.

'I'm not hungry,' says Gail. If she eats a single thing, she'll puke.

'I'm not getting the basket out again until we reach Kimberley, so you'd better have one now.'

'I don't want one.'

'I don't want one, *thank you*.'

Dad is sitting at the table. He eats an egg, and tells Ma how well they have done time-wise and how they ought to be in Kimberley by four o'clock. Ma pours tea from the thermos. Before she has to refuse that as well, Gail takes a walk down the road.

Next week she'll be in another bloody school ('Don't *swear*, Gail!') and they'll all stare at her. Tough. She doesn't care. Last year – Beaufort West. This year – Potchefstroom (Potch, they call it). Next year? Who knows. She doesn't care.

Geoff and Jessie Roberts, a bank manager and his wife, adopted Gail and her older sister Colleen as babies. Each time Geoff was promoted to a better position, they moved to a new town. There was no point in Gail's crying because she had just lost her best friend again – life was like that. She said goodbye, she shut up about it and started all over again, feeling nervous and lonely at a new school. It was okay for Colleen – she went to boarding school and never had to change.

The Beaufort West goodbye, however, was a particularly hard one. There the family had employed an ironing lady who had a small baby, Tony. He fell sick with gastroenteritis and nearly died. Gail would rush home from school to help care for him. She would

change his nappy, help feed him and see that he took his medicine.
Sometimes she would insist on letting him ride with them in the
family car, and her father would park a block away from his bank
and walk the last bit, in case any of the employees saw him with a
black child in the car. But when Tony got better, Dad made a little
wooden trailer for the back of Gail's bike, and Tony would sit in it
and she would ride around the garden, pulling him along, carefully,
carefully.

And in Potchefstroom there would be no more bathing Dr Marie
Alexander's babies in the house opposite. She'd got so good at it.
And who would care about the donkeys? The drivers in Beaufort
West beat them all the time, no matter how much she screamed:
'STOP THAT! YOU'RE HURTING THEM!' Her mother got cross and
tried to shut her up, thinking that people were staring. But Gail
didn't care. Let them stare.

Nkosi was very subdued at first, but it wasn't long before he began
to feel at home, especially with Alan. He was Daddy for Nkosi right
from the start, and they shared the same chair while they were
watching TV and Gail was busy cooking the dinner. It was their
time together.

Nicci occupied the sofa. Since Nkosi had come, she'd been
feeling rather as though her place in the family had changed. No
longer was she the main object of her parents' love and attention
(Brett, being ten years older, didn't really count). Someone smaller,
more vulnerable and very lovable, had moved in.

One evening, while Nkosi was in the kitchen, she went to sit on
Alan's lap. When Nkosi came in she said:

'This is *my* Daddy.'

Poor Nkosi burst into tears. He flung himself on the floor and
screamed and screamed. Gail came in to see what was happening.
She picked him up and held him tight.

'Alan is Nicci's Daddy as well, Nkosi. In this house you've got to
learn to share.'

Nicci ran to hug him. 'I'm only joking – I'm only joking!' she said. But it was a long time before he could be comforted.

After about eight months, Nicci figured that, okay, Nkosi wasn't going to live anywhere else. She began planning how to rearrange her bedroom to accommodate a permanent brother.

She felt okay about this on the whole, but there were some crazy things to get used to. One morning she and her Mom went shopping and took Nkosi along. In the Spar shop, they held his hands on either side so that he couldn't pull stuff off the shelves. She noticed that a lot of the folks were staring at them – a white mother and daughter with a black baby. It really bugged her. At first she let go his hand and walked a bit behind, pretending that she wasn't with them, but then she got the hell in, caught them up and swung Nkosi onto her hip. And when the next person stared she said loudly to Gail: 'What the hell is she staring at?'

'I don't know, darling. Because she's got no manners.'

When they got home and were putting the shopping away, Gail said: 'You know, there's going to be a lot of that. Just keep your cool and stare right back.'

It seems bizarre, looking back from the perspective of a new millennium, that a racially mixed family was almost never seen in South Africa before the 1990s. But the apartheid mindset that had paralysed everyone for so long was beginning to loosen up. Nelson Mandela had been released from prison in 1990, the African National Congress and other struggle organisations had been unbanned, and it was obvious that the country was heading for a black majority government eventually. At this time, latent fears of a violent outcome came to the fore, and many whites left. But a different attitude, which had been spreading imperceptibly through all but the most reactionary hearts and minds, was now strongly taking hold.

During the twelve years of Nkosi's life, there was to be, at least in some important areas of South African society, an almost complete transformation. As an example, the primary school in Melville where he was eventually to become a pupil was 100% white in 1989, 50% black when he first went there in 1997, and 95% black by 2001.

There were of course many people who had always been free and easy in this respect, even before the change of government. In the world of motoring, in which Gail and Alan moved, the family had lots of friends. They used to go to all the race meetings at Kyalami, and Nkosi, aged four or five, would love the bikes and the cars, especially the modified saloons. Alan was a member of the Guild of Motoring Journalists and they all used to sit up in the press stand, munching on *boerewors*[4] and mustard – Nkosi the most excited spectator of all, bouncing from Gail to Nicci to Alan to their friends and back again. On one occasion he was taken round the track in a racing car, almost invisible under his helmet. Nobody in those circles found it unacceptable for the Johnsons to be giving a home to a black child. Nicci's school friends, also, had no problem with it. It was from total strangers that a cold disapproving wind often seemed to blow.

On his arrival at the Johnsons, Nkosi was a very sick little boy. As well as being HIV-positive, he had TB and his sinuses were badly infected. On his 'Road to Health' chart at the clinic, he appeared underweight and undersized for his age, and this was never to change. He was put on a daily maintenance dose of Bactrim, a broad-spectrum mild antibiotic, and he was to take it for the rest of his life. Slowly the medication, proper meals and proper sleep – all the comforts of a middle-class home – brought the TB under control, banished the septicaemia and kept the AIDS at bay. Except that he was always weak-chested and later unable to do contact sports, Nkosi was able to lead a normal life.

Gail, however, didn't want him growing up with any illusions about himself. When he was still quite small she explained to him that he had 'baddies', 'funny *goggas*'[5] in his blood and that was why he must always fight them with medicine.

Every month she took him for a check-up at the JG Strijdom Hospital. This was the big state teaching hospital, afterwards to be renamed the Helen Joseph Hospital, in honour of one of South Africa's most indomitable fighters for freedom.

In 1992, when he first went there, there would be perhaps ten patients waiting on benches in the passage to see the AIDS specialist. The doctor would take blood samples from Nkosi each time, check his CD4 count, listen to his chest and check his mouth for thrush. He would write out a prescription and put it in Nkosi's hospital file. Gail would take the file and go to the dispensary department, place the file in the basket provided, and the two of them would sit down to wait their turn. This was a much longer wait, a much bigger queue. There was only one dispensary for the whole hospital. Sometimes Gail and Nkosi would still be waiting at three o'clock in the afternoon, having arrived there before nine.

During his first year with Gail, Nkosi stayed at home, being looked after by Irene, their domestic servant. In the house were also a young German Shepherd bitch called Kelly and two cats, Tiger and Ghost, who were almost identical. Gail had her public relations office, 'Gale Force Promotions', in a different suburb and Nicci was of course at school. Brett worked nearby for a desktop publishing company. But Alan was often at home, being between jobs at the time, and Nkosi loved being with him. Alan would tease him and laugh at him and call him funny names.

Irene was gentle and sweet and would watch Nkosi as he propelled himself slowly along on his yellow bike or sat with Kelly in the garden as she gnawed a bone. Irene wondered sometimes why he didn't run and shriek like the three-year-olds in the township. He always liked to sit on his own with one of his little cars, running it up and down and murmuring 'vroom-vroom.' He was never a child who demanded her attention all the time. He went down for his daytime rest and took his medicine after lunch when she gave it to him without protest.

The people living in Melville soon got used to seeing Nkosi trotting around with the Johnsons. In the local shops he became a favourite customer, so much so that Tula, the lady in charge at the Spar shop, gave him a new plastic scooter bike one day.

It became his most treasured possession. He liked to pretend it

was a car – open the door, turn on the ignition, fill it with petrol
from the garden hosepipe.

One evening he's riding his scooter round the swimming pool –
round and round on the hard brick path where it goes faster than
anywhere else. (Irene's always shouting at him to be careful, but he
knows he won't fall in – he's not such a dummy.) Kelly keeps
padding after him like a nanny. Gail appears at the kitchen door
and calls him: ''Kosi? Come see!'

He goes slower and slower and finally stops, making a
screeching brake noise like on TV. He gets off, takes out the
imaginary key and closes the imaginary door.

She takes his hand and he goes with her through the house to
the bathroom. She's bending down, looking into the bathroom
cupboard. Something funny, squirming.

He crouches down to look and then he can see it's Tiger, lying
on a blanket, and she's got a little lumpy thing lying beside her.
When he puts his finger on it, it moves, and he can see it's got a
head and legs.

'It's Tiger's baby,' says Gail, above him. 'You watch, you'll see
her making another one.'

Tiger begins to heave like she's making a big poo, and suddenly
there's this thing squeezing out of her backside. He doesn't like it
much, but when it's properly out she starts licking it and it turns
into a kitten like the first one. She's purring very loudly so he
knows she must be all right.

'So now you know where babies come from,' says Gail, and
laughs and coughs.

'Can I pick one up?' he says.

'Better not. Tiger might not like it. Tomorrow perhaps.'

Next day, Tiger's got four kittens, not just two. They haven't got
eyes and they've got very thin legs and claws that hook on his
jersey when he picks them up. They crawl all over Tiger's tummy
and suck on her titties.

'That's how they get their food, 'Kosi,' says Nicci. 'There's milk
in Tiger's titties.'

Three days later they are all watching the Portuguese Grand Prix on television. It is Sunday afternoon and although Gail watches from time to time, she is worried about Ghost, who is having her kittens in Nicci's wardrobe.

'How do kittens come out?' she asks Alan. 'Always head first, or can it be feet first?'

Alan downs half his beer and wipes his mouth. 'Head first. Why?'

'The cat's having its kittens, but one is coming out feet first.'

'But it's had its kittens.'

'No, the other cat.'

'What other cat?' He goes and looks. 'Do you know, all the time I thought it was the same cat!'

At the end of Nkosi's first year with the Johnsons, the family all drove down to Pennington on the KwaZulu-Natal South Coast for their annual seaside holiday.

Gail's sister Colleen had moved down there when she finally retired from her job as a school sports instructor. She and her friend Judy had found a home in a complex of 'townhouses' within walking distance of the sea, and it became a family tradition to go there every Christmas.

On Christmas Eve they had a big dinner, with all the friends coming in as well, and on Christmas morning – well, Nkosi could hardly believe his eyes!

There was Father Christmas (looking rather like Daddy), and there was a pile of presents so big and beautiful he was scared to even touch them at first. Father Christmas gave everybody some off the pile and they all began opening and shouting and laughing and thanking, and the red-and-green-and-gold paper got all thrown about and out of his parcels came trucks and cars and slipslops and T-shirts and a teddy bear and it was all bewildering and wonderful.

After that he went with Nicci and others down to the sea, wearing his new green Speedo. It didn't stay up too well because his tummy was the wrong shape or something, so Nicci had put

clothes pegs each side to make it tighter. They carried their towels
and his water-wings and they went across Colleen and Judy's
garden and through a little gate and across the railway line – 'you
must always look both ways, 'Kosi, in case there's a train' – and
through a jungly place where it was all thick bushes and trees.
Beyond that was the beach. Sand and shells and stuff, and off to
the right, the rocks. Beyond the beach was the sea. He'd been into
it already a couple of times but only so's the water was up to his
knees, and only holding Gail's and Nicci's or Daddy's hand. It was
very very cold at first and sometimes it felt as though his feet
were digging themselves into the sand as the water swirled
around, but after a while it didn't feel cold at all. It tasted strong,
though, not like ordinary water.

When Nkosi was about four, Gail would often take him to work
with her. Her PR consultancy was loosely associated with a group
of other consultants in the fields of media, graphic design,
advertising and so on. They operated out of a big house in
Wierda Valley, Sandton, which had a beautiful garden. Nkosi
could play there if he wanted, or he could sit with his crayons on
the floor of her office and make pictures. She did not need to
entertain him – as at The Guest House and at home with Irene,
he just fitted in with what everyone else was doing. Then Alan
got a contract to produce and present a TV programme on
motoring called *Drive Time*, and for a while Gail did his PR work
for him from home.

   Alan used to test cars for *Drive Time* and often there would be
a new and exciting-looking model in the driveway at home. Nkosi
was always the first to rush out and admire it, and always went
with Alan when he took it for a spin. Sometimes they filmed the
cars while they were there and Nkosi would help the cameraman,
Charl, to hold the big reflector.

   'Can I always be your assistum?' he once asked.

   Once he appeared on the programme himself when they did an

item on children's safety seats. He made a splendid model, strapped in his seat at the back, wearing a big smile.

Drive Time looked at cars subjectively – from the point of view of the man in the street. Alan's basic question was always: 'Is this a car I would like to have in my garage? If so, why, and if not, why not?' In the nine years that he produced the programme, he went all over the world, wherever a new car was being launched: America, Europe, the Far East.

Rather than children's picture books, Nkosi liked looking at Alan's motoring magazines. He recognised every single car, even though he couldn't read the captions. When a new one was pictured he'd say: 'What's that? I don't remember that one.'

In the evenings the family all came together. Gail had a rule: everyone who lives in the house must work in the house. So as soon as he was old enough, Nkosi had jobs to do. Firstly, he helped Nicci lay the table and put the dishes in the warmer, and secondly, he had to feed the dogs and cats. This would take him a long time ('The cats would be anorexic by the time they got their food,' says Gail), but it was good for him to be solely responsible.

He was also very slow when it came to eating. Everyone else would be finished and their plates carried out to the kitchen when Nkosi still had half his left.

'Come on 'Kosi – eat!' Gail would cry.

'Leave him – what does it matter?' said Alan.

'I'm switching off the TV. It's because he's watching and forgetting to chew.'

'For God's sake, leave him. Let him take the whole night!'

'Look – I've worked. I've done the cooking. I've washed up. 'Kosi's still eating so I've got to wash up again.'

At Gail's insistence, Nkosi always tried to eat every last thing on his plate, but he didn't have a very big appetite.

After supper was bath time, and this Nkosi really enjoyed. They had a big black bath. Alan would put his head round the door.

'Where's Nkosi, Nicci? I can't see Nkosi. There's only a set of teeth and two eyes in the bath!'

'He's been in there for hours, Dad, and there'll be no hot water for anybody else. Tell him to get out.'

Nkosi would climb out in the end, get into his pyjamas and settle down on Alan's knee to watch television.

At bedtime, he would say goodnight to each person in turn, as Gail had taught him, and Alan would take him to bed.

Gail was the one who dished out the discipline.

'If you're naughty, you get a smack. If you're good, you're rewarded. If you are given dinner, you eat it – and you appreciate it because other children haven't got any.'

Nobody argued.

It made no difference that Nkosi had AIDS. He was treated exactly the same as her other children – he was expected to toe the line.

At about this time, Gail had a woman friend who was a trainee minister in a church near Joubert Park. The Rev. Annelize van der Ryst had been a volunteer helper at The Guest House and had trained there as a bereavement counsellor. Gail had been one of her instructors, and once Annelize had shed her initial shyness, chiefly through the role-playing Gail made her do, they had become friends.

She was part of a team of ministers, headed by the Rev. Vernon Openshaw, at St George's United Church on the corner of Edith Cavell and Wolmarans Streets. (The church was 'home' to the Transvaal Scottish regiment, and the regiment's military regalia, including the flags from the Battle of Delville Wood, had been hung there until they were removed to the regimental museum.) St George's was a combined Congregational and Presbyterian church and had a large outreach ministry to the Johannesburg inner city. Every Sunday evening, for a long time, Gail had been providing a huge pot of soup for the church to give out to the street people of the area, and Annelize would come to fetch it from her house.

One evening it was suggested that Nkosi should be baptised. In general, they were not a religious family – as Gail says, it was 'not her scene' – but Gail and Alan thought it might be a good idea to link up with a church and do the right thing by Nkosi as far as religious ritual was concerned. At the back of their minds was the thought that perhaps he would not be around for very long. Gail's attitude to death was – when you die, you die, and that's the end of it, but it would perhaps be a good thing to leave the way open since sooner or later a funeral might be needed. This church was home to a largely black congregation – the local street people and many who came from nearby countries, Christians from Malawi, Zimbabwe, Botswana – all over.

They all went down to the church one Sunday morning for this ceremony. Gail and Alan, Nicci and Nkosi. During the morning service, the Rev. Vernon Openshaw called the family to gather round the font, and Nkosi was blessed and baptised with water in the name of the Father, the Son and the Holy Spirit.

Annelize also lived in Melville and when one night she found a little toddler running distraught down the middle of the road because she was lost, it seemed natural to telephone Gail for advice.

'Phone the police and report it,' said Gail, 'and if the mother doesn't turn up, bring the little one to me. I'll get a bed ready in the meanwhile.'

The mother was eventually found drinking with her boyfriend who worked at a local garage, so it had not been necessary to take the child to Gail, but Annelize had been glad that Gail's professionalism and immediate generous response were there for her to call on.

The friendship was fruitful for both of them: Annelize valued Gail's earthy sense of humour and Gail was able to confide to her friend her occasional frustration about being tied down by a sick child and her continual worries about money. (The Uno was repossessed from time to time and although she always managed to get it back, it was a struggle to make ends meet. She was desperately anxious to keep her house, the family's only security.)

Later, in 1995, Gail was to organise the festivities at Annelize's ordination as a minister in Westbury. The whole family attended this ceremony, which had to be held in a marquee as the church was too small to hold everyone who wanted to be there.

On Sunday nights, Annelize would often stay to supper at the Johnsons. Sometimes, moaning and groaning, Gail would make tripe because Alan and Annelize liked it, but she would cook chicken for herself and the children. There may have been very little money to throw around in that house, but there was always food, and some to spare for all the needy people who streamed in and out on a day-to-day basis. As Annelize says, Gail has a heart like a Soweto taxi.

Every so often, Mommy Daphne would telephone and then appear at the gate to fetch him.

'Granny is coming up from Newcastle,' she would say. 'I must take Xolani for the weekend.'

The fact that she and her child were infected was not spoken about in the family. Ruth had been told that Gail was looking after him and treating him for his TB, and when she came up for a visit, he would be taken to Daveyton. There he saw his Granny, and could play with his sister Mbali.

While they were there, Daphne would take him to visit her friends Paulina and Nombeko.

'*Sawubona*, Xolani,' Paulina would say, '*Unjani?*'[6]

'No,' he would reply, 'I'm not Xolani, I'm Nkosijohnson.'[7] And to Daphne: 'I don't understand that language they speak.'

'But you must understand,' said Paulina. 'I used to take you to the crèche and all the children used to speak that language. You too.'

Sometimes he would stay for longer than a weekend, and on his return Gail would see that his medicine bottle was still full. He often came back snotty-nosed and coughing.

That same year, 1993, an article appeared about him in the local *Northcliff/Melville Times*. Gail had thought for a long time before 'going public' with Nkosi. She felt that if more people knew about what she was doing, others might follow suit – they might even be able to attract enough interest to be able to open a proper care centre for HIV mothers and their babies.

She spoke about it to Edwin Cameron. He himself had AIDS, and although a senior member of the legal profession, had made the brave decision to speak out about his condition in public, in the interests of AIDS awareness. He said to her: 'If five other children can be helped because you go public with Nkosi, then it's worth it.'

But before doing so, she also spoke to Daphne. She told her what she was going to do and why, and gave her solemn promise that Daphne's name would never be mentioned, nor the area she came from, so that her AIDS status would be kept confidential.

The article in the paper was headed: 'AIDS AWARENESS CAMPAIGN – LOOKING AFTER AIDS TODDLER.' It was accompanied by a photograph of Nkosi, looking big-eyed and appealing. It described how Gail was looking after him and treating him like a completely normal child.

Then Cameron Hogg, who produced and presented a television programme on health, came to interview them. Four-year-old Nkosi didn't take much notice, just went on riding his scooter round and round the pool while Gail and Cameron talked in the garden. It was to be the first of many television appearances for him. It may have been because he attracted media attention from such a young age that Nkosi was never to be self-conscious in front of a camera. To him, a television crew was no different from family members taking casual snaps.

After that, other magazines took up the story of a black child with AIDS being kept healthy and happy in a white foster family. One of these was *Drum*, which had a largely black readership, and although, as promised, Daphne's name was never mentioned, it was probably from then on that rumours began to spread around Daveyton.

Over the years, Daphne had managed to save up enough to buy herself a plot of land in Zenzele, the informal settlement near Daveyton where her grandmother Sibongile Khumalo lived. On it she built a solid four-roomed corrugated-iron shack and furnished it. She then asked her mother whether she would like to come up from Newcastle and live with her in Daveyton on a permanent basis. As she had no job at the time, Ruth decided to make the move, and brought Mbali with her. This arrangement continued for quite a while. And then Daphne appeared at Paulina's house in tears.

'Daphne! What's the matter? Come and sit. I will make us some tea.'

Daphne comes into the house, Paulina busies herself with kettle and cups and they sit down together. By the time they are sipping the hot tea, Daphne has managed to dry her eyes.

'Now, tell me what's going on.'

'My mother doesn't want me to stay with her. She says the neighbours are pointing fingers because her daughter is sick. She... she doesn't want to touch me. When I was ill she... she sent someone to fetch Nombeko to wash me because I had sores all down my chest and arm. Now she says I have to go.'

Paulina is horrified. 'But it is your house! You bought the plot. You built the shack. How can you leave?'

'It is the community. My mother is scared of what they are saying.'

'And who's going to clean the house if you go? Your brothers and sisters won't do anything – Fika has gone to stay with his father and the others are too busy having a good time.'

'Mbali. She says Mbali will do the work.'

'Well, we'll think of a plan. But you're not going back there tonight. You're staying here, and sleeping with me. My husband will not mind. He will sleep in the kitchen. He loves you too.'

They talk long into the night. As they are drifting to sleep, Daphne says: 'If I was a guy, I'd want you for my girlfriend, Paulina.'

The next day they went to see Nombeko. At once she said: 'Come and live with me, Daphne. I will look after you.' So Daphne took her clothes, said goodbye to Mbali and went to stay with Nombeko in another part of Daveyton.

But from then on she was often very ill. Once Paulina received an urgent message that Daphne was at the hospital and wanted to see her friend. She went there and found Daphne trying to shuffle along, holding the back of a child's chair.

'Paulina, if I die I want to be buried by my father, down in Newcastle. The doctors say I've got double pneumonia. I want Gail to keep my son because she will give him a proper life. My mother says why did I give my son to this white lady? She says – Go and fetch your son and bring him back to us. I tell her where am I going to get the money to buy the medicines? He must stay with Gail.'

'That's all right, Daphne,' says Paulina. 'Of course he must stay with Gail. He's safe there and maybe he will live longer. The township doctors, they just give Panado and cough mixture.'

Daphne recovered that time and went back to stay with Nombeko. She was even able to work for a while at a panelbeater's.

She once said: 'Nombeko, if you didn't have children of your own, you would take Mbali to live with you, wouldn't you?'

Nombeko said: 'I would take her anyway, even though I have my own children. But your mother would never let me take your daughter.'

Fear of AIDS was not confined to the townships. Gail took Nkosi, when he was about five years old, to a party organised by Synectics, the group to which her PR agency was affiliated. Halfway through the party, the hostess came to her.

'Gail, we've got a problem.'

'What's that?'

'I feel so embarrassed about this. My maid doesn't want to stay in the same room as 'Kosi. She's getting hysterical. I'm terribly sorry.'

There was nothing for Gail to do but take Nkosi home.

A little way down the road from the Johnsons' house was the Foundation School. It functioned chiefly as a bridging school for black children to help them cope with being taught through the medium of English when they first went to school. It also had a nursery section, so Gail thought it would be a good idea for Nkosi to go there for a while before he was old enough to start proper school.

The teacher in charge at the time was an ex-Melville Primary teacher and knew the Johnsons, since Nicci had been a pupil there; she knew, also, that Nkosi was HIV-positive.

Gail telephoned her and asked whether she could make application for Nkosi. The teacher was noncommittal. She would first have to clear it with her Board of Governors, she said, and would let Gail know.

But she never came back to Gail about it, so the assumption was that Nkosi was not welcome.

Gail is going out this evening, she says, to be a policewoman.

'A real one?' Nkosi wants to know.

'Yes, 'Kos,' says Nicci, 'she's going to catch robbers and chase *tsotsis*[8] and rescue people in trouble. And you know what? She has to wear a bullet-proof vest and carry a 9mm pistol.'

'Like on TV?'

'Exactly like that.'

'Wow!'

Gail had signed on as a police reservist attached to the Brixton and Melville Police Station. She saw it as her time off when she could forget all her other responsibilities. Once a week, on a Friday or a Saturday evening, she would get into her uniform, book in at the station at 18.45, be issued with her bullet-proof vest and her handgun. By 19.00 she would have connected with the rest of her team and be on the road in a marked police car, cruising at random and answering any emergency calls.

It was a very mixed area the police reservists had to cover, from the more prosperous houses of Auckland Park, all the way down to the council houses (nicknamed 'Jurassic Park' by the police) and the squatter camps to the southwest. The reservists had to put in at least five hours each shift. As far as the public were concerned, they were the same as the police. They could make arrests and carry out crisis intervention. They often had to deal with family violence. Sometimes they had to do special duties such as roadblocks as well.

One night when she gets home she says to Alan: 'You'll never guess what I got into tonight. There's a call to say there's a wife-beating incident going on in "Jurassic Park", so we turn on the siren and go. When we get there the furniture and the potplants are all lying on the lawn and the window's broken, and the kids are sitting in the middle of the glass. And in the bedroom there's this little tiny guy and a huge woman on the bed and when we say "What's going on here, can we talk about it?" the little guy says "Excuse me while I put on my leg." He had an artificial leg. So I'm doubled up – I mean *hello*? Who beat who here?

'Turns out she threw him across the *braai*⁹ and took a baseball bat to his car, all because he chatted up some woman like a month ago. So I tell her we're going to remove her husband and the community worker will stay with her and the kids.

'So we take him off and before we get back to the station there's another call; we've got to go back to the same house. So I said – "What the fuck's going on? There's no one left to fight." Turns out she's taken an overdose and she's out. Well, we call the paramedics; she's too heavy for us to lift, and we leave them to it. "Cheers, guys," we say, "she's all yours". You have to laugh sometimes, you know.'

Gail was to stop, eventually, after six years of service, because Nkosi was not well, and needing her presence at home in the evenings. Also, her commitment to women with AIDS meant that she was spending more time with people in hospitals.

'If you're with someone at Coronation or Helen Joseph Hospital until four in the morning and you have to go out on police duty the next night, it becomes dangerous. You could fall asleep at the wheel or not be alert enough at a shooting scenario. I felt I had to give it up.'

On 27 April 1994, there was a General Election in which, for the first time in South Africa, all population groups voted. It was an anxious time. In the days leading up to the election, a bomb was set off by a militant far-right group at the Johannesburg airport. No one knew what to expect, but everyone feared the worst.

Gail, in her capacity as a police reservist, was one of those who did police duty at the polling station in Melville. It involved showing people where to go and what to do, and standing by in case of possible trouble.

There was no trouble. All over the country there was an unprecedented upsurge of goodwill and euphoria as people of all races stood together in long queues, chattered and laughed and kept themselves going with whatever food they had brought or could buy. So many went to vote that a second polling day was declared for the 28th. Even in the areas where they had to wait into the second day, the good mood persisted. People watched with elation as on the television newscasts that evening, image after image of orderly, cheerful queues flashed on to the screen. It was an experience that no one who was there will ever forget.

The African National Congress, which had spearheaded the struggle against apartheid, found themselves, triumphantly, heading a new Government of National Unity.

A National AIDS Plan had already been formulated two years previously by the National AIDS Coordinating Committee of South Africa (NACOSA), a body that was comprised of representatives from the then National Party government, the ANC, major unions, businesses, churches, civic organisations, and individuals and NGOs (non-governmental organisations) active in the field of AIDS. Now the Plan was finalised by a draughting committee and launched by the new Minister of Health, Dr Nkosazana Zuma, in August 1994. Implementing it, however, was to be a very difficult task. The government had to grapple with an epidemic that had now risen to an estimated 1.3 million infections in South Africa.[10]

The Plan covered every aspect of the problem in detail. Apart from the urgent necessity of making people aware of the spreading danger, there was the problem of training medical personnel and counsellors and deploying them where they would do the most good. There was the problem of understanding the right procedures to get this going and to access money for it at both national and provincial levels. The implementation of all this came under a newly created Directorate on HIV/AIDS and Sexually Transmitted Diseases.[11]

It is a hot summer's day. Nicci has been in and out of the pool several times since lunch and Nkosi is on his scooter, driving slowly round and round and watching her as she pops up out of the water and disappears again. He watches anxiously each time, just in case she stays under for ever.

She heaves herself out just where he has stopped and says: 'Come on, 'Kos, come in with me.'

He shakes his head, smiling.

'I'll teach you to swim. It's dead easy. Come on. You don't have to go in the deep end.'

He gets off his scooter, takes out the key, closes the door. He sits on the step and lets the water lap over his feet and legs.

'It's very cold, Nicci.'

'It's *lekker*.[12] Take hold of my hands.'

He does so, but tries to snatch them away immediately. Nicci pulls him gently to his feet.

'One step down. Come on.'

'No! I don't want to!'

His face is screwed up, his hands and arms like wire coat-hangers. She comes back and sits down beside him on the step. 'How's about you sit on the lilo? Then you can be like on a boat and I'll push you around.'

He doesn't look too sure. 'Okay.'

She splashes across to the other side of the pool and tows the lilo to the shallow end. 'There you are – sit on it and I'll push you.'

Slowly, he lodges his bum on the side of the bouncing bed she's trying to keep steady.

'Swing your feet up.'

'Don't let go!'

'I won't. Come on. Look, Dad! 'Kosi's sailing to Australia!'

Alan has come out to the pool in his swimming costume. 'Jolly good! We'll have him swimming like a fish in no time!'

'I want to get off!' says Nkosi. Nicci tows him to the steps and helps him off.

'Come in with me,' says Alan, 'and I'll hold you.'

Nkosi does so, but clings tightly to Alan's neck the entire time they are in the pool.

In spite of numerous attempts to teach him to swim, the family had to admit in the end that he was one of those people who just didn't take to water. When it came to enjoying himself, television was much more his style, apart, of course, from riding on his scooter.

Saturday morning in Melville. Crowds of weekend shoppers. Alan takes six-year-old Nkosi and fifteen-year-old Nicci to buy magazines, cigarettes, take-aways.

In the CNA, Nkosi gravitates towards the toy section. They have some new cars there he hasn't seen before. He takes one and goes back to Alan. He jiggles his arm.

'Daddy! Daddy! Can I have this one?'

Daddy? Everyone in the queue stares.

'Don't worry,' says Alan to them, 'my wife burns everything.'

Nicci rolls her eyes. 'Dad! That's such an old joke now.'

'Okay. Let's go. All right, 'Kos, you can have that. But don't show it to your mother. She already thinks you're a spoilt brat.'

'He is,' says Nicci. He looks quickly at her, but she's grinning, so he knows she doesn't mean it. Or only slightly.

Outside the shop the traffic is bumper to bumper, waiting for the lights to change.

'Merc, Ford, Toyota, Nissan, 'nother Toyota, Audi, BMW, BMW, 'nother BMW, Volksie,' drones Nkosi as they move off one by one and drive past.

Irene originally came from Zimbabwe. Nkosi liked her a lot and would spend time in her room with her while she got herself ready to go out at weekends. He liked the way she looked – pale – you couldn't really call her black at all. Every day she used to put cream on her face out of a fat round pot.

'What's that for, Irene?' he asked one day.

'It's to keep me beautiful,' she teased. 'Beautiful and white.'

'White?'

'Yes, of course. I'm going to be white like your Mom.'

'Wow! Can I put some on me?'

She laughs, bends down and puts a dollop on his nose. 'You can have this pot, Nkosi, it's nearly finished. I've got another one.'

Later, Nkosi finds Richard, the man who does the garden once a week, pulling weeds from under the bottle-brush tree.

'What you got on your nose, Nkosi?'

Nkosi rubs his nose and is surprised to find the cream still there. 'It's Irene's cream. She puts it on to be beautiful and white.'

'Oh, that cream. Yes – I use it for years and years.'

'You?'

'Yes.'

'You've been putting it on your face?'

'That's right.'

Nkosi looks hard. Richard is black. Black, black, black. He's the blackest person Nkosi knows. He runs, fast, to Irene.

'I don't want your cream!' he says, holding it out to her.

'Why?'

'Richard uses it. It doesn't work!' She laughs.

Later, he hears her telling Gail about it and they are both laughing.

Chapter
Four

DAPHNE DID NOT often have enough money to fetch Nkosi for the
weekend, but now when she did, she usually preferred to take him
to Diepkloof, Soweto, to the house of Mrs Mirtha Mlambo, the
mother of her cousins Billy, Busisiwe and Mavis. There a whole lot
of family members lived, and there were plenty of children to play
with. At first Nkosi felt very shy because they talked to each other
in isiZulu, and he could tell that they were talking about him. They
told him their names and laughed at him when he tried to
remember. There were the grown-ups: Mavis and Billy and
Busisiwe and Vusi and Butiza and Koseswe and Lindiwe and Mary
Jane, and there were the children: Njipile, Khomlano, and Thabo
and Thabane the twins and – oh, he would never remember.

Busisiwe – whom everybody called Busi – was very talkative.
She and Mommy Daphne chattered away and laughed and laughed.

'What's the joke?' he kept asking, 'Why are you laughing?'

'I'm remembering the night when we were just your age, Xolani,'
said Busi. 'We used to sleep in the same bed, me and your Mommy.
And one night I wanted to go to the toilet but I was frightened to
go out in the dark to the *donga*[13]; there were maybe bad spirits there
who would chase me – oooh! So I went to your Mommy's side of
the bed and I squatted down and relieved myself and then ran back
and went under the blanket. And in the morning everyone is saying

"Bad Daphne! Dirty Daphne!" And she was so cross. And I was saying it louder than anyone!'

When it is supper time they have stiff porridge and gravy and something that looks like thin pink snakes but is really meat.

He looks at it and he looks at the others, eating with their fingers, and he looks at Mommy Daphne.

'You don't like the *derms*?'[14] She's laughing at him. 'You want me to make you a fried egg?'

'No, no, I want to eat those snakes as well.'

But when he tastes it he is not so sure. He wishes he did like this food. He wishes, too, that he could talk this language. They watch TV for a while, and even that's a Zulu programme. Later, when it's bedtime, all the people are still there.

'When are they going home?' he whispers to Mommy Daphne.

'Hey, Uncle!' she calls to Billy, Busi's elder brother. 'When are all these people going home?'

At first he looks very surprised and then he sees her hand over her mouth. Nkosi is the only one who doesn't see the joke.

At last Billy says: 'This *is* their home, Xolani.'

'But where are they all going to sleep?' he asks.

'You're so funny – here of course,' says Mommy Daphne.

Nkosi suddenly has a picture of his small bed against the wall in Nicci's room at home. By now, Alan will be turning off the lights and Gail will be having her bath.

'Why are you crying, Xolani?' asks Mommy Daphne.

'I – I miss my family.'

'But this is your family – you're black.'

He shakes his head. He can't explain.

The next day he sees something that makes him very cross. There's a purse lying on the table. One of the children tiptoes over and takes out a coin.

'What you doing?' he asks. 'Why you doing that? You mustn't do that. You must ask!'

But on the whole it is better the second day. Mommy Daphne says: 'Tell the uncles how you go to Kyalami and race the cars.'

'We go all the time,' he says. 'My Daddy takes me. I like the motorbikes best. No, the Formula Ones. They let me ride in them. I wore a crash helmet. We did two laps. Once I went in a helicopter too. The pilot had to go and re-fuel at Grand Central and asked me to go with.'

They all stare at him – the children as well as the grown-ups, their eyes popping. And he feels a lot better. They follow him when he goes outside. They want him to play with them. When they say something he really needs to understand, he goes inside the house and jogs Daphne's (or Mavis's, or Busi's) arm. 'What are they saying?'

But he feels homesick again when he asks: 'What are they calling me?'

'*Mlungu*. Whitey. White man.'

It's Friday, and Nkosi is staying with Sharon and Dominic for the weekend. Nicci is there too, to play with their older children, Claire and Ross. Nkosi is just about a year older than Siobhan, their youngest. Sometimes Nicci fetches Siobhan from her crèche just down the road when she gets home from school, and they play together with Nkosi's toys.

Nkosi can't remember a time when he didn't know Sharon. She has been Gail's friend since forever, and she said she first met him at The Guest House before he came to live with Gail.

'Such a funny little toddler,' she tells him. 'I've known lots of toddlers but never one that was so calm.'

'Wasn't I calm?' demands Siobhan.

'You? Absolutely not. You were a princess from day one.'

Siobhan jumps up. 'Well, 'Kosi and I are going to play. We'll ride bikes and then we'll make something with the play-dough.'

'Perhaps Nkosi would rather do something else. He's the guest – ask him.'

'No, he wouldn't. He wants to do what I do. Come on, 'Kos.' She's out of the door, but he lingers, standing at Sharon's elbow.

'How are you, Sharon?'

'Actually, 'Kos, I'm all right today. I've been depressed, you know how it is.'

'I know. You've got a lot to cope with.'

'But today everything's hunky-dory. Must be a bit of the old Nkosi magic.'

He grins. 'Come ON, Nkosi!' yells Siobhan from outside. 'I'm waiting.'

He rolls his eyes at Sharon and then disappears too.

At the end of the afternoon he's back in the kitchen. 'Can I help you with the supper?'

'Sure,' says Sharon. 'Do you want to lay the table? Can you manage that?'

'I can manage. I do it at home. At home when there's visitors I put the serviettes in the wine glasses. I fold them and I put them in. And I put the plates to warm.'

'Good. The knives and forks and things are in that drawer. Glasses in the cupboard.'

Bit by bit, he brings them all to the table and arranges them carefully in order. 'Sharon, Dominic, Siobhan, me, Nicci, Claire, Ross. What a lot of us to cook for. It must be tiring.'

'Sometimes it is – you're right there. But what's happening in your life?'

'Daddy's testing a new BM for *Drive Time*. I went in it with him yesterday. It's very nice but it doesn't have much legroom in the back. Daddy says it's one of the first things you look for.'

'You're always on about cars, 'Kos. Are you going to be a racing driver?'

'Uh-uh. I'm going to be a cop. On a motorbike. "Pull over. Show me your licence".'

Sharon laughs.

After supper she is stacking dishes in the kitchen when she feels a little tapping on her arm. Nkosi, with his spoon and his medicine bottle.

'I have to take my *muti* now.'

'I'm sorry, 'Kos, I forgot. Come on then.' She measures it out. He opens his mouth and shuts his eyes. She puts it in and he swallows, wrinkling up his face. 'Nasty?'

'Ja.'

'Shame, 'Kos.'

'Will you tell us a story when we go to bed?'

'Sure. Which one do you want?'

'Can we have 'The Rainbow Fish'?' says Siobhan. ''Kosi likes it best, don't you, 'Kos?'

'Yes,' says Nkosi, 'I do like it.'

So once they are settled top to tail in Siobhan's bed, Sharon sits down between them and tells the story of 'The Rainbow Fish.'

'Once upon a time, there was a fish in the sea who was quite unlike any of the other fish. He sparkled and shone as he swam through the water. And this was because his scales were covered in – ?'

'Sequins!' shouts Siobhan.

'And all the other fishes were jealous of this fish because they were just plain colours and one day one of his friends came to him and said couldn't he have just one of his sequins – just one from underneath where it wouldn't show, so he gave the other fish one sequin. And the friend swam off happily. And when he met another fish he said – ?'

'Look what I've got!' shouted Siobhan.

'And the second fish thought – well maybe if I go and ask the rainbow fish he'll give me some as well. So he swam off and – Nkosi?'

'And that one met some more friends and they all wanted the rainbow fish's scales, and he gave them all away, one by one.'

'So he's just a plain fish,' says Siobhan.

'But all the other fish in the sea have one beautiful scale each,' finishes Sharon.

'Shame,' says Nkosi. 'But he probably felt better afterwards because he wasn't different any more.'

'And maybe he kept just one,' says Siobhan.

Nkosi gives Sharon a strangling hug. 'Can we have that story again tomorrow?'

One day, Nkosi finds himself going to a new hospital. It isn't the big one on the hill any more, it's one for women and children only, Gail tells him, and it's called Coronation.

There's a high wall all round and a gate that has to be specially opened for their car by a lady with a clipboard and a pen. She writes down their Uno's number and their name. They park in a long carport next to some others and then they have to go back out of the gate and into another one right next to it.

There's a long slope down to the hospital building, and a lady in a pink shiny dress is walking very slowly back up it towards them. She's holding up her stomach from underneath with both her hands.

When she's gone past, Nkosi says: 'She's pregnant, isn't she?'

'Probably going to have quins,' says Gail.

'What's quins?'

'Five at once.'

'Five babies? All together in her stomach?'

'Ja – you know, like twins. You know about twins.'

'Can I have a Coke?'

They are passing a little shop on the right with white plastic chairs and tables outside, and Coca-Cola advertisements.

'Not now, we have to go and see Dr Kelly.'

Suddenly, a baby starts screaming very loudly somewhere inside the building. It goes on and on.

'What's the matter with it? Why doesn't somebody do something?'

'Perhaps it had to have an injection. You can't explain to a baby that it's just a prick and it won't happen again. They have to get over the shock, too.'

'But why doesn't somebody – '

'Kos, I don't know. Here we are.'

They have arrived in a big hall, with lots of benches packed with people. Every last one of them turns and stares.

'Why are they all looking at us, Gail?'

'Well, they haven't got a television to look at, have they?'

They go to a small window where a lady directs them outside again and up a long ramp and round a corner to some glass doors. Inside there's another, smaller waiting hall with people on benches. All these seem to be mothers with children.

Gail goes to another window and talks to somebody and then they have to sit at the end of the last bench. When somebody is called to go out, they all get up and shift along and sit down again.

'Why do we have to keep moving up?'

'It's first come, first served. They want to give us exercise.'

Next to them there's a little girl of about two. She keeps burying her face in her mother's lap and peeping out. Gail nods and smiles and laughs at her until she's smiling too and even playing with Gail's watch. She's got bunches of hair sticking out all over her head, tied with red ribbons.

At last it is their turn to get up and go. Gail is given a brown folder and they go through another door into a passage where a nurse takes down their names and tells them to wait again. This time it's a cheerful room, sunny, with child-size blue plastic chairs as well as benches for the Moms, and a table at the side with a red and yellow truck on it and one of those easy puzzles where you have to fit shapes into holes.

Nkosi watches two brothers, one a bit older, one a bit younger than him, dressed in similar grey shorts and white shirts, take the pieces out of the puzzle and fit them back in again. A toddler in red comes and grabs one of the pieces, tries to put it in the wrong place. The brothers retire.

'Here,' says Nkosi, 'I'll show you.'

But the toddler doesn't want to know. He won't let go of the piece, so Nkosi has to give up. He doesn't feel like playing with the truck, it's for younger children really. He sits down next to Gail again.

Facing them on the wall is a picture of lots of different food. Cornflakes and bread and mealie-meal at the bottom and then pumpkin and beans and cabbage, and then bananas and watermelons and mangoes, and then eggs and steak and fish, and at the top a bottle of oil and a packet of sugar.

'It's showing how you should eat,' says Gail. 'The bottom of the pyramid is what you should have most of and the top what you should least.'

'It doesn't have any coffee,' says Nkosi, 'or wine.'

'Oh well, sweetheart, I'm fucked then, aren't I? Wish I could have a smoke.'

On the wall is a picture of two lions wondering whether to attack a porcupine. Nkosi jogs Gail's arm.

'Who do you think is going to win?' he asks, pointing.

'The porcupine.'

They are being called. Gail gets up. Nkosi pulls her arm urgently.

'Do I have to tell Dr Kelly about wetting the bed?'

'Yes, babes, and we'll get him to look at your mouth, even though it's much better.'

They go into a little room with an examination couch. Dr Kelly comes in, and shakes hands with them both.

He listens to Nkosi's chest, looks inside his mouth, takes his blood pressure and also some of his blood out of his arm with a needle, for testing. Nkosi hates this. It is very, very sore and he almost cries, but then he remembers that he is not a baby, that it will stop hurting in a moment and that the doctor won't do it again – not this time. He watches the blood oozing slowly, dark and dangerous-looking, into the syringe.

'How old are you, Nkosi?' asks Dr Kelly.

'Six and three quarters. I'll be seven in February.'

'Nearly seven. You seem pretty good for nearly seven. How are you feeling?'

'Very well, thank you.'

'No diarrhoea?'

Nkosi looks at Gail, but she seems to be leaving the conversation to him so he says: 'No, but I wet the bed this week. Twice.'

'Do you often do that?'

'No. I think maybe I had too much to drink.'

Dr Kelly laughs. 'Hit the bottle, did you? Well, if it goes on happening let me know.' He turns back to Gail. 'I want him to carry on with the maintenance dose of Bactrim. He seems to be in good health, on the whole. We'll know better when the CD4 count comes through. But I don't think we need to see him every month. Every three months is fine. If you have a problem, just bring him to Outpatients. I'll give you a script, which will see you through.'

As they make their way down to the dispensary, Gail says: 'The IC2 clinic is only open on Thursdays. If you get an ear infection or whatever I'm not going to take pot luck in Outpatients. We'll rather go to our Dr du Plessis.'

'What's IC2?'

'It's the specialist paediatric clinic for kids with AIDS. IC stands for immuno-compromised. They give it a fancy name to preserve people's confidentiality.'

'What's confidentiality?'

'Privacy. So other people don't know they're infected.'

'But you always say people ought to talk about it.'

'Yes, darling, and one day I hope it'll be like that.'

They sit in the queue in the dispensary, they get the medicine, they go back up the long slope to the gate. Before they are allowed out, they have to pay R2 to the lady sitting at a table. She gives Nkosi a silver coin, about the same size.

'It's not real money,' he says, turning it over. 'There's nothing written on it. What's it for?'

They find out when they try to drive out of the carpark. Before the gate will open, they have to put the coin into a slot at the side of the driveway. Up goes the barrier, another man opens the gate and off they go.

At about this time, the Johnsons acquired a new puppy.

'We're going to get a boy,' Nicci tells Nkosi, 'and then Kelly won't be jealous.'

'Why won't she be jealous?'

'That's just how it is with dogs.'

'Daddy is going to shits himself.'

Nicci laughs. Ever since she, as a small child, had said 'Daddy is going to shits himself' over the arrival of a new animal, it had become a family saying.

The new puppy was another German Shepherd. He was fluffy and black and frisky, and the tips of his ears flopped over.

'What's his name?' asked Nkosi.

'Something grand and important. He's going to be a big dog.'

'Duke,' says Gail. 'We'll call him Duke.'

While he was still a puppy, Kelly, the older dog, mothered him, but very quickly he got much too big for her to handle. When he tried to play with her she would often snap at him.

'Why's she always so cross with him, Gail?'

'Shame, darling, she's got hip dysplasia. The vet says that German Shepherds and other big dogs often get it. Their hip joints don't function properly. So sometimes she hurts and she's telling Duke not to be so rough.'

Duke grew and grew, and in no time it seemed he was bigger than Kelly, and very handsome.

One day Nkosi shouted from the garden: 'Gail! Gail! Come quickly and tell Duke to stop it! He's climbing on Kelly's back and she's hurting!'

Gail ran to see and found Nkosi trying to haul Duke away.

'Just leave them, 'Kos. He's trying to mate with her. You'll hurt him as well if you try to pull him off. She'll sort him out, don't worry.'

One day Gail sees an invitation to the launch of SAAB cars in South Africa on Alan's desk. At the bottom it says: DO YOU WANT TO TRY YOUR FIRST PARACHUTE JUMP?

It is a challenge she cannot resist. Alan is only too happy to pass on the chance to her if she will jump under the *Drive Time* banner. So off she goes one Saturday to Wonderboom Airport near Pretoria.

There is a large group of jumpers connected with the motoring world waiting to try the experience, but she is the only woman. Craig, the instructor, takes them carefully through all the steps – how they will have to get out one by one, hang onto the wing for a moment, throw themselves backwards in a roll, lean one way and then the other to balance everything and there they will be, floating down calmly and safely, having the experience of a lifetime. There is no need to pull a ripcord, he says, the force of the jump does it for you. Just as well, thinks Gail, in all the excitement she would never remember to do it. When they land, they will have to fold up their parachutes very carefully so that next time they will unroll with no snags. Parachutes, he says, are very valuable.

At seven o'clock that evening, the phone rings in the Melville house. Nicci rushes to answer it.

'Mom! How was it?'

'Well, darling, it was okay. I think I've broken some ribs, but my nails are cool.'

'Mom! What happened?'

'Well, I got out okay and jumped, but nobody said your legs should be parallel and of course my radio was fucked. The guy was probably screaming at me to do this or that. Anyway, everything was calm and beautiful but I couldn't remember what the trees were supposed to look like at a thousand feet. So I went way off course and came down in a residential area. First there were some trees and I thought, Jesus – there goes the parachute – but then there was this magnificent mansion and I couldn't decide whether to try for the lawn or the swimming pool. Actually, I came down on the servants' quarters and there was a flat roof with nails sticking out all round the edge and I thought God, I'm going to be impaled.'

'Mom!'

'So I sort of kicked back as I came down and the parachute got caught on the nails but I landed on a heap of rubble. And then a labourer came out of the *kaya*[15] and said "Hello, Madam." I said "Please help me get out of this crash helmet." I was feeling a bit traumatised, but my nails were fine. So there's this guy hanging onto my bum and legs while I'm trying to unhook the parachute. And, meanwhile, Craig was wondering whether he should phone the insurance company – they'd taken out half-a-million on the jumpers – or whether he should phone Dad and say we've lost your wife. I told him Dad would say "Thank Christ – send the insurance money".'

'So did they find you all right?'

'Oh yes, I walked along carrying the parachute for a while but there was a farm with a bull and an electric fence so I sat at the side of the road with the parachute all bundled up but still tied to me. Up screams this *bakkie*[16]. They'd been driving up and down all over saying "Have you seen a woman in a parachute?" The guy leaps out and says "Are you bleeding?" and I say "No, and I haven't broken a nail either," and he says "Never mind the fucking nail." And when we got back I had to tell Craig I hadn't folded up the parachute properly.'

'So where are you now, Mom?'

'We're at some place in Dullstroom. Crotch Hackle, or some name like that.[17] Stunning. We're just going to go and have dinner. I've got a four-poster bed. I came in the SAAB convertible. Hell of an adrenaline rush. I had the cameraman with me and he says "Look out, there's cops – forget it, Gail, you're past them," and I said "Are you cold? Shall I put the top up?" and you should have seen his face – he thought I was going to put the top up at 220 ks.'

'So how's Mom?' asks Alan, as Nicci gets back to the lounge.

'Fine. She says she's broken some ribs but her nails are all right.'

By the end of 1995, there were approximately 1.8 million South Africans who were HIV positive.[18] The implementation of the National AIDS Plan was not going smoothly. The chief difficulty was that much of the intended funding was never allocated in the national budget. Even money that had been allocated was left unspent, as the AIDS Plan was submerged under all the other priorities of the health department. And then, in the interests of public awareness, the Minister of Health, Dr Zuma and HIV/AIDS and STDs Director Abdool Karim discussed the idea of an AIDS awareness play with playwright Mbongeni Ngema. Ngema had written a very successful play, *Sarafina!*, some years earlier, which had championed the struggle against apartheid, and now they suggested to him that he might write another one, championing the struggle against AIDS. '*At the time, Ngema gave an off-the-cuff estimate of R800 000; Zuma subsequently set the ceiling at R5 million,*

but Health Department officials ultimately signed a R14.2 million contract with Ngema.'[19] The project caused a furious outcry because of the huge expenditure of public funds involved, while the play, called *Sarafina 2!,* was criticised for emphasising existing attitudes of fear and rejection rather than enlightening people as to how they should change them.[20]

When Nkosi was seven years old, Gail was invited to fly to Rio de Janeiro, to join her friend Rob Black and sail back in his catamaran, *Tigress,* together with two other friends, Tertia and Derek. *Tigress* had taken part in the Cape To Rio yacht race. It was a romantic trip that was supposed to take twenty-eight days and ended up taking fifty-six.

Firstly, they had terrible weather. Rob decided to take the so-called 'southern route'. They encountered heavy seas and considerable cold. Gail, on her first sailing trip ever, put on jerseys and oilskins and took her turn crewing the boat. She also made bread, roasted chicken and cooked cordon bleu vegetables in the galley. When the seas got too high for comfort they put on safety harnesses and did their best to keep the yacht going. Then the hydraulic steering system failed. They managed to substitute manual steering, but things looked pretty bad. Then after a couple of days they made contact with a passing South African fishing trawler, which gave them some help, but in the end they had to stop off at Tristan da Cunha, while the broken part was welded.

Alan and Nicci held the fort at home. Nkosi was all right as long as he continued taking his medicine, but he was a little perplexed because Alan was cooking the food now. However, Nicci was there and going to school as usual, Irene was there and doing all the things in the house she usually did, and the atmosphere was certainly calmer when Gail and Alan were not under the same roof. For a long time their relationship had been strained, and exchanges between them were acrimonious and often angry. They did not hold back in front of the children and Nkosi, who hated friction, became quieter and quieter.

Gail's going to Rio on a romantic trip and being away almost double the expected time marked the final split in the marriage. Things limped along for a few months but it was obvious to them that they needed to part, and Alan moved out in September 1996. He found a place to stay nearby, but at first he kept away from the family.

This was very hard on Nicci and Nkosi, of course. Gail telephoned and suggested that he should at least see them, and gradually the children started to visit him for meals and outings. He would make *braais* in the garden for them and let Nkosi play with his collection of miniature cars. Once or twice he took Nkosi on a 'shoot' for *Drive Time* with him. When he travelled overseas he brought back mementoes for them – caps, T-shirts, toys – whatever he thought might amuse them.

Only Nkosi knew what the loss of Alan meant to him. Daddy was the one who never shouted at him, who let him climb all over him like a spider, who loved him and laughed at him and took him out in the cars and gave him fun. Nicci was busy with her new boyfriend and Gail – well, Gail was busy with all the other people who needed help and who seemed to fill the house at all hours.

If Alan's moving out was a big blow to Nkosi, it was equally so for Nicci, then aged sixteen. But it was just at the time when Vincent Pienaar first came into her life, a person outside the family who could take an unbiased view and who was there to give her emotional support when she most needed it. They had first met in July, and by the time Alan left in September they were going out on a regular basis.

At Christmas, Alan asked Nicci what he should get as a present for Nkosi.

'He's seen Scalextrics advertised on TV,' she said, 'and he's crazy for a set.'

Alan picked her up one Saturday morning and off they went to choose it. They all set it up on the dining room table at Pennington on Christmas Day for Nkosi, and they raced and raced. Later on, Alan got him another track with Formula One cars on it. He was not the sort of child, however, who would set it up and race against himself, so he would wait until someone else was around to play

with him. If no one was available, he would watch TV, sit at the
pool, sleep. He never showed a desire to learn to read for pleasure,
and even at school, never got very far with it.

Brett had emigrated to Israel after a two-year stint at desktop
publishing. He was now twenty-six, and he came home for a while
at the time of the divorce to support his mother. A couple of
months later his girlfriend Nira, who had stayed behind in Israel to
take exams, joined them. The two of them went off on a back-
packing trip around South Africa.

When they got back to the house in Melville they said: 'Guess
what? We're going to get married!'

'Cool,' said Gail. 'When?'

'We thought Valentine's Day,' said Brett.

'Three weeks' time. Oh well, we'd better start organising.'

'Brett is so romantic,' said Nira. 'On the beach at Cape Town, he
gave me an oyster. And I opened it and was just about to eat it
when I saw – a ring!'

'Oh wow,' said Nicci, 'that's seriously romantic.'

Brett had been born when Gail was twenty-one and unmarried. She
had met his father, Peter, a man from Salisbury, Rhodesia, during a
spell working at the Victoria Falls Hotel. Peter had begged her to
marry him, even making a terrible scene in front of all the guests
in the restaurant where she worked as a cashier. But Gail did not
see herself settling down so soon. Peter went 'down south' and she
followed shortly afterwards, ostensibly to join him on the Natal
South Coast where he said he had a job. They ended up in
Pietermaritzburg, but not together. Gail's parents were living there
by then, and her mother set up a twenty-first birthday celebration
for her with all the relatives.

Colleen came home from her teachers' training college for the
occasion, and Gail informed her that she was going to be an aunt.
In their teens, Gail had been jealous of Colleen, who was always
their father's favourite, but now Colleen became her ally in a crisis.

Their parents decreed that Gail should go into a Home for Unmarried Mothers, since it was too late for an abortion (which in those days was illegal in South Africa, and which Gail declared she would not have had, anyway), and they chose one in Pretoria, well away from local wagging tongues. Gail and her parents travelled up from Pietermaritzburg by car, Ma sitting tweezer-mouthed and Dad silent with embarrassment. On the way, they stopped in Johannesburg and collected Colleen from the home she shared with five other women in Observatory. During the stop-off, Colleen had taken Gail aside and said: 'Look, you can come and live with us here. There's a flat at the side of the house. I've spoken to the others and they agree.'

The Home looked to Gail exactly like a boarding school. It was run by nuns and had religious statues in the garden and a chapel. The mothers were expected to get up at six, to attend Mass and take their turn at cooking and cleaning.

'We try to persuade the girls to give up their babies for adoption, Mrs Roberts,' said the Sister in charge.

Gail's parents arranged for her to go there when she was six months pregnant. Colleen and Gail went along with the story to keep their parents happy, but Gail moved in with Colleen at No. 33, Urania Street, Observatory, and in spite of frantic telephone calls from her mother when the six-months deadline came and went, stayed there.

Brett was born at the South Rand Hospital on 3 January 1970. It was a traumatic birth. At the last moment, it was discovered that the umbilical cord would obstruct the baby's breathing and a caesarian section had to be performed. The nursing home in Hillbrow into which Gail had been booked did not cater for this, and the nearest government hospital that could take her was miles away, so it was an emergency rush in her gynaecologist's car. Gail has an awful memory of struggling along the hospital corridor on her knees.

She ended up in a ward with a girl who was giving up her baby to be adopted, and was therefore not permitted to see it. She watched Gail suckling Brett with tragic eyes.

'What's your baby's name?' she asked.

'Brett.'

'May I hold him? Just for a moment? *Please?*' she said.

'Are you sure you want to?'

'Oh yes, I'm sure.'

As this girl was about to leave, a baby went on sobbing and sobbing in the nursery. It could have been anyone's, but it was terrible for the deprived mother to hear. She came from a very conservative home, and there was no question of her being allowed to keep her child.

After a week, Gail took Brett home to Colleen's place, and it was there, with seven doting women, that he spent the first few months of his life.

Gail could never have offered him up for adoption, however much her mother urged it. She herself had felt from as young as three that the family in which she found herself was not right for her. They were conventional, they cared what the neighbours thought, there were constant clashes with her mother, and Gail would get angry and sulk, sometimes for weeks.

Once, as a teenager, she went to stay with a friend, Pat Stubbs, on her parents' farm. She was amazed by (and envious of) the warm, friendly relationship Pat had with her mother. So much so that she sat down while she was still there and wrote her mother a letter of seventeen pages, trying to explain that she couldn't talk to them properly because she felt they were always criticising her – her hair, her miniskirts, her make-up ('only whores pluck their eyebrows!'), and she always ended up being made to feel like a criminal.

Her mother's response was to pick up on one point only. 'How dare you say we make you feel like a criminal?'

'So, okay,' she said to herself, 'I'll never try again.'

At Brett's wedding, Nkosi was to be a pageboy. Nicci coached him in his task.

'You will have to carry the ring on a cushion,' she said. 'Walk behind the bride and groom, and when the pastor asks, you give him the ring. Don't pick it up – just hold out the cushion.'

They hired a tuxedo for him and he looked very spruce and proud, walking behind, with Nicci the bridesmaid. The wedding took place in a friend's garden and was conducted by the Station Commander of Brixton Police Station, who was also a Presbyterian padre.

Chapter
Five

IN JANUARY 1997, Gail applied for Nkosi to be enrolled at Melpark Primary School. This, under the name Melville Primary School, had originally been for white children only, but when pupils began to be integrated it had become a so-called 'Model C' school – a school where the parent body had some say in the running of the school – and had changed its name.

The application form Gail had to complete asked whether your child was suffering from any disease, so she put 'Yes, AIDS', because Nkosi was known around Melville and she thought if there was going to be any difficulty she should sort it out at the beginning. He was number fourteen on the waiting list because she had left it so late, although as they lived in the immediate area he should have been in the first five. She kept telephoning to find out whether he was in, but the answer was always: 'Well, he's moving up to number one, but we need to sort out a few things.'

On 19 February she received a phone call from a reporter on *The Star*. 'What do you think about the outcome of the meeting?'

'What meeting?' she said.

The governing body of the school had been thrown into a quandary by her application because there was absolutely no official government policy on children with AIDS attending school. The school governors and the Headmaster, Mr Badenhorst, were scared. They felt that while Nkosi himself had the right to go to school, other children had rights too, and maybe the parents would feel that there was a risk of infection. Eventually it was decided to take it to the parent body and a meeting was called. The parents were divided 50/50 on the question: ('No, I don't want that child sitting next to my child.', 'Well, if you say it's not contagious, what's the harm?', 'If my child goes there he's got to wear plastic clothing.') But before any decision was taken, someone leaked their dilemma to the press, and Gail's struggle to get him into school became a political and public issue.

WE DON'T WANT YOU, NKOSI! shouted the headlines. *PANIC AS AIDS BOY TRIES TO GO TO SCHOOL,* and Melpark Primary was blamed, very publicly, for not taking him in.

The *Pretoria News* reported on 26 February that the Minister of Health and the Minister of Education had made a joint statement that included the following: *'We are disturbed by the reaction of some members of the public to an 8-year-old HIV-positive child's attempt to exercise his democratic right to attend a public school. We want to state categorically that no governing body has the right to deny a child access to a public school.'*

Gillian Anstey, writing in the *Sunday Times* on 23 February, reported: *'The national education ministry said yesterday that it had no policy on the issue... A spokesman for Professor Sibusiso Bengu, the Minister of Education, said yesterday that it was up to the provinces to draw up regulations in terms of the Constitution and the Schools Act.'*

Melpark Primary School therefore applied to the Education Department of Gauteng Province. Mary Metcalfe, the MEC for Education in Gauteng Province, then passed the responsibility straight back to the schools. She was reported in *The Star* of 28 February as saying that *each and every school in the province would have to develop a policy on AIDS because 'the reality is that schools are going to deal with this issue.'* However, she said that an education task team would be constituted to draw up guidelines to help the schools.

'When am I getting to school, Gail?'

'Darling, there's a problem. They don't know how to deal with you.'

'Why?'

She puts her arm round him and pulls him onto her lap. 'Because you're HIV-positive. People don't know how to deal with it.'

The family in Diepkloof are sitting around the table one evening shortly before supper. Suddenly, there are screams from the direction of the toilet. 'Who?' 'Who is there?' 'It's Christina.' 'Hau! Christina! What's the matter? Are you all right?'

She comes out, waving a sheet of newspaper.

'Look – look here! I was just going to use this when I see the picture. That's our Xolani! It says he can't go to school because he's got HIV/AIDS!'

The family is dumbfounded. Nobody knew. Daphne had not said a word.

'Is that why he's staying with Gail?'

'Because he's HIV?'

'No, it's because of the TB.'

'But how did he catch it?'

'Is that why Daphne's sick? Has she got it too?'

'She's been losing all that weight.'

'And she's often sick.'

'She's never told us.'

'She's often got sores on her left-hand side.'

'And her mother's come from Newcastle to look after her.'

'No, she's not staying with her mother any more.'

A little later the TV is switched on. It is time for the news. Busisiwe drops her knife. 'Look – that's our Xolani again!'

'They're saying he's HIV positive.'

'Gail's saying. Gail's telling everyone.'

'She's saying he must go to school.'

'Yes, look, Gail's fighting with the school.'

'What will Daphne say?'

Next time she comes they will all feel very awkward. Maybe they will catch it from her. It said on the TV and on the pamphlets at the clinic that you can only catch it through contact with an infected person's blood, or through sex, but who knows for sure?

But in the little time she had left, Daphne never said anything. At the end of March, she packed her things, borrowed R60 from her friends for transport, and told them she was going to Newcastle, to her father.

Melpark Primary School, the Gauteng Education Department and representatives from the Department of Health and Welfare came together to deal with this sudden, very public crisis. They organised workshops for the teachers and any parents who wished to attend. People learned what they might expect in the way of emergencies in dealing with an HIV/AIDS child; they were even told how to cope in the event that he died suddenly at school.

Nkosi was thus accepted at Melpark Primary School for the beginning of the second term.

'Badie' Badenhorst remembers it as a terrible time. Apart from the adverse publicity, it was a difficult time for his teachers also. None of them had known exactly how infectious AIDS was and whether they would have to take special precautions. In those days, most people were rather hazy about the danger. The media were reporting that there was a worldwide epidemic, but nobody at Melpark Primary had any personal experience of it.

Miss Hastings, teacher of Grade One, said she was willing to take him. 'I am a single person, I've got no children at home, I'll take him into my class.'

Gail decided to write an open letter to the Minister of Education and the Minister of Health. It was published in the *Sunday Times* on 9 March, under the heading '*Learn from my AIDS child's example*':

'The AIDS status of my son Nkosi Johnson threw a school, their governing body, parents and the Gauteng Department of Education into total turmoil recently. Why? Because, while it is agreed that all children have the right to education, there is no established national policy specifically compiled to address the issue of admission of HIV/AIDS children to schools.

'This incident should never have happened. As HIV/AIDS is a national problem, a specific policy for infected children should have been on every principal's desk at least two years ago (if not sooner). I do not believe that each province should be left to draw up its own policy – this could lead to confusion and discrimination, depending on the particular MEC for Education's attitude towards HIV/AIDS.

'I understand that policies are being drawn up around "children with special needs" - great! However, HIV/AIDS should have its own specific policy as the ramifications and issues that arise from the infection are huge, varied and confused. This is where the Minister of Health, Dr Nkosazana Zuma, should come in.

'While it is all very well to state that HIV/AIDS children have the right to education, Zuma should have taken the initiative and *worked hand in hand with the Minister of Education, Professor Sibusiso Bengu, to design and compile education brochures/ pamphlets (in support of the policy and to support those affected) targeted at pupils, parents and teachers.*

'All this should have been done ages ago and should have reached every school in the country. I challenge both Professor Bengu and Dr Zuma to create the policy and have it established nationwide by the end of April, as well as to have brochures/ pamphlets printed and distributed nationwide.

'What happened to Nkosi must not happen to another child in this country. Although I am glad that, through him, every other infected child will enjoy the right to education, people cannot be forced to accept a condition they know nothing about. It is only through education that they can be informed and enlightened and reduce their fears and prejudices.

'We have a golden opportunity to educate our most important generation – the little ones, who are not yet sexually active – to inform and arm them with HIV/AIDS information, that through them we will have a future generation who will be AIDS-friendly and accepting, that through them there will be no more discrimination. But, most importantly, they will be so completely prepared that the rate of infection among the youth will drop drastically.

'May the school that Nkosi will be attending be the role model for every other school in the country. I understand and accept those parents who are concerned and have fears, but hope they understand that if there were any chance of cross infection, I would never, ever have jeopardised the health of my children five years ago when I brought Nkosi into my home.

'I admire Nkosi's courage and hope he enjoys school.' – Gail Johnson, Johannesburg.[21]

However, it was to be another two years – in August 1999 – before the National Policy on HIV/AIDS for Learners and Educators was finally launched by the government. Edwin Cameron (by then a judge in the Supreme Court) was involved in drawing it up and Peter Busse of the National Association of

People Living with HIV/AIDS (NAPWA) sent it through to Gail for her comment. She suggested that bereavement counselling should be included.

During 1997 the number of South African HIV/AIDS infections had risen to an estimated 2.8 million.[22] A number of new AIDS initiatives were started. An inter-ministerial cabinet committee was set up, chaired by the then Deputy President, Thabo Mbeki, to broaden the responsibility for the AIDS epidemic to include other government departments. Two campaigns were later to be unveiled by the government: 'Partnership against AIDS', and 'Beyond Awareness', both of which were aimed at raising public awareness of the AIDS crisis and prompting companies, churches and civic organisations to tackle HIV/AIDS.

With the Medicines Act No. 90 of 1997, parliament passed legislation to enable patients to get prescriptions for generic medicines for the treatment of AIDS. It allowed for parallel importing, so that if a drug was sold more cheaply in Brazil, for instance, South Africa could import from that country. It also created a mechanism for government to involve itself in the pricing of drugs. This legislation was contested however by the pharmaceutical industry both in South Africa and overseas, which claimed that it would threaten its intellectual property rights, and the Pharmaceutical Manufacturers Association took the South African government to court. It was to be almost four years before the matter was finally resolved.[23]

Just before Nkosi starts school there is a phone call from his aunt Dudu, Daphne's younger sister. He takes the call and she asks to speak to Gail. Gail comes, has a conversation with her, and puts the phone down.

' 'Kosi? My love – you know your Mommy's sometimes been very sick?'

He nods.

'Well, now she's died, darling, and you've got to be very brave about it.'

She holds him tightly while he cries and cries.

'But you know the nicest thing about death? You don't have to wait for a phone call. You don't have to wait for Mommy Daphne to come knocking at the gate. You can talk to her any time you want.'

Dudu had explained that her sister had become very ill and gone down to her father's place near Newcastle. She had been there only a day or two when she had been taken to hospital at Madadeni and died there during the first week of April.

It was important, Gail felt, for Nkosi to be present at his mother's funeral, both as a mark of respect and as an opportunity to say a final goodbye to her. It would also be good for him to experience a significant event in his family's life.

Sharon offered to drive them down in her car and be with them at the funeral, so they set out for Newcastle at 5.30 in the morning, arriving at the town for breakfast at about 8.45. They stopped at a restaurant for coffee and bacon and eggs, and they talked about what to expect at the ceremony. Not wanting to be at a loss, Gail had telephoned a police sergeant who was a Zulu to ask him about the traditions and observances, and he had told her what to do and what not to do.

'Now, when we go into the vigil room, 'Kos, I've got to take off my shoes and my jewellery. The coffin will be there, with Granny Ruth and the other relatives.'

'Will we see Mommy Daphne in the coffin?'

'I don't know, darling – the policeman said they may leave it open so we can see her, and if so you can kiss her goodbye if you like. I'll lift you up so you can do it.'

Dudu came to fetch them at the restaurant and show them where the funeral was being held. Near the main road was a petrol station, and behind it they could see a big marquee. They parked the car and approached slowly. Several men were standing near the marquee, so Gail asked where they should go. They pointed out a *rondawel*[24] off to the side. She took one of Nkosi's hands and

Sharon took the other and they went up to the doorway, where Gail bent and started taking off her shoes.

'It's all right,' said a man standing by, 'you don't have to.'

Inside the *rondawel* it was dim after the bright sunlight. There was the coffin on the floor – not on a table as they had expected – and there beside it sat Ruth Khumalo and other elderly women of the family, wrapped in blankets. The coffin was open, but all they could see of Daphne was her face, looking very small.

Gail squatted down on her haunches to offer condolences, and Ruth started to cry and leaned towards her. Somehow, Gail lost her balance and knocked into Nkosi and he in turn lost his balance and nearly toppled into the coffin. In fright, he burst into bitter tears. Quickly, Sharon picked him up and took him outside while Gail stayed talking to the family members. All thought of kissing Mommy goodbye had to be abandoned. He was too distraught to go back inside the hut, but his sister Mbali joined them and he soon began to calm down.

Then they went into the marquee. They were told to sit at the long table at the head, with other close members of the family. It was crowded and very hot – so much so that eventually the sides of the marquee were rolled up so that a breeze could blow through. There were many speeches in isiZulu, homilies from Methodist ministers and traditional African priests, and other tributes. Towards the end of the speeches, an interpreter gave the meaning in English, and when the next woman got up to speak, Gail heard her own name mentioned. Daphne, said the speaker, always hoped that Gail would take responsibility for Mbali as well as Xolani.

The cemetery where Daphne was to be buried was at the top of a koppie about two kilometres from the vigil. The coffin was placed on the back of a small truck. Some people went up by bus, some walked, and Gail, Sharon and Nkosi went by car. It was a rocky place, and planks had been laid down around the open grave. Gail and Sharon stood back, while Nkosi was taken forward to the graveside by his uncle Fika and his aunt Dudu. There were more speeches in isiZulu, and this time no one translated.

The coffin was lowered into the grave, a blanket placed on top of it, and then members of the family, Nkosi included, threw down handfuls of earth. Large pieces of timber were lowered in before the men filled in the grave with earth.

'Is that part of the tradition?' Gail wanted to know, and was told that they were put there to make it difficult for anyone to steal the coffin.

When burials are completed, it is necessary for everyone to wash their hands. As well as a practical cleansing after handling the earth, this is a ritual cleansing from the malevolent entities that hover around a burial. So Gail and Sharon and Nkosi queued with the rest to pass by the bucket of water and cleansing herbs that had been provided for the purpose.

As they were doing this, Ruth said: 'You must take Mbali. You must take her now.'

Gail said: 'Ruth, my cause is infected people. Nkosi is with me because he is sick. I don't have the money to take on healthy children who have families.'

Someone else said: 'There's the father.'

Gail looked up and saw two men watching them. One was thin and frail-looking, in a suit with big lapels, the other well built, in a beautiful leather jacket. She bent down and said to Nkosi:

'Do you want to meet your father? He's here.'

'Yes,' said Nkosi.

As they approached, the thin one fell to his knees and tears streamed down his face.

'My son!' he said, 'My son!'

His friend in the leather jacket said to Gail: 'What about the sister? Who's going to look after Mbali?'

Gail had had enough. 'You'd better ask the father!' she snapped.

Shortly after that, having donated money towards the funeral, they were on their way back to Johannesburg. The man claiming to be Nkosi's father never made contact again.

Members of the family, however, declare that this was the father of Mbali only, not of Nkosi. Nkosi's father was commonly presumed to be Zenzele Mthethwa, who had been Daphne's boyfriend when she was in Standard Nine at school, where he was the athletics champion. He was to become gravely ill towards the end of 2001, and was to die shortly afterwards. However, in an article in the *City Press* on 3 June 2001, his mother denied that he was Nkosi's father, saying that he had never reported Daphne's pregnancy to his family.

When she saw the photograph of Zenzele in the newspaper, Gail did not think that it was the man who came up to them at Daphne's funeral. But Nkosi remained convinced that he had met his father, and even mentioned it in the speech he made at the World AIDS Conference.

Later, Fika was to say: 'I was angry because Daphne reconciled with Nkosi and Mbali's fathers, but they never did anything for Nkosi and Mbali.'

After Daphne's death, Nkosi slowly began to realise that people die when they have AIDS. She had had 'baddies' in her blood, just as he had. Gail and Nicci and he were sitting in the living room one night eating supper, and they were talking about it.

'You see, 'Kos, sometimes the "baddies" eat up all the "goodies" in people's blood and they can't go on living any more.'

'Why?'

'Well, they just get too sick, that's all.'

'That's why you came to live with us, 'Kos, 'cos your Mommy got too sick to look after you.' Nicci leaned over and gave him a chip from her plate. 'Not because she didn't want you, or anything like that.'

'It's called a virus,' said Gail, 'and we're all trying to fight it. You and me and a whole lot of other people. I'm going to start a special home for mothers and their babies who've got it.'

'Really, Mum?' said Nicci, 'Where?'

'Don't know yet, but I'm going to do it.'

'Does everyone who has AIDS die, Gail?' asked Nkosi.

'Well they do, but they also die of other things.'

'And lots of people go on for years and years, even though they are infected,' said Nicci.

When he took his plate out to the kitchen, he asked Irene what she thought about it.

'Everybody got to die of something, Nkosi,' she said. 'They get gunshot wounds, car accidents – all that.' Somehow, this was not comforting.

When Nkosi went to bed that night he pulled the covers up round his ears and shut his eyes. When Gail came to kiss him she said: 'You all right, 'Kos?'

'Mmm.'

'Sure?'

'Mm.'

But he wasn't. He was grappling with two ideas that had come together in his mind. One was that his Mommy was dead because she had AIDS. And the other was that he himself had it.

Later in the night he woke, crying. Nicci came over to him. 'What's wrong?'

'Had a bad dream.'

'Shame, 'Kos, what about?'

'My Mommy.'

'Okay, 'Kosi, it was only a dream. Look, I'll sit on your bed and talk to you until you go to sleep.'

Not many eight-year-olds have to face the terror of knowing they will soon die. For Nkosi, it was the beginning of a journey that was to take him to a lonely place.

In the event, very few parents took their children out of Melpark Primary School because of Nkosi. In fact, some of the parents who had raised the loudest objections were among those whose children stayed on – even some who were members of South Africa's extreme right-wing reactionary political movement, the Afrikaner Weerstandsbeweging.

Nkosi enjoys the prospect of school because he will be able to have lots of friends and play.

'Whoa, 'Kos,' says Gail, 'school isn't just playing with friends. There's sums and school books and having to sit still at a desk.'

She tucks him into bed and sits down beside him.

'Kosi – what are you going to do if you hurt yourself at school?'

'I'm going to go to the teacher.'

'Supposing there's no teacher around? Supposing you fall on the playing field and your knee is bleeding and there are only kids around?'

'I'm going to... I'm going to ask them to take me to a teacher.'

'All right, but you've forgotten the first thing.'

'Ja! Ja! I'm going to tell them not to touch my blood.'

'That's right, that's the most important thing. You cover up the wound with a tissue, you go to a prefect or the teacher and you ask them to help you. If you're really bleeding like you're going to die, then they must run like hell. But you don't let them touch you; you go at once to the sick room and whoever's there will put on rubber gloves and attend to it. Okay? Tell me again – what are you going to do?'

Nkosi counts on his fingers. 'Don't let them touch my blood – cover it with a tissue – fetch the teacher – go to the sick room.'

'That's right, darling. Now I've explained it to the school so they know what to do. But you must be prepared too. You must take responsibility for yourself.'

On the morning of Nkosi's first day of school, it is the usual chaos in the Johnson household. Nkosi has put on his new uniform tracksuit, green and charcoal. He is wandering around the kitchen with his bowl of Pro-Nutro. He can't possibly sit down at the table and eat it, his legs feel too restless. Duke is also in the kitchen, his nose questing the table top, Nicci is leaning against the fridge drinking her tea, and Irene is at the counter making his lunch. It feels very crowded, more crowded than usual, especially when Gail comes whirling in, demanding coffee.

'If you get milk on that uniform, I'll kill you,' she says. Nkosi looks down at his chest and sees a small dribble. But Gail hasn't seen, she's off into the dining room, winding up her hair into a knot, the clip between her teeth. He takes the damp cloth Irene is holding out to him and dabs at the dribble. Now you can't really see it.

'Where's your school bag?' shouts Gail.

He goes into the lounge and gets it from the sofa. He checks inside. Zip bag of pencils and crayons. Tissues. Apple. Plastic box with lunch. Gail has gone clattering upstairs again so he wanders into his bedroom because he can't stand still.

Back she comes. 'Nkosi? Where are you? Shit – we're going to be late!'

Everybody comes crowding into the yard to see them off: Nicci, Irene, Duke – even the cats.

Outside the gate, Gail takes his hand.

'Come on, darling, and if there's a whole lot of press fucking around, we'll just smile nicely and then go on walking.'

There are. On both sides of the road, cars are drawn up, and people are waiting to see Nkosi Johnson arrive for his first day at school. Flashbulbs, TV cameras, people shouting questions. Mother and son pose briefly for the cameras and then keep on walking, because the point is that Nkosi must begin his education, never mind all the hype. They can see Mr Badenhorst waiting for them at the front entrance, and once Gail has handed him over, he can disappear into the school building where no media people will be allowed.

All the way along DF Malan Drive, the billboards on the streetlamps shout: AIDS BOY GOING TO SCHOOL! On her way to her own school, Roosevelt High, Nicci sees them and thinks – how easy would it be to steal one of those posters? They could put it up on the wall at home. There's one right outside her school gate. But it's late already, and she decides to get it after school.

'I tried to steal one of the posters,' she tells Gail when she gets home.

'So what happened?'

'Well, I went to get it down – the one right by the school gate – but what I didn't realise was one of the kids' fathers was there who's a traffic cop or something; he's there to fetch his kid. And I'm like trying to get the scissors to cut the string and this traffic cop comes and he's, like, 'No, no, you can't take it.' So I'm, like, 'But it's about my brother – this is my brother.' And he said no, but it's government property and he showed me the little luminous orange sticker and when that's there it's the property of the municipality, you can't touch it, so I'm, like – "Okay."'

It is the second day of Nkosi's big adventure, and this time he's walking to school by himself. Not quite true. Gail has told Irene to walk with him, but since it is only two and a half blocks and he isn't a baby, he can walk a few paces behind her and imagine that he is alone.

In the morning, it's all uphill. Once out of the sliding gate, he turns left and takes care to jump over the bit of grass with the dog turd on it. It's been getting smaller and dryer each day, but it's still there. Duke, probably, one of the times he got out and Gail had to shout at him.

Two blocks, and they are almost at the top of the hill. Past the high concrete wall with the extra bit of wire netting, and there's the red church with the funny spire that looks like an assegai on the opposite corner. Over the hill in front of him pokes the top of the Brixton Tower. All the TV gets beamed out from there, his Dad told him. If you climbed to the top, you could see all the way to Pretoria.

He turns the corner at the beginning of the sports field. Through the wire fence he can see some children already playing around there, climbing on the spectator stands, kicking a small red ball around, shrieking as it whizzes through the soccer posts. Their school bags and anoraks litter the grass. One guy is wearing his green jersey pulled over his head like a hood. One is standing at the side, talking on a cellphone, while a friend jabs his arm excitedly, trying to interrupt.

They have started walking early so as to be sure to be on time, but already the buses are there at the kerbside and children are pouring out. There are lots more coming up behind him and soon he's one of the crowd. Everyone seems taller than he is and for a moment he wishes he were at home still, playing with the cat. He looks back and sees Irene at the corner, waving.

Someone suddenly calls out: 'Hi, Nkosi!' It is one of the biggest girls and her friend giggles and nudges her. But then someone else says: 'Hi, Nkosi,' and then lots of them are saying it. 'Saw you on TV,' ventures one, and 'Ja, what's it like to be famous?'

'Okay,' he says. But then the school bell shrills above the crowd. Like a hungry mouth, the school gate sucks them in and they clatter and shout to their classrooms, pushing, cackling, their shoes loud on the passage floors.

At first, Nkosi can't remember which way to go, and then the headmaster comes up behind him and puts a hand on his shoulder. 'Come along, my boy,' he says, 'you're in Miss Hastings' class. Round the corner and down the stairs. Thandi, take Nkosi with you, and show him where to line up.' A girl, almost as small as he is, says '*Woza*[25],' and soon he finds himself standing in a long line of children outside a classroom. It's got a red door.

Thandi leaves him and goes to stand with the girls. Here comes Miss Hastings. He remembers her from yesterday. She's got yellow hair, not as long as Gail's. Yesterday she said something to him which he didn't hear, and he said 'I beg your pardon?' She said 'Do you hear that, Grade Ones? Here's a boy with manners.' And they all stared at him.

The girls have finished filing in and now it's the boys' turn. Nkosi finds himself beside the same desk he had yesterday.

'Now, I want everybody to sit down and fold their arms. We're not running around on the playground now. We're here to learn.'

Nkosi sits down at once, but some of the other children don't seem to understand. At last, with a lot of clatter and kicking the chairs around, everybody is sitting down with folded arms.

All the desks are facing the blackboard, and on it there's a lot of writing. Nkosi knows what it is because Miss Hastings did it yesterday. It says DOG and PIG and COW. It gives him a good feeling to see it there, he belongs, he has started to learn.

'Now, has everybody put their pencil cases and their blackboards in the chairbags? Has everybody forgotten what we do now that you've had holidays?'

Nkosi unpacks his satchel and debates what to do with his

lunchbox. Perhaps he'd better leave it where it is. The chairbag is long and dark blue and hangs behind him. Now it looks quite fat and bulging. Then Miss Hastings calls them to come and sit on the floor in the front. When they are settled and quiet she tells them a story.

It's all about a poor mother who, it seems, doesn't have enough money to look after her new baby properly so she takes him down to the river and sets him afloat in a cradle woven out of bulrushes. Nkosi wonders how that would be, to just send your child off, not knowing what would happen. It could drown, and there were crocodiles in the river, Miss Hastings said. Anyway, the baby's sister hangs around and watches to see where it goes and Miss Hastings says she'll go on with the story tomorrow.

'Now, get out your workbooks,' she says, 'and your pencils, and we're all going to write today's date. What is today? I want hands up, please.'

One of the children stands up and says: 'Tuesday.'

'That's right – Tuesday. And Tuesday begins with a... ?'

'T!' shouts everyone.

'And how do we write a T?'

One or two of them don't seem sure. Miss Hastings writes a big T on the board. There's a lot of talking and getting out of cases and unzipping. Miss Hastings gets quite cross. 'Quiet, please!' she says, and then she has to shout it again, very loud. One of the children is still standing up, arguing with his neighbour.

'Daniel, are your ears sewn shut, or something?'

Nkosi catches her eye and giggles, but Daniel doesn't seem to see the joke.

The morning goes on, and he begins to feel quite tired. He has learnt what b and c and d say. He can call out DOG when Miss Hastings points to the word on the board or holds up a card. Now it's break time. Miss Hastings tells them that they must go outside to eat their lunch, and they can play until the bell goes again.

He takes his lunchbox out of his case and follows behind as the others all rush for the door. They're all running down the steps over to where the climbing frame stands. At first, he sits on the wall in the sun and has his sandwiches and juice, but when he's finished he gets up and climbs on to the jungle gym. It's scary, but nice up there. He'd better not fall, though. Better not make a fool of himself like yesterday. Yesterday he had tripped on the steps up from the quad, fell and cut his lip. 'Don't touch my blood!' he'd cried to the unknown faces crowding round him. 'Don't touch my blood! Call the teacher!' They had helped him up and taken him to the office, where the lady had put on rubber gloves and cleaned him up with damp cotton wool and disinfectant.

From the top of the jungle gym, he can see over the fence to the houses across the road. Maybe he can see the roof of his own house, but he's not sure.

There's the bell again, and this time there's a very cross-looking senior girl yelling at him to be quick and get down and go back to his classroom. She's got hair tied back in lots of little plaits.

When they're all back inside and sitting down again, Miss Hastings writes up on the blackboard: $2 + 2 = 4$.

'Who remembers what this is? That's right, Tracy, this is how we add. Now I'm going to give you all some counters. I want you all to take two blue ones in your left hands. Which is your left hand, children? Okay. Now, add two red ones to the blue ones. How many do you have?'

'Four!' most of them shout.

'Right,' she taps the board. 'And this is the way we write it. Two plus two equals four. If I've got two sweets and somebody gives me another one, how many do I have?' Nkosi joins in the chorus of 'Three!'

'That's right. And this is how we write it. $2 + 1 = 3$.'

They do the same with four and five, and they copy it into their workbooks, and then it seems time to be singing, because a new lady comes into the classroom and tells them they're going to learn to sing the National Anthem properly, because the school sings it every time in Assembly and they must sing it with the others. Nkosi really enjoys this. He knows the tune and some of the words, too.

And then suddenly it's the end of school and they all have to say 'Goodbye, Ma'am' in a chorus, and then they are grabbing up their school bags and running out to the bottom gate.

In the road, there are a lot of buses parked, with children piling in, and there are two big boys with long poles with STOP on them. Nkosi watches them. Every so often they march out into the middle of the road with their poles and all the cars have to stop and wait while the children cross on the zebra crossing.

'Who are those boys?' he asks a child next to him.

'Scholar Patrol,' she says. 'You a dummy?'

There's Irene, coming along the path. He goes to meet her, suddenly glad that home is waiting.

By the end of the first week, Nkosi is beginning to feel as though the classroom belongs to him. He doesn't have to wonder what's going to happen next; he knows just where to line up, just where to stash his bag against the wall at the beginning of the day, and he knows that before anything else happens they all have to stand up and say 'Good Morning, Miss Hastings, Good Morning, Friends' when she says 'Good Morning, Grade Ones.'

And he knows all about what happened to the baby in the river. The sister followed along behind on the bank as the cradle floated down, and then some girls who were swimming grabbed it and found the baby and took it to the king's palace. One of them was a princess. And she was allowed to keep the baby and give him all nice clothes and food and stuff and his name was Moses.

Nkosi has his own special desk. Beside it is a long cupboard against the wall with a curtain in front. It's really nice. It's got a pattern of blue camels. He starts counting them, but after twelve he loses it and has to begin again.

'Nkosi Johnson! Are you listening to me?'

Everybody else is facing front, their arms folded.

'Yes, Ma'am,' he says.

'We are going to go out to break five minutes early because then you can all have a chance at the tuckshop before the big ones come out. So now you can all go – no pushing, please!'

Nkosi follows them. It seems he's always at the back of the

queue. But – a tuckshop! Maybe they've got sweets. And ice-cream. Much better than sandwiches. He'll have to try and get some money.

It is at News Time that he shines. When it comes to talking to the class about what he has done in the holidays or over the weekend – like staying with Sharon and Dominic and all of them – he really enjoys standing up and describing it all. His vocabulary is excellent for his age, and where Miss Hastings has to help others along with every sentence, mainly because English is their second or third language, Nkosi has no difficulty.

During his first year, Nkosi acquires a friend. He is sitting down by himself at the edge of the small field at break time. The others are running and shouting and kicking a ball around and he doesn't feel like joining in. It's funny, although it's quite a long time since he went to Mommy Daphne's funeral, whenever he is by himself for a bit, he always begins thinking about it. And about having AIDS and all that. This is one of those times. It seems as though people can suddenly just stop. Not be there any more. Where are they? What is it like, to be dead? Like sleeping? Gail has told him that no one is very sure. But she seems to think that they are still around somewhere, or how could he go on talking to Mommy Daphne like she says, if she isn't anywhere at all?

He watches a boy coming towards him across the field. Bigger than him, with hair the colour of Nicci's.

'Hello,' says the boy, when he gets up to him. 'Er – I saw you sitting all alone and thought I would come and introduce myself. My name is Eric. Eric Nicholls.'

Not to be outdone, Nkosi stands up and says: 'Pleased to meet you. I'm Nkosi Johnson.'

'I know,' says Eric. 'I've seen you on TV.'

They both sit. There is a pause. Nkosi slides his eyes sideways without turning his head. Eric is chewing a piece of grass.

'So, how do you like school?' asks Eric.

'It's okay.'

Eric's hands are rather dirty, and there's a piece of Band-Aid around one finger. He keeps that finger hidden in his other hand, as though it is cold.

'Are you in Miss Hastings' class?'

'Ja.'

'How do you like her?'

'She's okay. She's *lekker.*'

'Ja. When I was in Grade One, I thought she was *lekker.*'

'What grade are you in?'

'Grade Two. I've got Mrs Hendricks. I went to another school at the beginning of this year, but I didn't like it. I asked my parents if I could come back to Melpark. I just turned eight. How old are you?'

'I turned eight in February,' says Nkosi. 'My birthday's on the 4th.'

'So we're both eight,' says Eric, 'but you're older than me.'

'And you're bigger than me!' They laugh.

There doesn't seem anything more to say just at present, and in any case there's the bell.

'Well, I'll see you around,' says Eric, and starts running back across the field.

But the next day at the end of school, and often after that, Eric is waiting for him at the bottom gate, and they walk together as far as the corner.

In the July holidays, Nkosi's sister Mbali comes to stay for ten days. Nkosi feels shy about this, but when Mbali arrives he sees that she is even more shy than he is, even though she's nearly three years older.

He takes her hand when Granny Ruth has gone, and says: 'Come on, come and see my racing track.'

The big problem is that she doesn't speak English, so they can't really talk to each other. He tries to teach her to use a knife and fork, like he does, because she eats with her fingers in the traditional African way. She picks them up and has a go, but she looks very funny trying to do it, and they laugh a lot.

Nkosi, of course, had been taught to use a knife and fork from the time he arrived at Gail's. When she insisted on good table manners, Alan used to say: 'For fuck's sake, Gail, he's never going to get to Buckingham Palace.'

'Just because a child's got AIDS, you don't make allowances,' said Gail. 'I'm not going to be embarrassed by my son's table manners.'

In the room next door is the other Grade One class – the Blue Class. Both rooms look out onto the grassy playground where the roundabout and the climbing frame and the seesaw are. One break time during the third term, Nkosi is twirling slowly around the roundabout on his own. One of the Blue Class boys comes up to him. Nkosi hasn't seen him before – he must be new.

'Do you want to come and play with us?'

'What you playing?' asks Nkosi.

'Marbles.'

Nkosi doesn't have any marbles, but he'd like to watch them anyway. 'Okay.' He gets off the roundabout.

They join a little group crouched in a corner by the fence. They are all Blue Class boys. The game is that you have to throw your marble and try to hit the other guy's three, and if you hit them you get them.

Nkosi's new friend has his turn and gets a big one – a goon. 'Wow!' he says, 'Cool. Go on, Nkosi, you try.'

'I haven't any marbles.'

'I'll borrow you some of mine.'

He finds himself with three marbles in his hand. He throws, but misses. Throws again. And again.

'Shame,' says the guy, whose name turns out to be Aubrey Dube. 'You'll soon get better.'

After that he sees Aubrey often at break time and they play together. He discovers that Aubrey also lives in Melville. Mrs Dube works at night in a local steakhouse and she says that Nkosi can come and play at their place any time after school. Nkosi is thrilled. He's going to ask Gail if Aubrey can come to his house too.

'But we've got two big scary dogs,' he says.

'I'm not afraid of dogs,' says Aubrey.

'Of course he can come,' says Gail, 'but remember the rules. Uniform off and eat lunch before you start playing.'

On Mondays and Wednesdays they have Assembly first thing in the morning. Everybody has to file into the hall and stand in straight rows, grade by grade. Because he's in Grade One, Nkosi stands in the front. They have to keep to the white lines that are painted on the floor.

One particular Monday, Mr Badenhorst tells them about something called Mister and Miss Melpark. A lot of the bigger children begin to whisper among themselves. It seems that it's a bit like Miss South Africa, only it's just for the school and it's for the boys as well.

'It's to choose the ones who can present themselves the best,' Mr Badenhorst says, 'the ones who can be a credit to the school. Not necessarily the best-looking ones. And, of course, if somebody's got dirty shoes we're not going to choose him!'

There's a Mister and Miss Melpark Junior for the lower grades, and a Mister and Miss Melpark for the higher grades, so four people are going to get a chance. It will be in front of an audience of parents and friends, and there will be outside judges, maybe TV people and stuff.

'I'm gonna do it,' Nkosi decides, there and then. 'I'm gonna win it.' And all the time they are having the prayer he isn't really listening, and when one of the Grade Sevens does the reading out of the Bible he is seeing himself walking down the ramp, swinging his hips, showing off his jacket, pulling it out so's they can see the lining, turning around, smiling, just like he's seen on TV, walking back up and everybody clapping – the whole nine yards, as Nicci would say.

In the event, he didn't win it, but as Gail said to him afterwards when he was feeling really disappointed: 'Never mind, you gave someone else the chance to win.'

The 'someone else' was his friend Eric.

Nonhlanhla Daphne Nkosi, mother of Xolani Nkosi.

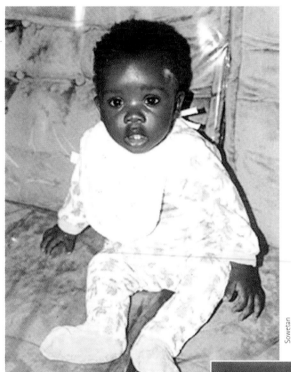

Sowetan

Xolani Nkosi at about seven months.

Nkosi at two and a half. Three months previously, he couldn't walk and was starving because he was unable to eat.

Femina (Giselle Wulfsohn)

Nkosi – the three-year-old toddler. Even at that age he had the ability to draw people to him.

'Look at me – swimming!' Nkosi enjoyed the sea every Christmas at Pennington.

His black scooter was five-year-old Nkosi's most treasured possession.

Nkosi with Tiger. Nkosi began learning the facts of life when Tiger's kittens were born.

'Wouldn't you rather have had a truck, Gail?' Another Christmas at Pennington.

Helping Daddy with the braai is a serious business. Seven-year-old Nkosi with Alan Johnson.

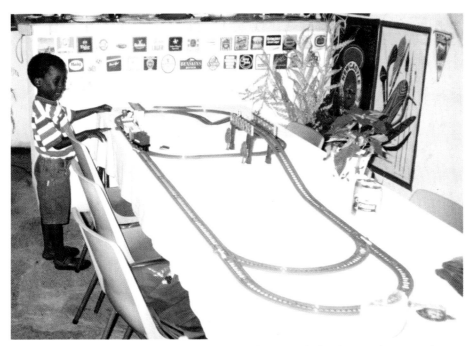

Alan's present to Nkosi for Christmas 1996. Everyone helped to set it up on the dining-table at Pennington.

Brett is home from Israel: late 1996. The family celebrate. Brett, Nkosi, Gail, Nicci.

February 1997: Brett's wedding. Best man Wilfred, Nira, Brett, Nicci. Nkosi in front in his cool tux.

Melpark Primary at night.

Nkosi Johnson   Grade 1 H

Nkosi's chalk drawing of Melpark Primary School at night which he did in Grade One. It still hangs in the school entrance hall.

Mister and Miss Melpark Junior 1998: Alicia Barnard and Nkosi. Behind stands Eric Nicholls, Nkosi's friend.

The opening of Nkosi's Haven: 14th April, 1999. Miss South Africa, Sonia Raciti, Nkosi and Miss Universe, Wendy Fitzwilliam of Trinidad and Tobago, pose in the garden.

Nkosi and Mommy Gail – 2000.

Sowetan (Makgotso Gulube)

April 1999 – Nkosi meets Madiba.

Nomonde Gongxeta, Nkosi and Sowetan Editor Aggrey Klaaste at the launch of National Youth Power against HIV/AIDS (NYPAHA) 23rd July, 1999.

Gail and Nkosi listen intently at the Durban World AIDS Conference, 12th July 2000.

Nkosi's Haven and Friends

NKOSIS HAVEN

Associated Press (Themba Hadebe)

20th November 2000 – Nkosi and actor Danny Glover at the gate of Nkosi's Haven. Danny Glover is the Goodwill Ambassador of the U.N. Development Programme (UNDP).

Eating pasta with Robin Williams in San Francisco, October 2000. Robin signed a copy of *Jumanji* for Nkosi.

Nkosi surrounded by some of the children of Nkosi's Haven (some faces have been blurred because the children's families could not be contacted for their consent). Top row: 15-year-old Elizabeth with her 2-year-old Joanna. 2nd row: Nkosi with baby Hope and to his left, baby Jo. Front row: Ismael, Tsfundo and Tsidiso. Guess which is their favourite movie!

Nkosi with headmaster Badie Badenhorst. His last day at school: December 2000.

In the Mayor's Parlor, San Francisco, October 2000. Gail, Nkosi and the Mayor of San Francisco, Willie Lewis Brown, Jr. The certificate celebrates 'Nkosi Johnson Day in San Francisco'. The Mayor is holding an embroidered panel made by the women of Nkosi's Haven which Nkosi and Gail have just given him.

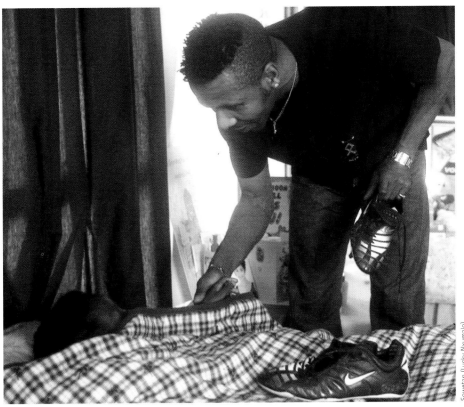

Sowetan (Lucky Nxumalo)

1st January 2001. Lucas Radebe, South African soccer star who captained top British club Leeds United, visits Nkosi and gives him his soccer boots. It is not certain whether or not Nkosi was aware of his visit; he had not spoken since 29th December.

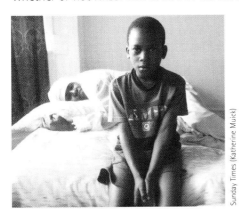

Sunday Times (Katherine Muick)

Feroza and her son Ismail. Nkosi felt very close to Feroza. She and he were able to support one another emotionally.

Sowetan (Lucky Nxumalo)

Kwaito musician, Mdu has committed himself to being a *chomi yabana*, children's friend. This was his second visit to Nkosi. He turned up one day unannounced with his wife to see if there was any improvement in Nkosi's condition.

2nd February 2001: Nkosi's 12th birth-day celebration at Melpark Primary School. He was too ill to be present. Granny Ruth Khumalo, DJ Fresh, Gail.

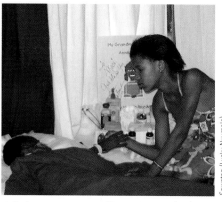

9th January 2001. Sister Mbali (16) at Nkosi's bedside. Sometimes he would squeeze her hand.

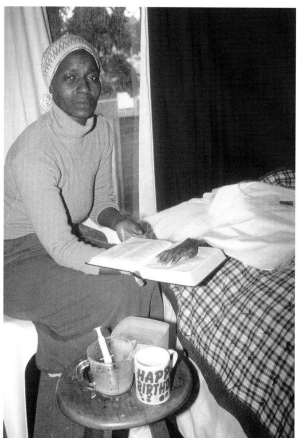

Grace sits at Nkosi's bedside with her Bible.

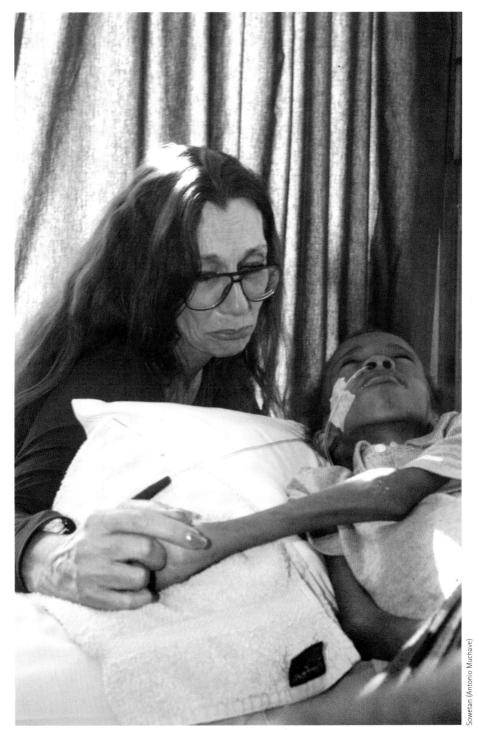

31st May 2001, Gail holds Nkosi's hand on the day before he died.

Sowetan (Antonio Muchave)

Granny Ruth Khumalo and Gail
light candles together at Nkosi's
Memorial Service, 6th June 2001.

Sowetan (Pat Seboko)

Former President of Zambia, Kenneth Kaunda,
comforts Gail after Nkosi's burial, 9th June
2001. Dr Kaunda also lost a child from AIDS.

Ayanda, one of the
orphans at Nkosi's
Haven with Oscar
Martin at the grave on
the occasion of the
commemorative stone
laying.

Chapter Six

THEN CAME 'THE Virodene affair.' This caused great excitement in the media and among the public. At last it seemed as though there had been a real breakthrough in the treatment of AIDS – a locally developed treatment, affordable and effective.

Gail discovered more about it when she was invited to a meeting by the AIDS Consortium to talk about Nkosi's problems with regard to getting into school. At this meeting the main speaker was an attorney who gave a presentation on Virodene. It sounded very hopeful, but Gail, among others, was concerned about the apparent lack of trial protocols and surprised that several high-profile members of government, including Deputy President Thabo Mbeki and Health Minister Zuma, championed it so quickly. She met the team who had pioneered it in Pretoria, and found them enthusiastic, eloquent and absolutely convinced of its value. But there was widespread doubt in many circles; the members of the Medicines Control Council (MCC) had misgivings concerning testing procedures, and they banned clinical trials. The drug was later found to contain an industrial solvent that was harmful to humans and the project was dropped.

As a result of all the publicity that surrounded Nkosi's getting into school, on World AIDS Day, 1 December, Radio Metro asked Nkosi and Gail and Mr Badenhorst to take part in a public phone-in programme at their studios. Nkosi was an instant success with the listeners; he was quite unselfconscious about being on air, and enjoyed himself very much talking to all the callers. It was the first sign of the instant rapport he was able to develop with the wider public.

Nicci and Vince and Nkosi are sitting in the lounge one afternoon when Gail comes in flourishing a newspaper.

'I've just read this stunning article! It says the police Child Protection Unit and Childline are opening up a safe house project for abandoned and abused kids. And what it is, is instead of them being removed from a bad home environment to an institution, they'd be moved first into a temporary home pending court cases etcetera etcetera. What do you think? Shall we sign up?'

'Slow down, Mom, slow down. Explain it properly.'

'It says this head of CPU, whoever, was once in his car over the weekend with a raped child, the rapist, and an abandoned baby. The only one he had accommodation for was the rapist because he could put him in a police cell. But Child Welfare and all the institutions close at 4.30 on a Friday and don't open again till Monday morning. And hospitals, because of the high level of abandonment, will only take in children who are physically damaged. So there's a need to train private individuals in their homes to take children in at short notice.'

Nicci and Vince look at each other. And then Nicci says: 'Look Mom, we know you're gonna do it anyway. Let's go for it.'

They had a family discussion about it first, in which Vince and Irene and Nkosi were included, because they would be very much involved in seeing that this whole project went smoothly. Luke Lamprecht of Childline came round to the house and explained to them how it worked, and then Gail and Nicci and Vince attended a course run by Childline. At the end of it, their house was registered as a safe house.

Over the years, many children found refuge with them. The first of these were two little blonde sisters, six and two, called Toni and Terri.[26]

The day before Gail is due to take the little girls for their physical check-up, Nicci comes to her mother with a worried face.

'Mom, when you take Toni to the Teddy Bears Clinic and they see a bruise on her bum, just tell them it happened here – she slipped on the bathroom floor.'

'Oh, okay.'

At supper that night, Terri tips out of her high chair and gets a lump like an egg on her head. Next morning, Toni comes running naked out of the bathroom. 'Terri's bleeding!'

Gail flies to look. She's chewing on a razor blade. 'Oh fuck,' says Gail.

At the Teddy Bears Clinic, she tells the doctor: 'The bruise on the bum, the lump on the head and the cut lip all happened at the safe house.'

It was the doctor's first encounter with Gail Johnson: he seemed to take it in his stride.

Most of the children who came to them had never been bathed in a built-in bath with running water before; at first they often screamed the place down, but they soon got used to it, and to life with the Johnsons. And just when they began to get a sense of belonging, off they had to go somewhere else.

It's January 1998 and it's the first day of the new school year.

'I've got to be there early today,' says Nkosi over his bowl of cereal. 'I can't wait for Irene. In any case, I'm not a baby. Can't I go by myself? Only the babies in Grade One have to come with a nanny.'

Gail is in bed, having her first coffee and smoke of the day. She looks at him over her specs.

''Kosi, you can go by yourself, but you've got to promise me you'll go straight there; you'll keep to the path, you won't talk to any strangers, you won't get into any cars, you won't accept any sweets.'

'No. You don't have to worry.'

'Come here and give me a hug.'

He does so, and two minutes later he's out of the gate and heading up the hill. It's a hot morning, and his bag is heavy. He ought to get one of those fancy ones with little wheels like the old ladies trundle around at the Spar shop. The guys at school would think it was a bit weird, though. He drops the bag and pauses for a rest.

Not for long though, he must get on. He wants to wait for Aubrey at the corner before school. They haven't seen each other since before Christmas and there's a lot to talk about. Why's this hill so steep? He hefts the bag again and starts off. Left, right, left, right. If he keeps his eyes on the path, suddenly there he will be at the end of the block without knowing. Last term he did it in six minutes flat, gate to gate. WHY'S this hill so steep?

Gail was not a 'morning person', so it fell to Nicci to make sure that Nkosi got himself up and ready for school, but it took him a very long time. So much so that sometimes he had no time for breakfast.

'But Gail,' said Irene on one such occasion, 'he would have been late for school.'

'I don't care. Let him get crapped on by his teachers – he's got to learn. Breakfast is an absolute must – especially for an infected child. He does not leave for school until he's had his breakfast – ever!'

In Grade Two, Nkosi's teacher is Mrs Serrao. It's a big change from Grade One. In the first place, they have to learn to do cursive writing. Mrs Serrao tells them to write with their fingers on the air, and it doesn't matter if they make mistakes because no one can see. And then they practise on their small blackboards, with chalk. When she lets them make the shapes of the letters with their own bodies they fall apart, laughing. Capital H, for instance, can only be done by two people, and they don't bend in enough places for W. Finally, they are allowed to write in their workbooks. Nkosi has one workbook which is only for handwriting.

He wants to use a pen, but Mrs Serrao won't hear of it. 'No pens till the end of Grade Three,' she says. 'Too many mistakes to rub out.'

The Maths they have to do in Grade Two is much more difficult. Now it's a case of having to add and subtract and multiply in double digits. It's okay when she lets them do it on the abacus or with beads, but when it comes to writing it down and working it out in his head, he can't seem to get it together so well.

There's a lot more sitting still and writing in Grade Two, so he's really glad when Mrs Serrao tells them a story and lets them act it out. They do Noah and the Ark and Joseph and his brothers and even Moses again, which he remembers from Grade One.

After break they put the chairs in little groups and read to each other out of the Beehive Readers. Nkosi enjoys the stories and can always relate them to Gail at the end of the day, but when it comes to reading word for word by himself he finds it very difficult. He also likes it when they do Comprehension – Mrs Serrao reads them a piece that has a word missing from it, and they have to guess what the word should be.

Sometimes they do Environmental Studies. One week it's all about Johannesburg. They look at pictures of people in the street – all different people just walking along – and Mrs Serrao says they are from different population groups. There's the biggest group, the black people, who could be Zulus or Xhosas or Tswanas or whatever (he himself, Nkosi knows, is a Zulu), and then there are the Asian group, who mostly come from India and China, and then there are the White group from Europe and the Coloured group who come from – well, he's not sure, but they are mixed in some way. All these different people live in Johannesburg and they speak different languages. Well, he knows that already. Yack, yack, yack on the playground, and he wishes sometimes he knew what they were saying.

And this starts him thinking.

Over supper, he will say to Gail: 'You and Rob and Nicci and Vince are all another Population Group.'

And she will make that little snort in her nose and say: 'Really, sweetheart, why did nobody ever tell me?'

One day Nkosi came home and said: 'Gail, guess what? I came second in a race today!'

'You WHAT?'

'Second last!'

Gail laughed. 'Well, I don't know who came last, then – must have been in a wheelchair!'

Other children didn't seem to think any the less of Nkosi because he wasn't good at sport. But when everyone is running and kicking balls around on the playing field and you can't really join in – it makes you feel isolated.

Gail had told him that if he ever had a problem with another child relating to his infection he should tell her at once and she would sort it out. All went well – until he had a bad dose of oral thrush, with cold sores on his mouth. He knew it didn't look very nice, and was left in no doubt when somebody said 'EEYUK!'.

So she kept him at home until the infection cleared up. He was not encouraged to feel sorry for himself, however. When he complained to her that somebody wouldn't play with him because he had AIDS, she suggested that it might be for quite another reason. 'But, sweetheart – maybe he just doesn't like you. I didn't play with everyone at school. You get to like different people. Maybe this guy's got other friends.'

The school was very good about letting Gail know if there was anything infectious like measles or chickenpox around, so that she could keep him at home. They were learning by direct experience how to handle children with HIV/AIDS.

During Nkosi's second term in Grade Two, Pauly came to stay with them under the safe house project. He was a four-month-old baby to whom the family became very attached, as he stayed longer than any of the others. Nkosi, now aged nine, took his position as 'elder brother' very seriously.

'No, Pauly,' he would say, 'If you want something off the table – don't just grab!'

When his friend Aubrey came to play, they would usually incorporate Pauly into their games when he got a bit bigger, and the three of them would be busy in Nkosi's room for hours with his boxes of toys. One day the Child Welfare people let them know that a prospective foster family had been found for Pauly, and that the mother would be telephoning Gail to make an appointment to visit him.

Mrs W. arrives with a friend and an assortment of children. Pauly is on the floor, playing with one of Nkosi's cars. Nkosi is on the sofa, watching the scene. The prospective mother tells Gail she bakes *koeksusters*[27] and sells them on street corners with her children.

One of them clamours for her attention and she says: 'All right, ask the Auntie if you can pick him up.'

'Auntie,' says the child to Gail, 'can I pick him up?'

'Go ahead,' says Gail.

The child goes to Pauly and hauls him into her arms. Pauly lets out a howl and the child puts him down. The mother does not seem to want to pick him up.

'Can we go in the yard and play with him?' asks the bigger child.

'I don't think so,' says Gail, 'better stay inside where I can see you.'

When the family had gone, Gail says to Nicci and Nkosi: 'I get the impression they want him just as a toy for the kids. Did you notice she wouldn't even pick him up?'

'He mustn't go there,' says Nkosi.

Nothing more was heard about that family for months.

The procedure with a safe house and the responsible care-giver is as follows: within the first ten days of a child's arrival, the court officially places the child in the custody of the care-giver. Every six weeks thereafter, the care-giver has to state, in court, that she is prepared to keep the child for a further six-week period. Ideally, the

child should only be in a safe house for a short period of time, to
prevent him from bonding too strongly with the family there, only
to be taken away again and placed with strangers. In the case of
child molestation or abuse, however, the period is often extended
beyond a few weeks, due to the child's enhanced need to be in a
stable, comforting environment while the investigative and judicial
process is being concluded.

That same year, 1998, Alan bought a house in Hermanus on the
Cape coast, and in the April school holidays he flew Nkosi, Nicci
and Vince down to stay for a few days. It was Nkosi's first flight
and his first visit to the Cape, and he was seeing his Dad for the
first time in quite a while, so on the way to the airport he was
almost too excited to talk.

When they get there he follows along behind Nicci and Vince while
they pile the luggage on a trolley and make their way through
hundreds of hurrying people. They stand around in a queue and
then hurry off again and at one moment he has to clutch onto
Vince's jacket because it seems he and Nicci will disappear in all
these crowds. Then suddenly they are on a bus, zooming along
behind a line of parked aircraft.

'I thought we were going to fly on a plane,' he says to Nicci,
sitting on her lap, swaying and jolting.

'We are,' she says. 'We've got to go on the bus to the plane. It's
too far to walk.'

'Wow,' says Nkosi.

The bus makes a sudden tight turn and stops. Everybody piles
out and then they are walking up a gangway into the plane. This is
the real stuff. A very smiling lady says hello at the doorway and
Nkosi would like to stop and talk to her, but Nicci gives him a little
push and they are struggling along a narrow aisle between rows of
high-backed seats. Everybody seems to have huge bags, which they

are trying to heave into the cupboards overhead. What happens if they fall out again? But Nicci is helping him into a seat next to the window. He sits down and she sits down next to him and clips a big belt across his middle.

'You have to keep that closed while we take off,' she says. 'It's for safety. Like the belt in Mom's Uno.'

He snaps it open and shut a couple of times to see how it works. The smiling lady stands up in front like a teacher and shows them how the oxygen mask works. And then puts on a life jacket, which you have to use when the plane falls into the sea.

'Can I try?' he says to Nicci, 'I want to practise.'

'No,' says Nicci. 'You aren't allowed to touch it until they tell you.'

Then suddenly the buildings begin sliding past them. 'Are we flying?'

'Sort of,' says Vince, 'but the wheels are still on the ground. We have to get up speed first.' He winks at Nkosi from the seat the other side of Nicci.

They roll along and roll along for ages and then they stop again. And then it's making the most terrible roaring noise.

'Here we go,' says Vince, and Nkosi sees that he and Nicci are holding each other's hands tightly. There's a big surge forward and they are rushing along, roaring and shaking, and he feels as though something is pressing him hard against the seat-back. And then it all calms down and the ground and the buildings and everything have disappeared. His ears feel very strange; he keeps feeling he needs to swallow. Everybody is smiling and snapping open their seatbelts and there is a man in a uniform leaning across and asking whether he'd like something to drink. He has a big trolley with bottles and things on it.

'Coke, please,' he decides, and Nicci shows him how to unfold a little table from the back of the seat in front. Nicci is also having a Coke, and Vince is drinking out of a can of Castle.

'Are we nearly there?'

''Kosi, we've only just started. It takes two hours. Like from the beginning of school to break,' says Nicci.

'I need to go to the toilet.'

'Come on,' says Vince.

They have to go right to the back of the plane, past all the people. Some are reading newspapers, some are asleep. A lot of the awake ones stare as Vince leads him past. The toilet is very, very small. When he is finished, he can't find the lever to flush. He calls through the half-open door to Vince.

'Leave it, I'll do it,' says Vince.

He doesn't wait for Vince, and goes back to his seat by himself. This time he smiles at some of the people, and every single one of them smiles back. Nicci's got her eyes closed.

'I don't feel too good,' she says as he squeezes past.

On the little table is a plastic box. 'What's this?'

'Lunch. Just eat it if you want it. You don't have to.'

Inside the box there's a container with stew and mashed potato and carrots and plastic forks and everything and another little round dish with trifle. Nkosi looks at Nicci. She's taking no notice at all so he decides to eat the trifle first. Halfway through, he feels very tired himself. He stares out of the window but can only see sky and it's white and boring. If he stands up and squints down he can see the earth but it's just sand-coloured and sort of misty. When he sits down there's only the back of the seat in front. He lies back and closes his eyes. He'll finish the stew when he wakes up.

In a moment, it seems, Nicci is leaning over him and closing his seatbelt. 'We're nearly there,' she says, 'We're beginning to go down.'

'Wow,' he says. The plane is tipping down towards a white shining mass beneath them. 'We're going to hit that cloud!'

'It's okay. We'll go through. You'll see.'

All the blue sky in the window turns to grey fog. And there's something wrong with the plane. It shivers and slips sideways and goes up and down. 'What's happening?'

'Just a bit of turbulence,' says Vince, 'Nothing to be afraid of. It's always like this in a cloud.' The plane seems to leap and sway about.

'The pilot can't see!' shouts Nkosi.

'He flies on his instruments,' says Vince. 'In a minute we'll be through.'

The fog outside thins, turns to flying wisps and then it's all sunshine again.

'Look, 'Kosi – the sea!' Nicci is leaning over him, looking out the window. 'And there's Table Mountain. There's the cable car! Look at the ships, 'Kosi!'

He looks, but before he has time to take everything in the plane is turning again and they have to sit back quietly as it skims along just above the houses and then a big green field.

Crash! Roarrrrrrrr! Nkosi grips the armrests of his seat for dear life. But everything seems to be all right. They're going much faster than they were going in the air. Poles, buildings, everything is rushing past. And then slower and slower and at last they stop. Snap-snap-snap, people are undoing their seatbelts, standing up, opening cupboards, pulling down luggage, shoving their way along the aisles. They have to wait for ages before it's their turn to move along and get out.

'Where's Daddy?'

'He'll be waiting inside the terminal.'

This time there's no need for a bus; the plane has parked right by the entrance. In they go, and there's a little wall with lots of people waiting on the other side.

'There's Dad!' shouts Nicci, and all at once they are hugging, and Daddy is lifting him up and saying 'Hello, Nkosi, howzit?'

Then they are in his Dad's car and driving out on a long road. Suddenly, Nkosi feels very sleepy. He yawns, and yawns again. He dozes off and then wakes to hear Nicci saying; 'What's that place?'

'It's the edge of Khayelitsha,' says Daddy.

They are driving past some terrible shacky-looking places. Not even shacks, some of them, just bits of corrugated iron and cardboard leaning together. 'They must be the poorest in the world,' says Nicci.

'Ja,' says Nkosi, 'shame.'

Soon, in the distance, they can see a line of mountains. 'The other side of those,' says Daddy, 'is the sea.'

It's a long drive through places with names like Rooi-Els and

Betty's Bay and Fisherhaven, and sometimes the road runs along beside the sea and sometimes it doesn't. When at last they get to Hermanus, Daddy's friend Desiree is waiting to welcome them at their house. All Nkosi wants to do is sleep.

'You've got a room all to yourself,' says Nicci. 'How's about that, 'Kos?' It doesn't have a bed in it, but there is a sleeper-couch, and that's okay.

For the next few days they are quite busy helping Daddy to paint the house. Firstly, they paint the room where Nicci and Vince sleep, yellow and green, and then they do his room blue. But Daddy also takes them down to the harbour so that they can look for whales. The first time they go Vince shouts that he can see some, but they are very far out, and all Nkosi can see are one or two black lumps heaving themselves up in the water. Once there's a big forked tail that suddenly rears up and waves in the air, but it's gone almost immediately.

'Wow! Did you see that, Nkosi?' says Daddy. 'It's the biggest animal in the world, did you know that?'

'Why isn't it called a fish, if it lives in the sea?'

'Fishes lay eggs. This has babies like the land animals.'

'Why don't they drown?'

'I reckon they're designed not to,' says Daddy.

The holiday seems to be over so quickly. Just five days and they are on the plane back to Johannesburg. This time, Nkosi feels like a seasoned traveller. Nevertheless, this journey is different. When they arrive, he can hardly wait to get into the terminal building. 'Gail! Gail! I went in the cockpit! I sat in the pilot's seat! I wore his cap – hey, Nicci? I was driving the plane!'

'Good heavens, darling, how did you manage that? The other passengers must have been *kakking* themselves!'

Nkosi has arrived home from school. He has taken off his uniform. He has had some lunch, sitting at the kitchen table (soup, with small bits of carrot and onion and some bread), he has been upstairs to say 'Hi' to Gail. She's on the phone as usual, but she blows him a kiss. He hangs around a while to see whether the conversation is interesting, but it's all about some meeting she's setting up so he has come back down the stairs and switched on the TV. Power Rangers. Cool. He settles down in the armchair with Fluffball. Two minutes later Gail is down the stairs.

''Kosi? Let's do some maths.'

'Now?'

'Of course now. You need lots of practice.'

He gets up slowly and drags his school bag out from his bedroom. Maths workbook. He follows her back up to the office and they settle down on the couch.

'All right, show me. What did you do today?'

'All these on this page.'

'All right. Did you understand?'

He shakes his head.

'What's the first one? Eight take away three. Okay, 'Kos, you can do that. Count on your fingers. Show me eight fingers.'

He counts and then holds them up.

'Okay, now take away three.'

He thinks about it and then puts one hand down.

'So what's left?'

'Five.'

'So write it down.'

He looks at the page and at the pencil in his hand. His eyes go past her shoulder to the screensaver patterns sliding across the monitor.

'You know the answer, 'Kos, it's five. So write it down. We went through this whole scenario yesterday for fuck's sake. And don't start crying at me. Go get the bullet shells.'

He brings a handful and they spread them out over the table. He sniffs and wipes the back of his hand across his nose.

'Okay. Give me five. And another three. How many have I got?'

He looks into her hand and counts. 'Eight.'

'And if you take the three away again, how many have you got? No – tell me without looking.'

'Er...'

'Well, what did I have first?'

'I don't know.'

'Of course you know. Christ, Nkosi, you're not a blithering idiot, so don't carry on like one. You can look at a car and know exactly what car it is – why can't you grasp the concept of numbers? Three fingers, three bullets, three Ferraris – it's all the same thing!'

He bends down to run his hand along the cat's tail as it brushes his legs.

'That's it. I'm not wasting my time helping a child who doesn't want to concentrate. I mean – *hello?*'

Thereafter, Nicci and sometimes Rob were the ones who helped with homework. As Gail says, they had far more patience. Also, once or twice, Nkosi's Uncle Fika. He was a student at the University of the Witwatersrand by that time, and came on a Friday when he had finished his classes.

'What's your problem at school?' he would say. 'Maths? Oh, that's simple. Come, bring your paper and I'll show you.'

Nicci also tried to help him with comprehension. She would read the beginning of a story: *'In a beautiful part of the country lived a little girl called Susie.* Now then, 'Kos, where did Susie live?'

But he could never grasp it. It was as though certain connecting links in his mind didn't work. Whether or not this was the effect of the virus no one seemed able to tell. He enjoyed school but again, possibly because of the virus, he was enthusiastic without being energetic. He wanted to learn, but didn't want to make an effort when things became difficult. He would perhaps have benefited from a remedial class, especially later in his school career when it became obvious that he was just not coping.

Sharon went to check on the kids. They were okay, playing in her bedroom. Funny how they always seemed to cluster round Nkosi, even though he wasn't doing anything special, even though he was the quietest of them all. She'd noticed it several times, whoever the children were. They seemed to need him to like them. Well, it wasn't surprising. He had only to walk into her kitchen and say 'Hello, Sharon,' for her day to lighten up, no matter how hectic it had been.

Today was fairly hectic because there were 'gazillions' of cousins and other friends around and the dads were making a *braai* outside.

When it was ready, one of the mothers went to call the children. She came back looking very upset and talked urgently to her husband. The children began to arrive in twos and threes and stood around looking awkward, some shamefaced, some scared.

'What's the problem?' said Sharon to the husband and wife.

'They've been doing inappropriate things in the bedroom.'

'Inappropriate things? What do you mean?'

'The black child must go home.'

'Nkosi? Why him?'

'Sharon – I've said it all along. You never know what you're letting yourself in for with one of them.'

'And he's sick. He's infected, Sharon. And they're playing those games in the bedroom.'

'Nkosi would never do anything "inappropriate" as you call it. It just isn't in him.'

'Well, we think he should go home.'

Sharon went to the telephone and dialled Gail's number.

'Gail Johnson.'

'Gail. Something's come up. And I don't know what to do.'

'What's come up?'

'Well, apparently the kids have been playing in the bedroom and it's you show me yours and I'll show you mine type of thing and some of Dom's relatives are feeling very uncomfortable. Look, I know it's not Nkosi, but... '

'That's fine. I'll come and collect him right now.'

She came, she took Nkosi, and they left.

Sharon picked up her glass of wine and went and sat on the stoep by herself. No way could she handle a *braai* with the others right now. Nkosi should not have gone home. He would never ever do something like that. Okay, Dominic's extended family still drew a certain line from the racial point of view, but in Dom's case Nkosi had turned that around – he'd turned it around without even talking about it. When he first started coming to stay, he would hug Sharon and Claire and Ross and Siobhan, but instinctively when it came to her husband he would shake his hand. By the end of a year, Dominic and he were hugging just like the others. Look at the way he was cool about Nkosi and Siobhan bathing together. That had been a major triumph. And never in all the years Nkosi's been visiting has she ever walked in and found him doing something with Siobhan he shouldn't be doing.

The next day, Gail phoned. 'It wasn't him, you know, Sharon, it was the oldest boy – the twelve-year-old. Nkosi took no part in it. He's told me and I know when he's telling the truth.'

'Of course it wasn't Nkosi, Gail, I knew that all along. I've been feeling terrible about sending him home. Can I have a word with him?'

'Of course.'

Nkosi says: 'Hello, Sharon?'

'Darling, I feel so bad that you had to go home last night. I want to apologise. I knew quite well it was nothing to do with you, but, well, those parents wouldn't see it.'

'It's all right, Sharon, don't worry. Some people are like that.'

One September evening Nkosi is busy in the kitchen feeding the cats while Gail makes the supper.

It seems to be taking him very long, much longer than usual, and any minute now Gail is going to make her usual crack about the cats being anorexic by the time they get their food. His hand, holding the fork, doesn't want to connect properly with the food in the tin, and he's having such difficulty breathing it's suddenly very scary. He drops the fork and the tin.

'What's the matter, 'Kos?'

'I can't... I can't... breathe...'

Suddenly she is there beside him, picking him up. She carries him through to the lounge and sits with him on the sofa.

'Am... am I letting you down, Gail?'

'With what, babes?' She's wiping the tears off his face.

'Because you've got to do the cats now.'

'What you should be saying to yourself is "I've been doing it for six years, thank fuck she's doing it and I can sit on my arse and watch television".'

Dr Steven Miller diagnosed pneumonia and wanted to admit Nkosi to hospital, but Gail said no, he'd never been away from home since he was two, and at home there were her and Nicci and Irene to take care of him and he'd be better off there.

Just walking to the bathroom exhausted him, he had no breath, so for four or five days he sat tight, either in bed or, when he felt up to it, in front of the television. Gradually his chest loosened up. In a few weeks he felt strong enough to go back to school.

Sometime during the third term, Mr Badenhorst announced the Mister and Miss Melpark Junior competition again. The previous year when Nkosi had gone in for it he'd only been in Grade One. Now it was different. He knew it all from A to Z now. This time he'd get it for sure.

When Nicci came home from school, he told her: 'I'm entering for Mr Melpark Junior again.'

'Okay, if you want to do it, let's do it. Have you got the entry form?'

She filled it in for him and the next day he took it and remembered to hand it in.

A few days later she's changing after school again and Nkosi's lying on his bed. 'It's Mr Melpark tonight,' he says.

'WHAT?' she yells 'So what you gonna do?'

He shrugs. 'I don't know.'

'Well, we better try to teach you something. Come on. What time's it start? Mom! It's 'Kosi's Mr Melpark tonight!'

'Fuck!' comes Gail's voice from upstairs in the office. 'You better practise. You've got less than three hours.'

'Right, 'Kos,' says Nicci, 'we'll do it here in the bedroom. Let's put on some music – here, this'll do, this has got a good beat. Now, you walk down the ramp, you strut your stuff, you do a bit of a pose, whatever, and you walk back. Go on, do it.'

He does, and she claps. 'Okay, now do it again. More of an attitude. That's it. You got it.'

'They're going to ask me questions,' he says.

'Okay, well, they'll ask you, I don't know, something easy like what are you going to do when you grow up. Doesn't matter what they ask, just talk so's they can hear you. Try it again.'

It looks good.

'Now, go in the lounge and we'll call Mom down and show her.'

'Right,' says Gail. 'Let's see. Not too quick. Give them time to take you in. Don't smile till you get to the end of the ramp, and then give them the works. That's it. Stunning!'

He has a bath, and Nicci puts some deodorant on him and some of Vince's cologne. He puts on his favourite jeans and *tackies*[28] and sweatshirt, and off he goes to school.

'We'll be there later,' Nicci assures him, 'we'll be there cheering for you.'

The hall is already packed when they get there. First on the programme are the entrants for Miss Melpark Junior, and the little girls do their stuff most professionally, some shy, some not at all. The judges write busily. Then it is the turn of the boys; the seniors will come later.

When Nkosi does his act, the audience loves him: everyone claps and laughs – he really has exactly the right cheeky, charming attitude.

'He's gonna win, I know it,' says Nicci to Vince.

And when they announce that Mr Melpark Junior this year is – NKOSI JOHNSON – everybody stamps and cheers.

He gets a trophy and a big sash with Mr Melpark Junior on it and a red-and-grey school bag nearly as big as himself, with a pencil case and chips and sweets. A little blonde girl with a face like a flower wins the Miss Melpark Junior.

Afterwards, coming out of the hall with all the rest of the crowd, Nkosi says 'I'm hungry!' In all the excitement, nobody had thought about supper.

'Okay,' says Nicci, 'Vince and I will go and get takeaways. You choose, 'Kosi – it's your night!'

In October 1998, the Medical Schemes Amendment Bill was tabled. This prohibited medical schemes from excluding people with HIV/AIDS. Gail decided, however, not to have Nkosi included on the scheme to which they belonged, mainly because it would have made the premiums too expensive.

It is raining. It's been raining all night and most of the morning, and the children eat their sandwiches crowded into the covered walkways instead of on the playgrounds. It's Tuesday so there are hot dogs on sale and Nkosi decides he will get one. Hot dogs are his second-best – not quite as good as pizza, which is on Fridays.

Aubrey nudges him and says: 'We're going to get wet going back to your place.'

Aubrey has been in the same class as Nkosi since the beginning of Grade Two, and their friendship has flourished.

Nkosi looks out at the dripping jungle gym, the sodden jacaranda tree dipping its branches low, so heavy with the wet, and says: 'We'll go in my room and play with the Formula One cars.'

This thought keeps them warm all the rest of the morning in spite of the rain now throwing itself against the windows, and when the last bell rings they pack up their books and hurry down to the bottom gate with their jackets over their heads.

'I can drink the rain!' shouts Aubrey, opening his mouth and tipping his head back. Nkosi does it too, and feels it cold on his face.

'Come on, we'd better hurry. Gail's gonna kill me if I get sick again.'

Off they go down the hill, and it's not long before they are peeling off their wet jackets and settling themselves at the kitchen table for instant noodles and rolls.

'You not playing outside today,' says Irene, clearing the plates away. 'You want apples?'

'We'll take them with,' says Nkosi. 'We're going to set up the Scalextrics.'

Kelly, the old German Shepherd, is lying in the passage. Aubrey nearly falls over her.

'She can't see,' says Nkosi. 'The vet says she's got cataracts in her eyes. Gail says we have to put her to sleep but Nicci doesn't want to.'

'Shame,' says Aubrey.

(Although Nicci understood really that it was the kindest thing to do, she was inconsolable when they finally had Kelly put down. She wrote in Gail's diary on 28 November: *Kelly died today with her blood on your hands.'*)

In the bedroom, they have to lay out the track between the two beds. It's quite easy to fit it together and to get the two cars going. The trouble is that they only have a single track, so unless the first car goes too fast or bashes into something and falls off, the other car has to stay behind all the time. But it's fun, and indeed there are enough terrible accidents to keep them happy most of the afternoon. More than once Gail has to shriek from upstairs that she can't hear herself think because Aubrey is yelling so loudly.

On a Friday afternoon in November, seven months after Pauly's arrival, Child Welfare telephoned Gail and said they were just letting her know about the procedure for the following day.

'What procedure?'

'Paul is being placed tomorrow.'

'Are you telling me that Pauly will not be sleeping in my house tomorrow night?'

'Yes.'

'Like fuck! How dare you let me know only twenty-four hours in advance? I will not hand over a child to a total stranger. Who is he going to?'   ·

'Mrs. W.'

'The last time I saw that woman was in April, and you want me to give Pauly over to her tomorrow?'

'Yes.'

'I'll see you in court.'

Already, Nkosi was howling his eyes out in the kitchen. 'Pauly mustn't go to that family, Gail – he mustn't.'

'Don't shit yourself, 'Kos, he won't if I can help it.'

Gail telephoned the Child Care Commissioner, and said she would not bring Paul to court, she did not care whether she was had up for contempt. She would not release him, she said, because for the child's sake there had to be a slow handing over. The prospective family could visit, could bath and feed the child in her house and get to know him. But he was not going to be ripped out of her home without warning.

So she went to court and sat there with the social worker and the welfare supervisor and the prospective mother Mrs W., and the supervisor said: 'Where's Paul?'

'I didn't bring him,' said Gail.

'Why?'

'Because I don't believe what you are doing is right.'

'But we always do it like this.'

'I beg your pardon? A child can be with a family for seven months and you just take it away?'

'Yes.'

In court, the Commissioner asked if Gail was prepared to have Paul for another six weeks and she said yes, and that Mrs W. could visit at any time to get to know the child. The Commissioner stipulated one supervised visit per week with the social worker.

Not once did Mrs W. turn up.

So the Welfare people finally agreed that this was not a suitable family for Pauly to go to, and they also agreed that it had not been the right way to go about it.

In the end, Pauly was placed with Denise who popped round and bathed him and fed him and really got to know him. Gail, Nicci and Nkosi still found it difficult to give him up but they knew he'd be all right with Denise. Gail and her family have stayed in contact with him ever since.

Among the other children who came to Gail's safe house was a big six-year-old who would shoulder Nkosi out of the way, even though Nkosi was the elder and permanent member of the family. After that experience they decided to take only considerably younger children.

The government gives an allowance of R11 per day for each child in care. This is the equivalent of two cups of coffee in a restaurant. At any time of the day or night, Gail may get a call from the Child Protection Unit to say that they are bringing a baby in half an hour, and out must come the folding cot, the blankets and the bottles.

There could be confusion. Sergeant X might call to say they are bringing a six-month-old baby girl found abandoned in Alexandra township. It arrives sopping wet and they change its nappy, only to find it's a much younger baby boy. A Form Four must come with the baby because if there isn't, it means he hasn't been documented and could get lost in the system and be stuck at the safe house for ever. Babies without a Form Four get a change of nappy and a bottle and are sent straight back to the police station.

During December, Gail's PR company, Gale Force Promotions, was contracted to sell the corporate tickets for the annual AIDS Benefit Concert put on by the South African Artists Fight AIDS group. These actors and musicians give their time free to rehearse and perform at the concert each year

The 1998 concert was held in the Johannesburg Civic Theatre and Gail and Nkosi went to the show. At the end, all the members of the cast danced on stage around Yvonne Chaka Chaka, the star, and Nkosi was up there also, boogieing with the best of them.

Also in December, the National Association of People Living with AIDS (NAPWA) launched the Treatment Action Campaign. The short-term goal of this campaign was to pressure the government and the pharmaceutical companies into giving anti-retroviral therapy and formula feed free to pregnant mothers for the prevention of mother-to-child transmission (MTCT) of the HI-virus.

'This would mean that babies wouldn't get born with AIDS, hey, Gail?'

'That's right, darling. At least, it would very much reduce the likelihood. It's effective in about 50% of cases.'

'So why aren't they doing it?'

'Well, the government says it's too expensive. It's not just the drug itself, it's having enough money to formula feed the babies afterwards, and to pay for people to be trained to counsel the mothers. It's no good if they get the prevention *muti* and then they breastfeed, because the babies could get infected all over again.'

'But why hasn't the government got enough money? They've got all the country's money.'

'Because they've got a lot of important things they have to spend it on.'

'What's more important than saving the babies?'

In the Christmas holidays, it was decided that Nicci and Nkosi and Vince should again go down to Hermanus to Alan and Desiree. Nicci had just written her matric exam, and reckoned she deserved a good holiday. There was a big crowd: Desiree's mother, her daughter Leanne and her husband and two little boys, Desiree's sister Marilyn with her boy Darren, and her friend Margaret with her son Marcel. As Alan said, it was wall-to-wall mattresses in the dining room, where the five little boys slept. Leanne and her husband camped in the garden, as did Nicci and Vince, who had taken their tent.

This was the year that the huge theme park Ratanga Junction opened on the outskirts of Cape Town, so they decided to go and check it out.

Nkosi went on the Ferris Wheel and took a miniature train ride with Vince, but when he saw the enormous snaking roller coaster called The Cobra and heard the screams, he decided to let Vincent do that one on his own. He and Nicci and Marilyn and Margaret and Marcel and Darren all watched and waited for Vince to fall out, but of course he came back safely to the starting point.

'Was it scary?' asked Nicci.

'It was scary,' said Vince.

Most days Alan took them to the beach in his car, and they played games and had a picnic lunch and went in the sea and came out and lay down on the towels to get a tan.

'You're so lucky, 'Kos,' said Nicci. 'You don't have to try.'

Nkosi had water wings and an inflatable belt, just to be on the safe side, but he never went in very far, just splashed about in the surf. After all the fresh air and sunshine, he simply could not keep awake in the evenings. He would nod off in front of the TV and they had to carry him to bed.

An elderly lady in the local newsagent was a great fan of Nkosi's. All she could see of him over the counter, she said, was a pair of huge eyes. 'I always try to find some little thing to give him,' she told Alan.

At the beginning of 1999, Nkosi is promoted to Grade Three.

This seems to be a big jump up from last year. In the first place, he's in a classroom upstairs now, not down near the jungle gym with the babies. Mrs Pitchers is his new class teacher. She has the sort of voice you have to listen to.

'Are you allowed to talk?' she asks, and everyone answers: 'No, Ma'am.'

He and Aubrey sit together quite near the front, facing the blackboard.

'How many children left home without having breakfast this morning?' demands Mrs Pitchers.

What a funny question. The children look at each other and one or two giggle.

'Come on! I want to know.'

Several hands go up.

'All right. A lot of you live in Soweto, right? What time do you leave? Five-thirty? Six?' They nod. 'Well, I don't have time to eat breakfast either. But I can grab four dry Pro-Vita biscuits and eat them on the road. And you can grab a slice of bread and eat it while you're waiting for the bus. There's no such thing as no time to eat. Nobody said you've got to sit down and have fried eggs and bacon and a bowl of cereal and yogurt. As long as you put something in your tummies. Make a sandwich the night before and eat it on the journey. You're old enough now to be responsible.'

Responsible. That's a word Gail often uses. 'You have to be responsible for yourself, 'Kosi, as an infected person.' 'We've got to be responsible for these children, 'Kosi – *someone* has to look after them.'

Outside, through the small high windows on the right, he can see the red-tiled roof and the funny little tower on top of the old school building. It's like they're up in the sky here, much brighter than the classrooms downstairs. Some pigeons alight on the tower and start stalking each other, all puffed out. A brown one, a white one and two grey ones. He nudges Aubrey and points. 'They're mating,' says Aubrey. 'Shall we go back to your place after school?'

'Okay. And listen – Gail told me to ask you if you can come to Carnival City tomorrow. It's my birthday and we're going to have clowns and hot dogs and everything. I'm going to ask some of the others as well. Maybe – '

'Aubrey Dube and Nkosi Johnson! Excuse me for interrupting your conversation. The rest of us are doing Maths.'

When Nkosi arrived home from school one day in March, he found that the police had brought a tiny baby they called Mickey, who had been abandoned in Yeoville, one of Jo'burg's inner suburbs. The cop who brought him said 'There's a bit of a problem when he tries to drink.'

There was. Two sips and he was already choking. At one o'clock in the morning Gail rushed him through to Coronation Hospital because he was dehydrating badly. There he was diagnosed as having full-blown AIDS. They brought him home again, and Gail and Nicci and Nkosi tried their best.

'You have him on your lap, Nkosi, while I get on with the cooking,' said Gail. 'Try feeding him some more. If he chokes, sit him up straight.'

Nkosi and Nicci took turns trying to give Mickey his bottle, but he could take so little at a time, he never got enough food to keep him going. Gail had him in her room at night and got hardly any sleep. By the following weekend, he was suffering badly from diarrhoea and again dehydrated, so they took him back to hospital.

Gail telephoned Welfare and said she just could not keep him – he needed specialised care, perhaps in a hospice. Eventually he was taken to Chris Hani Baragwanath Hospital, where he soon died.

They were all very sad. They had loved little 'Squeak', as they called him. He couldn't even cry, his lungs were so infected; he could only squeak faintly. But he never stood a chance.

Chapter
Seven

HIV-POSITIVE MOTHERS and babies should be able to stay together, thought Gail. A sick baby needs its mother, a sick mother does not need the added stress of wondering whether her child is being properly cared for. There should be homes where mothers and babies could live together, where mothers could be trained and counselled in how to cope with their disease and look after their HIV-positive babies; where they would be given proper food and be made to feel safe in their environment. New mothers would learn from their sisters already in residence, and maybe the idea would spread and grow in all directions through the country. Gail began to talk.

The project was first publicised back in 1997 when she enlisted the support of the Rotary Club of Sandown and UNAIDS. A site in Muldersdrift, northwest of Johannesburg, was decided on at first, and together they chose a name – Nkosi's Haven. But the deal fell through. Then in November 1998 a friend of a friend, over dinner one evening, offered Gail a house in Berea, a shabby, once genteel suburb, very close to the centre of the city. He said she could have it rent-free for five years. It had become very difficult to sell houses and flats profitably in Berea by then; together with neighbouring Hillbrow, it was the first area to become 'grey' when blacks and whites at last began living in an integrated way. Whites – those who could afford to – moved out into more distant suburbs, more and more blacks came in from the townships and occupied the vacant buildings, and Hillbrow and Berea became the haunts of street children and the unemployed. Though shabby, the area was full of life.

Number 23 Mitchell Street was an old house by Johannesburg standards, built between the two world wars, a double-storey with a walled garden, overlooked by blocks of flats. There were four bedrooms upstairs, one bathroom upstairs and one downstairs; there was a big lounge in the middle of the house downstairs and another big room that could be used as a dormitory; there was a courtyard surrounded by outbuildings. They could put swings and a jungle gym in the garden. There were lots of possibilities.

Gail talked about it to Shaun O'Shea, director of AIDSLINK. AIDSLINK was a well-established NGO whose main aim was to support destitute people living with HIV/AIDS. It provided counselling, food, clothing and financial grants, and started support and empowerment projects such as Thandanani, a women's craft group. It was instrumental in raising funds to open a number of care centres in the early 1990s. It had raised funds for The Guest House in 1990 through one of its very first benefit concerts, and it was then that Gail had first met Shaun. It had also helped with the cost of Nkosi's medication when Gail was struggling financially. Now Shaun said to Gail: 'Why don't you become a director of AIDSLINK, and we can get Nkosi's Haven going?'

As well as organising repairs and renovations to the house, they needed to get furniture, appliances, cutlery, crockery, blankets and so on. All Gail's experience and expertise as a public relations consultant swung into top gear. She decided to hold a kitchen tea with a difference at 23 Mitchell Street during March 1999. They drew up a 'wish list', publicised it in the media and invited everybody they could think of who might be interested in contributing.

At the tea, she told the guests that applications for residence had already exceeded the house's capacity.

'We have room for nine mothers and their children so far,' she said, 'when we get larger premises we'll take more. Eventually, we hope to open up more shelters – this is just the beginning. Women must have an alternative to silence and rejection. I'm starting

Nkosi's Haven because of Nkosi. He was separated from his Mum because she was sick and couldn't afford to keep him. I feel very strongly that the health status of the mother shouldn't mean separation from her children.'

She went on to explain that Nkosi's Haven would offer a kibbutz style of living. Everyone would look after everyone else; they would all take their turn at cooking and cleaning and caring for the kids. There would also be AIDS counselling for the mothers; this was essential if they were to cope emotionally with the stress of the disease. She estimated that running costs, to start with, would be about R28 000 a month.

The kitchen tea yielded wonderful results. Among other donors, a casino/entertainment complex gave R45,000-worth of discounted furniture and equipment to Nkosi's Haven; a bookshop collected a thousand second-hand books, an office equipment firm donated R30 000 to equip the children's dormitory and nursery, and an electrical company gave their services free of charge.

Oscar Martin, one of the AIDSLINK employees, was given the task of helping Gail with administration. Sandra Dismore, who ran the Thandanani project, helped out by painting walls, sorting through clothing donations. and helping to make the home ready for the opening ceremony.

The Mission Statement of Nkosi's Haven is as follows: '*Our dream is to establish care centres for HIV/AIDS mothers and their children (infected or not) to ensure that they are able to live in an environment of acceptance and understanding. Here they will learn to care for themselves and their children and cope effectively with the new challenges that HIV/AIDS will present to them.*'

Friday. End of the school week. Nkosi walks down the hill, kicking a pebble as he goes. When it's a good kick it goes straight in front of him, but most of the time it skids off to the side so he has to zig-zag and it's rather tiring. When it flies into the road he gives it up. He's just about there anyway. Duke's nose is poked through the bars of the gate and he gives it a scratch of greeting. He rings the bell twice. Irene comes to the doorway and presses the remote to open the gate.

In the dining room he drops his bag. Thump. He listens. Gail's voice, upstairs in the office. A deep voice, answering. Oscar. He goes through to his and Nicci's room, sits down on the bed and then slowly lets himself topple over until he is lying flat, gazing at the ceiling. Irene is in the doorway. 'Lunch is ready, 'Kos.'

'What is it?'

'Some nice potato salad and tuna.'

'Okay.'

He rolls off the bed. He changes out of his school uniform and then hears Gail's voice from upstairs.

'Hello 'Kosi? How are you?'

He mounts the stairs. There they are, Gail at her computer, Oscar going through a heap of files on the other desk. 'I'm fine. I'm going to have my lunch.'

'Come and talk to us when you've finished.'

Fluffball jumps up on the table while he's eating.

'No, Fluff, you can't lick the butter.' He pushes it out of reach and the cat licks its backside instead. When he's finished lunch he goes to the fridge and takes out the box of white wine. He fetches a glass and carefully fills it from the little tap. Then he takes it upstairs.

'I've brought you a glass of wine,' he says to Gail.

She looks at the clock. 'It's a bit early for me to start, but seeing it's you, I'll have it.'

'Not for me,' says Oscar, 'I'll go straight to sleep.'

Nkosi settles himself on the couch. 'Oscar,' he says, 'what's the Immorality Act?'

Oscar and Gail look at each other. Gail's doing that funny thing down her nose, which means she's suppressing a laugh.

'Well, you see, Nkosi, it's very simple,' says Oscar. 'There were three Acts – the Group Areas Act, the Group Separation Act and the Immorality Act. The Group Areas Act meant that we could sleep together but we couldn't stay together, the Group Separation Act meant that we could work together but we couldn't sit together, and the Immorality Act meant we could stay together but we couldn't sleep together.'

Nkosi gazes at him. Is he being funny? His face is dead serious. Gail is snorting down her nose again.

'I don't understand,' he says.

'Nkosi, I'll tell you all over again. I'm a black person and I work with a white person. Under the Separation Act we couldn't share the same office. And under the Immorality Act we couldn't share the same bed. And under the Group Areas Act we could share the same office and the same bed but we couldn't live in the same town. Get it?'

'Yes,' says Nkosi, but it all sounds mad to him.

Brought up as he had been in the way of white South African children, there was much about black culture that puzzled him, and Oscar, himself a one-time freedom fighter, became his mentor for such things. Also, Oscar was a powerful advocate for Gail and his support of her was proof of her credibility in the wider black community.

Before the house at 23 Mitchell Street was ready, Oscar worked in Gail's office in Melville and he and Nkosi would sometimes have lunch together and sit talking beside the pool.

'Are you married, Oscar?'

'Me? No, I'm not married.'

'How come you have a son if you're not married?'

'Well...' Oscar gazes up into the bignonia flowers, seeking inspiration. 'I'm old enough to be a father.'

'What happened to his mother?'

'Nkosi – it's like when you go and choose a puppy. People give you the puppy because you are responsible enough to look after it. You don't take the mother as well. The only difference is a child isn't a puppy. But because they know you are capable of looking after it, they give it to you.'

'Is that like my mother and father?'

'Do you know all about that?'

Nkosi looks up at him. 'Yes. I've discussed it with Gail.'

'Exactly like that, then. People fall in love and then, as time goes on, they get tired of each other and take their separate ways.'

'Is that right or wrong?'

'It isn't right and it isn't wrong. As long as there's someone looking after the child – or the puppy, for that matter. What's wrong is to dump the child.'

'Like Pauly?'

Oscar breathes again. For a moment he thought Nkosi was going to say 'Like me?'

'Exactly like Pauly. We don't all have mothers who care, like you and me.'

On 14 April, there was a grand opening at Nkosi's Haven. No fewer than three beauty queens were present: Miss Universe, Wendy Fitzwilliam from Trinidad and Tobago, the reigning Miss South Africa, Sonia Raciti, and Kerishnie Naicker, Miss South Africa in 1998.

When she became Miss Universe, Wendy committed herself to joining the fight against AIDS in Africa. She opened Nkosi's Haven, visited Thandanani (the craft group run by AIDSLINK), took part in patient visits at the Johannesburg Hospital (arranged by the Reach for a Dream Foundation), and attended a fashion show where four designer garments were auctioned in aid of Nkosi's Haven.

They had also invited various people from the City of Johannesburg AIDS programmes, community-based organisations and local government to the opening.

The opening ceremony and lunch took place in the garden. Shaun O'Shea welcomed everybody on behalf of AIDSLINK and thanked everyone who had contributed to the project. By now, there was an impressive list of donors. He added that this home was just the beginning, and that in a couple of years, when they really started seeing the effects of HIV/AIDS on the destitute, there would be a dire shortage of accommodation and care facilities. He invited Nkosi, Wendy Fitzwilliam and the MD of Carnival City, which had made the magnificent donation of equipment, to cut the ribbon Sandra Dismore had strung across the entrance, and the media cameras flashed. Everyone drank pineapple punch and started in on the lunch. Nkosi was very interested in Wendy's tough-looking bodyguards. They showed him their two-way radios and let him have a go.

After lunch, Oscar, now installed in the house as Administrative Manager, retired to his office for a little peace and quiet. He had eaten well, he had drunk well. The phone rang.

'Hello?'

'President Mandela's office here, Pillay speaking. The President regrets that he will be unable to see Miss Universe and Gail and Nkosi Johnson as requested. Please convey his apologies to them.'

'Oh,' said Oscar, made perhaps less discreet by the punch, and thinking moreover that the conversation was over, 'it's only the three most beautiful women in the world who are here. Who is Madiba[29] anyway?' And he replaced his receiver.

Twenty minutes later the phone rang again.

'The President will see Miss Universe and the other visitors for a few minutes at four o'clock.'

'Thank you very much,' Oscar was careful to say this time, and then he leaned back in his chair and laughed.

He went outside and called everyone's attention, and told them that the President would see them that afternoon.

This expedition had been arranged by Diane Stevens, an African-American businesswoman who had approached Gail through AIDSLINK, as she wanted to make a connection with a South African AIDS organisation to help raise funds. She, together with Shaun and Gail, had invited Wendy Fitzwilliam over from Trinidad to do some fund-raising. So Nkosi, Gail, Wendy, Shaun O'Shea, Diane Stevens and her associates drove off at great speed down the M1 to the presidential residence in Pretoria.

They arrive, only to find that the President is not there. He will be coming soon, they are told, by helicopter. In the meanwhile, they are shown into a very grand reception room.

'Where's he gone?' Nkosi wants to know. 'Do you think he's having lunch with some friends? Does he always go by helicopter? Much quicker than a car.'

'No,' says Shaun, 'he's out campaigning.'

They wait and they wait, and at last the door is flung open and there is Madiba, tall and smiling. He looks tired, and his shoes are dusty. But he shakes hands with everyone and talks like he knows them. When he comes to Nkosi he says: 'And what would you like to be when you grow up, young man?'

'I don't know,' says Nkosi.

'Don't you want to be President?'

Nkosi looks at him, hesitates and then says: 'No, it looks too much like hard work.'

He's worried, at first, that it might have sounded rude, but everyone packs up laughing, especially Madiba. And then he says: 'Let's all go outside for a photograph,'

So out they all go into the garden and line up in a row. The President stands in the middle and beckons Nkosi to stand in front of him. Nkosi can feel his hands, warm on his shoulders. Click, click, go the cameras, and then they can stop smiling.

Gail tells one of the bodyguards that she has brought her copy of Mr Mandela's book *Long Walk to Freedom*. She asks whether he might perhaps sign it for her. Madiba overhears this and does it straight away.

And then the visit is over.

In the car on the way home, Nkosi says: 'What did he write in your book?'

Gail opens it and reads it aloud.

"To Gail Johnson and Nkosi,' she reads, 'Best wishes to a lady who cares and to a very brave young man. N. Mandela.'

'That's quite something, hey?' says Nkosi.

Monday morning, and it's back to school for Nkosi after all the excitement of the weekend. He thinks perhaps it's going to feel rather flat, but Mrs Pitchers has a surprise for them.

When they have settled down in the classroom she says: 'Now we're going to learn all about what happens to water when it gets very hot. And the easiest way to do this is by boiling a kettle. Who has seen a kettle boiling?'

Hands are waving and everybody is shouting: 'Me! Me!'

'And what happens when a kettle boils?'

'We have tea,' says some joker, and they all fall apart.

'We have tea, but what happens to the water before we pour it out?'

'It bubbles?' says Nkosi.

'It bubbles, and something else happens too.'

'Steam comes out?'

'Exactly. Some of the water turns to... ?'

'STEAM!' they all shout.

'And what happens when your Mum puts the potatoes on to boil and forgets about them?'

'They get burnt.'

'Right. And they get burnt because all the water has turned to...'

'STEAM!'

'Right. And we call that process evaporation. Can you guess where we're all going to see some evaporation? Into the kitchen. One group at a time.'

She settles the class with worksheets and takes the first group to the kitchen, where the urn is simmering, giving off little puffs of steam.

'Now, I'm going to hold this dry sponge over the steam, and we'll watch what happens.'

Nkosi stands on tiptoe to watch. Slowly, the sponge is getting darker.

'Now, you must all imagine that this sponge is a cloud, and all the water in the urn is the sea. The sea is evaporating all the time because the sun is shining on it and heating it up. We don't call it steam, because you can't see it. We call it vapour.'

As they watch, the sponge begins to drip a little.

'Now, our cloud gets blown along till it's over the land.' Mrs Pitchers moves the sponge away from the urn. 'It rises and gets a bit cold, so what happens to the vapour?'

No one seems very sure.

'If making water hot turns it to vapour, what does making vapour cold do?'

One of the girls thinks she knows. 'Turns it back into sea?'

Mrs Pitchers squeezes the sponge gently, and small drops fall. 'What is it called when drops fall out of clouds?'

'Rain! Rain!' they all shout.

After school, Aubrey and Nkosi are walking slowly along the road beside the wire fence skirting the playing field. Some of the Grade Sevens are practising soccer. Aubrey and Nkosi stop to watch.

'D'you wish you could play?' asks Aubrey.

'Nah. Maybe when I was in Grade One.'

'Did you see the Orlando Pirates match on Saturday?'

'Ja. But I like Kaizer Chiefs best.'[30]

'I keep telling you. They're a rubbish team.'

'Bet you next time they play Chiefs win hands down.'

'Let's go to the Spar.' Aubrey is feeling in his pocket for change. 'You got any money?'

'No,' says Nkosi, 'I got a pie today.'

'Well, I got enough for chips, or shall we get sweets?'

'Maybe the Auntie will give us for free.'

'You ask her. Tell her Gail will pay next time.'

'She won't. She'll kill me.'

They loiter outside the Spar shop for a while, looking at the advertisements for cut-price goods.

'How come they never offer anything anyone really wants for cheaper?' complains Aubrey. 'Like it's always Omo or mealie-meal or floor polish.'

'Ja,' says Nkosi. 'Let's tell them to do Coke or chocolate. Bar Ones. I bet they'd have people queueing up for Bar Ones.'

'Magnums,' says Aubrey.

'Let's get some Coke anyway.'

'It's my money, I'm gonna choose,' says Aubrey.

'So what you gonna choose?'

'Coke,' says Aubrey.

Inside the shop there are cards of plastic whistles and hairclips on a stand by the tills. And lower down a row of penknives, held in place by elastic bands.

'I'd like one of those,' says Nkosi, fingering a green one.

'Well, ask the Auntie. She gave you a plastic scooter once, didn't she?'

'It's not the same one.'

'I'm gonna get a penknife on my birthday,' says Aubrey. 'No, on Christmas. But a better one than this. A Swiss army knife. It costs hundreds. What's your Dad gonna give you?'

'Dunno,' says Nkosi. 'A computer, or something like that. He's in Hermanus. Maybe we'll go there for the holidays. If we don't go to Pennington.'

'Where's Hermanus?'

'By the sea. You get waves this big.' Nkosi holds his hand high above his head. 'And whales. Lots of them. We saw hundreds last time.'

'Let's go and play chess at my place,' says Aubrey.

'I can't play.'

'I'll teach you. It's easy.'

'Okay.'

Gail is driving back from Nkosi's Haven through the rush-hour traffic. She is hot, she is tired, she is nearly out of petrol and she's dying for a cup of coffee. She pulls up in the driveway. Irene, calling from the door.

'Gail, Nkosi hasn't come home from school.'

'What? What's the time?'

'Mmm – something to five.'

'Christ. You start walking up to the school, I'll phone them, if anyone's there to phone.'

'I already went up there.'

'Well, go again. And go around all the roads.'

The secretary, just about to leave, says no, there are no children left on the premises.

Gail puts on the kettle, spoons coffee into the mug. Three spoons of plain, one spoon of decaffeinated. When were those girls abducted? And the paedophile committed suicide? Stupid to jump the gun like that. He's out, stealing sweets at some shop. She gulps the coffee. What's his teacher's name? Pitchers? Is she in the phone book? It's not only girls they molest, it's boys too. She should know. She's been a police reservist for six years. When he comes home she's going to kill him.

The game of chess at Aubrey's house has degenerated into a sort of checkers. Aubrey has become impatient with Nkosi, who can't remember how the knights jump and makes his behave as though they are queens. They push the pieces around and knock each other out and then Aubrey says 'Let's see if there's any cake.'

'Are you allowed to?'

'Sure.'

'Listen. I must phone home. Tell them I'll be late.'

'We haven't got a phone.'

'What's the time?'

'Ten past five.'

'I gotta go.' He is struggling into the straps of his school bag. Gail is going to be furious.

Aubrey comes down the steps of the block of flats with him. 'See you tomorrow, hey?'

'Ja.'

'Bye.'

It's one of those times, like in a dream, when you know you've got to hurry but your legs just won't do it. When he turns the corner into Fourth Street and sees the Uno in the driveway he wants to turn tail and run – anywhere but home.

Inside the house Irene says: 'Your Mummy's very cross with you.'

He goes slowly up the stairs to her office.

'Where have you been?'

Her face looks like a stone face.

'I... I've been playing with Aubrey.'

'Why didn't you phone and tell us where you were?'

'He hasn't got a phone.'

'Why didn't you phone from a call box?'

'We tried, we really did, but it wasn't working.'

'What time does school come out?'

'Half-past one.'

'And it is now half-past five. In four hours, you could have come past the house a dozen times and told us where you were. And don't tell me lies about phones not working. You know I can't stand lies. You can have your supper by yourself in the kitchen. I don't want to see your face. It's no use crying, I'm not interested.'

Later, when he is going to bed, she says: 'Nkosi – you never, ever, come home late without letting us know where you are. In the first place, you ask whether you can go; in the second place, you tell us where you are going, even if it's one of the mothers taking you; and in the third place, I want to know what time you'll be back. Understand?'

'Yes. I'm sorry, Gail.'

One day Nkosi said: 'Gail, can I call you Mommy?'

'Of course you can, sweetheart. You can call me what you want – except fucking bitch.'

'I wouldn't say that, Mommy.'

'I know.'

His reluctance to use swear words was amazing, considering the language he heard in that house. If he had to relate a story with one of 'those words' in it, he'd squirm with embarrassment. When he was a very small child, the lights fused one evening and Gail was scurrying about saying 'Fuck... fuck...' Nkosi trailed after her saying 'Don't *say* that, Gail, don't *say* that!'

Gail makes no apology. 'My kids have to fit in with me, not me with them.'

There had been another incident, also involving Aubrey, some while previously. Gail had received a frantic phone call from Mrs Dube. Where was Aubrey? Nkosi had gone to Siobhan's sleep-over birthday party at Sharon and Dominic's house. Gail telephoned them to find out if he knew anything.

'Oh,' said Sharon, 'yes, Aubrey's here. He's invited himself along. We were all surprised when he pitched up.'

Afterwards, Gail said to Nkosi: 'Was it your idea that Aubrey

should go to the party? You can't do that, Nkosi. Just because he's
your friend doesn't mean he's Siobhan's friend. His mother's been
out of her mind.'

It was about this time that Nkosi acquired a proper bicycle. A friend
of Gail and Rob's had a child's bicycle that was not being used, and
passed it on to them for Nkosi.

There's not much room in the garden for practising, but Rob holds
it steady and he gets on. Eventually his feet find the pedals and he
pushes.

'Don't let go!'

'Don't worry, I won't. You just worry about your feet. And steer.'

Slowly they go round and round on the grass. Every time Rob
lets go, the bicycle falls sideways.

'Why does it keep falling? Don't let go!'

'Don't worry, 'Kos, it's just a question of practice. You'll be doing
it one day and suddenly you'll find you can ride.'

Nkosi starts again. And again.

'No, I can't do it. It's too hard.'

'Yes, you can,' says Nicci. 'It's easy. Just keep practising.'

But anything that required sustained effort was hard for Nkosi,
and he never mastered the trick of remaining upright on his
bicycle.

In his bag he's got the new Pokemon card. At break he shows it to
Emmanuel and Charlie.

'Wow, that's beautiful. Don't you want to swop? I'll give you two
of mine.' Emmanuel's voice is husky.

'I'm not swopping.'

'Aw, come on, Nkosi. I'll give you three of mine just for this one.'

'Uh-uh.' He sips his hot chocolate, swinging his legs.

'I'm gonna play soccer down the big field,' says Charlie. 'You coming, Emmanuel?'

Emmanuel shakes his head, riffling through his cards again and again. 'Tell you what – I'll give you six of mine – just for this one.'

'Uh-uh. This one is from overseas. It's valuable. I love it.'

It's bigger than all the others and it's shiny on both sides. Yesterday Aubrey had offered him ten of his and he had still said no. Slowly but finally he puts it away in his bag.

'Okay,' says Emmanuel, 'do you want to come and play?'

'I'll just watch for a bit,' says Nkosi.

There is a mystery about the Pokemon cards, however. Some of Nkosi's school friends were later to insist that he had lots of them and loved them. If so, he must have kept them at school and never taken them home, because his family never saw them. Aubrey was later to say that Nkosi had had several boxes of them but they were stolen from his bag one day.

It is seven o'clock. Outside it is dark and Nkosi and Nicci have been sitting together on the sofa watching TV. As the ads come on, Nicci says: 'Cats, 'Kosi.'

He gets up and goes to the kitchen. Fluff and Ginger and Gizmo and Smudget are already winding round his legs, expectant, miaowing. On the shelf there are no tins of catfood. Again. Gail is going to go crazy. It's his job to warn her when the food is running out and last time he forgot it was also when the shops were closed and there had been a major scene. When there's no catfood, there's no catfood. He moves all the other tins around to make sure. He goes back into the lounge and sits with Nicci.

'That was quick,' she says. But *Isidingo*[31] is on and she doesn't say any more.

In a little while, Gail comes down from the office and goes into the kitchen. Nkosi can hear her talking to Emily, the new maid who had replaced Irene. (Gail had fired Irene, eventually, for constantly taking too much time off during working hours). Soon she is in the doorway.

'Why aren't the cats fed?'

'I reminded him,' says Nicci.

'There's no catfood,' he says, very quietly.

'WHAT?' shouts Gail.

'Sorry,' he says.

'Say that again.'

He's already beginning to cry. 'There's no catfood,' he sobs. 'I'm sorry, Mommy.'

'Sorry doesn't feed the fucking cats. How many times have we had this scene, Nkosi? Jesus Christ. There's such a thing as responsibility and this is your responsibility. You know that. All you've got to do is tell me when you're down to the last three tins. NOT when it's all finished. I'm not going out again. In any case, Spar's closed.'

'I'm sorry, Mommy.'

'Don't keep saying that! Listen, 'Kosi. You've got to remember. You are ten years old – I mean – *hello?*'

'Can't we, like, make a chart?' suggests Nicci, 'make a tick or whatever when he starts a new tin?'

'I don't care what you do,' says Gail, 'as long as you remember to warn me in time, not when it's too late.'

'Go and get your crayons and a sheet of paper from Mom's office, and we'll make a chart,' says Nicci.

This is better. Quickly, he goes for his school bag.

'Say Mom gets fourteen tins at a time,' says Nicci, 'that'll last x number of days. Put a big X on the last one, and when you see the cross tell Mom it's time to get more.'

'Not the last one,' says Gail. 'Shit, then it'll be the same story all over again. No. You'll have to number all the tins and put a cross against tin number twelve. And when he sees the cross he tells me.'

'He'll have to use them in the proper order,' says Nicci.

'We'll use stickers. Can I stick them on?' says Nkosi.

'Yes,' says Gail, 'but, darling, you've got to remember to tick off on the chart every time you start a new tin, okay?'

Next day, there are fourteen tins of catfood among the groceries. Gail has also bought him some stickers.

'One on each tin, 'Kosi, and then you can write the numbers.'

So on the lid of every tin he puts a sticker, taking care to get it in the middle, and then he gives each one a number – one to fourteen. They are all arranged on the shelf in numerical order and the chart is stuck up on the kitchen wall. Nicci gets a pink koki and puts a cross on the chart against No. 12. She looks sternly at him.

'All you've got to do is, when you get to No. 12, tell Mommy. Easy-peasy.'

But it wasn't. Next time Nkosi got to tin 12 something interesting happened or he was in a hurry to get back to the TV or whatever, and he threw the lid away without noticing that it was tin 12. So two days later Gail was even angrier. They tried everything. 'Leave the tin on the table,' they said. 'And when Emily sees it she'll tell Gail to get more.'

But he never did. According to Nicci, he remembered to tell Gail to get more catfood before it ran out only about four times. It just wasn't the sort of thing he was good at.

Coming out of the school gate, he sees a familiar car parked at the kerb. Sharon, waiting for Rosemary, the little girl who lives with her now and is also going to Melpark Primary. As he comes level with the car, Sharon winds down her window.

'Nkosi!'

'Hello, Sharon – you waiting for Rosemary?'

'Ja – she's never where she's supposed to be.'

'Shall I go and find her?'

'No. Come and sit in the car and talk to me for a minute.'

He gets in and smiles up at her. 'How are you, Sharon?'

'Oh, you know, full of the usual dramas.'

'How's Claire? Is she going to cope?'

'How do you mean, 'Kos?'

'With this baby. Gail said she's pregnant. She's going to make a marvellous mother.'

'Oh yes, 'Kos, she'll cope all right.'

'Hope so. Give her my love. I miss you all.'

'Well, we miss you. We really do.' Nkosi doesn't say anything and she turns to look at him more closely. 'What's the matter? Are you crying, 'Kos?'

He nods, sniffs and wipes his eyes with the back of his hand.

'So tell me what's the matter.'

'Gail doesn't like me.'

'Don't be silly. Of course she likes you.'

'She doesn't like me 'cos she's always so cross with me now.'

'What do you mean she's always so cross with you?'

'I don't remember the catfood and she gets cross.'

'You know she's going to be cross about that, 'Kosi, and it doesn't mean she doesn't like you.'

'I wish she would stop shouting at me.'

'Well, mothers always get cross with their children. Sometimes we have to shout.'

When Rosemary arrives he gets out of the car regretfully, waves goodbye and sets off for home. It's sad that Gail and Sharon aren't talking to each other any more. They've had some sort of quarrel. He doesn't know why it's happened, but Sharon never comes around any more, and he doesn't go and stay with them either. Feels like he's lost part of his family. It was with Sharon and her kids that he went to the zoo, on picnics, to their Gran's farm and so on. He really misses all that. Most of all, he misses them. Of course, Siobhan could be difficult, but that was okay. As he once said to Sharon, kids of her age were often difficult.

When Nkosi gets home he's in trouble again. Bad trouble. Gail's been out shopping and is in the kitchen putting it all away.

'Kosi? Remember that five rand I couldn't find this morning?'

'Ja.'

'Did you take it?'

'Nnh-nnh.'

'You sure?'

'Ja.'

'Don't lie to me, Nkosi. Emily told me she saw you taking it.'

There's nothing he can say.

'I cannot tolerate lying, 'Kosi. You know that. I'm not an arsehole, so don't treat me like one. Be honest and I'll crap on you for the thing you've done – but lie about it and you'll be in even more trouble. And being dishonest with money is the worst.'

One of the new residents at Nkosi's Haven was Grace. She had been married for fourteen years and lived with her husband and ten-year-old son, Mpho, in Orlando West, Soweto. Her husband was a sickly man and went for regular check-ups to the hospital. He had been diagnosed as having TB, he told Grace.

In 1998 she herself started to develop unpleasant symptoms. She had thrush, she had sores on her body, she lost her appetite. She spoke about it to her mother. Her mother told her it was because she needed to have another child, so she stopped taking contraceptives. Very soon she fell pregnant, but the symptoms persisted. At the hospital clinic they advised her to have an HIV test. She thought it was unnecessary, but she agreed, because the doctor was insistent. It was positive.

'But I have no boyfriend,' she protested. 'There's only ever been my husband! No! I don't want counselling. I don't want anything. I want to go and talk to my husband.'

When she got home and confronted him, all he said was: 'I'm sorry. How could I tell you I had AIDS?'

His condition deteriorated, and so did hers. He told her to lock the door, to let no one in. She gave birth prematurely, and her baby was born with sores in his mouth, and a bad cough.

'God!' she cried, 'Why? What did I do?'

Her baby was still very young when her husband died. His family came and accused her: 'You are sick. You killed him. You've both got AIDS. You should both die.'

Grace went to the police who said they could not protect her all the time. His father, his sister, his brothers – at any time they could come. She took her two children, she left the house, and went to sleep like a vagrant in Joubert Park. She had no money left for medication, no money even for food or renting another place. Every day she tramped the streets, going into shops and asking for work.

For three weeks she slept in doorways, holding baby Thabiso close, hugging Mpho against her side.

Then Thabiso became very sick. In despair, she went to the hospital and sat in Outpatients. The sister there said: 'What's wrong?'

Grace said: 'I'm sick and the little one is sick. I need a job to get money for medicine.'

The sister looked at her thoughtfully and then said: 'I'll phone someone who might help you.'

The 'someone' was Gail Johnson.

In June 1999, Grace became a resident of Nkosi's Haven.

'This woman, Gail,' Grace was later to say, 'is feeding my children, is sending my son to school. We have a place to stay. I'll do anything for her. I'll cook, I'll clean. I told her I'd look after Nkosi for her if she wanted to go out. He became my child too. I fed him and he slept with me in my room.'

All the other mothers who came to live there had similar stories of rejection by their families, of fear and abandonment and near starvation. Elizabeth (who was only thirteen and had a baby of six months), Sibongile, Eunice, Samantha, Feroza, Zodwa and many others owed their continued survival to Nkosi's Haven.

Oscar Martin was to say later that it was not only the good food and shelter that contributed to the long survival of most of the residents. It was the peace of mind.

'This is the only place where they feel welcome. Here they can sit down and talk to each other and no one keeps reminding them of their status. They feel more welcome than they did in their family homes... and when they have problems, we listen to them.'

'Don't any of them have families to look after them, Gail?' asks Nkosi.

'No, darling, That's the whole problem. Their families don't understand about AIDS. So all the mothers have been rejected, and of course their babies too. We have to find a way of making everyone understand that there's nothing to fear.'

'So I was lucky.'

'You were lucky because your Mommy found a way of giving you a good home when her community rejected her. So it's because of you that we're giving some others the chance.'

'That's why it's called "Nkosi's Haven" – hey?'

It is the beginning of break time. Badie Badenhorst is about to get up and go and have some coffee in the staffroom when there is a knock on the door. The child who enters has a troubled face.

'What's wrong, Nkosi?'

'Can I have my painting back?'

'Which one's that, my boy?

'The one on the wall outside.'

In Grade One, Nkosi had done a painting of Melpark Primary School at night. It was a beautiful, atmospheric picture of buildings with lit-up windows against a black background. Badie had taken it to hang on the wall outside his office.

'Now, Nkosi, why do you want it back?'

'I want to sell it and buy Gail a present.'

Badie sits back in his chair. 'I can't give it to you to sell, Nkosi, because you gave it to me and I want it to stay in my family.'

'Okay.' Nkosi is about to go and then stops just inside the door and rubs one foot against the other leg.

'Come here.'

He goes around the desk and Badie encloses him in his arm. 'Now what's wrong?'

'I'm hungry.'

'Hungry? Don't you have any lunch?'

Nkosi shakes his head and scrapes the edge of the desk with his thumbnail.

'Did they forget to give you lunch?'

Nkosi nods. His eyes are big and tragic.

'Well, I'll tell you what. I'll give you a bit of change and you can go and get yourself a pizza at the *lapha*[32]. Okay?'

The face isn't troubled any more. It is shining and grateful. He's off, clutching his coins, careful to shut the door quietly. A lot of kids would let it bang. Badie smiles to himself as he goes through to the staffroom.

Next morning in the Johnson household Emily comes to Gail. She holds out a limp parcel of sandwiches in clingwrap.

'What's this? Where did you find it?'

'Under 'Kosi's bed.'

When Nkosi gets home, Gail is waiting for him.

'Did you enjoy your sandwiches yesterday, Nkosi?'

He looks at her, opens his mouth and shuts it again.

'Yes, you'd better not say anything. If there's one thing I can't stand, it's lying. If I find bananas that are ready to walk out of your case and sandwiches hidden under your bed so the mice think it's Christmas – why should I make lunch for you? Why should I? I'm not prepared to provide food that's wasted. So tomorrow you'll go without. End of story.'

The next day, Nkosi is in Badie's office with a long face again. Badie chuckles, reaches into his pocket and pulls out some coins. He reckons that Nkosi is probably up to something but, well, what's the harm? He's a special kid and needs a bit of TLC. And Nkosi is off to get pizza for the second time that week.

Badie did not know that although pizza was Nkosi's favourite food, it was also the worst thing for his diarrhoea, which was troubling him more and more. He was sometimes even caught short before he could get to the lavatory.

Nkosi loved the afternoon soaps on TV: *Loving, Days of our Lives, The Bold and the Beautiful*. He would watch them, curled up on the couch in the TV room, Duke collapsed on the floor beside him. As soon as Gail got home, he would try to fill her in on the latest episodes. Unfortunately, he could never remember the names of the characters. He would trail around the house after her as she unpacked the shopping, opened the mail and had her coffee.

'...and the one with the brown hair, you know, Mommy, the one that's married to the dark man, well, she was kissing the other one – not that one, but the other one who's got the girlfriend with the white hair, you know Mommy, that one. And she's going to have a baby, no, she was in labour all the week and she hasn't had it yet, she's lying in the hospital and the dark man, you know the other dark man, not that one, he... And Mommy, now there's going to be trouble because the other one just came along the passage and saw that one waiting outside her room – not that same one like last time, but the one who...'

By this time Gail has had her coffee and is lighting up her fourth cigarette and it's time to start getting the supper.

The family agreed that certain TV programmes would be sacrosanct. No one interrupted Gail when she was watching the news, *NYPD Blue, Murder One* and other American cop series.

Gail's bath time was her time to relax. In theory, anyway. Usually, one or other member of the family would perch on the lavatory and chat; often Nkosi would bring her a glass of wine to enjoy while she lay back in the warm water, and would recount the latest joke he'd heard at school. He'd tell it very slowly, with many giggles – and then forget the punchline. When they watched movies, such as *Panic Mechanic,* he'd be beside himself. He would see something funny coming and start shrieking with laughter.

He also loved *Gladiators* (Shadow was his favourite), the Sunday morning cartoons, and the cricket, especially when Jonty Rhodes, his favourite player, was in the team. Over and over again, they would watch *101 Dalmatians* and *The Lion King,* which they had on video.

During the July 1999 holidays, Granny Ruth came to fetch Nkosi for a visit with her and Mbali and his aunts and uncles at her place in Daveyton.

When he came back he told Gail: 'They killed a chicken on the grass outside the house. I saw it. They cut off its head and then they started pulling its feathers off. They said would I like to do it and it was still kicking! I didn't want to pull off the feathers and I didn't want to eat it afterwards!'

'Sweetheart – this nice chicken we have here all wrapped in plastic has been through exactly the same, I promise you. They have to pull out the feathers because they taste fucking awful.'

Two months later, in September 1999, Butiza Mlambo of the family in Diepkloof married Nonhlanhla Dlamini from Newcastle. Butiza was brother to Billy and Mavis and Busi, and there were to be big celebrations in Diepkloof. Again, Granny Ruth came to fetch Nkosi from Gail's.

'Do you want to go?' Gail had asked the night before, when she was kissing him goodnight. 'You don't have to, you know.'

'It's only that you don't like it when I go there.'

' 'Kosi, I don't object to your seeing your family. What I object to is that you always come back sick as a dog. God knows what you pick up there. Just remember to take your medicine, that's all.'

'I will, Mommy, I always remember. I hope they don't kill any chickens.'

Already on Saturday morning when he got there the place was buzzing. Thabo and Thabang, Busi's eight-year-old twins, grabbed him and they went off to play with the others. Later they brought a cow into the yard. 'It's specially for the wedding,' said Busi. 'Poor people have to use a goat or even a chicken, but a cow is better.'

'What is it for?' said Nkosi.

'We're going to eat it, of course,' said Busi.

'But it's not dead!'

Busi laughs. 'We slaughter it in a special way and then we cook it.'

'You're going to kill it? Right now? Here?'

'Of course. We always do that at weddings. It's traditional. But you don't have to look. You can go inside.'

'No, I want to look. I want to see what happens.'

'Come and help,' says Billy, 'then you'll know what to do.'

'How you gonna kill it?'

'With a knife. We cut its neck.'

'No. I'm not doing it. Yuk!'

When Fika arrived later, Nkosi ran to him and said: 'They slaughtered a cow. It was absolutely gruesome!'

Fika laughs and rubs his head. 'It's OK. You'll get used to it.'

'Uncle, when they get married, they're going to do love stuff, hey.'

'Sure.'

'What's it like? I mean, I know what they do and all that, but what's it like?'

'You wait and see.'

'I saw Nicci and Vince. They said they were tickling. They were under the blankets.'

'Well, that's not your business. When you grow up you'll know.'

'When I grow up I want to be a policeman.'

'You! A policeman! You're so small, the *tsotsis* will run off with you, not the other way round!'

Nkosi has a solemn conversation with one of his girl cousins, just turned nineteen. She is going out with a lot of boyfriends. Her name is Mbali, the same as his sister's.

'You must only have one boyfriend, Mbali,' he says. 'It's very dangerous to sleep around, you know. And you must tell him to use a condom.'

Mbali thinks it's very funny, to be told by a ten-year-old how to conduct her sex life, as though he is an old granny, and the story goes all round the family. It is not considered correct, in African culture, to confront an older person as an equal, so Nkosi's habit of talking straight to everybody surprises them all.

When it is almost time to go home again, Nkosi says: 'I wish I could join you guys. You have fun here. When are you getting married, Fika?'

'It's all right for you,' says Fika, 'you're a white guy. When I get married I've got to pay *lobola*.'[33]

If it was really Nkosi's wish to join his black family, however, he never voiced it to his foster family or to Oscar, with whom he spent long hours discussing things he would talk about to no one else.

At some time during that visit to Soweto, the family began talking about a proposed trip to Newcastle at Christmas time. They would all go to Daphne's grave, they said, at which time a mandatory cleansing ritual would be performed. It was suggested that Nkosi should go too, and apparently he said that he would like to.

He came home to Melville after this visit and said to Gail: 'Mommy, Granny asked me to go to Mommy Daphne's grave with them at Christmas. Can I go?'

'Cool, sweetheart. If you want to.'

But she doubted whether he really wanted to go. Over Christmas? She didn't think it would be his cup of tea at all. There certainly wouldn't be thirty presents under the tree in Newcastle. However, nothing more was said on the matter until mid-November. Then Nicci came to her.

'Mommy, he doesn't want to go to Newcastle. He doesn't want to tell you because he knows you'll hit the roof.'

'I knew this was going to happen. I knew it. Now I'm going to be in shit with the family. They'll think it's me stopping him. Why doesn't he want to go?'

'He says it's because the other kids call him Whitey.'

'Well, he knew that before. All right, I'd better let them know.'

She faxed Dudu and explained that Nkosi wouldn't be coming with them. But she also wrote that she would be happy to bring Nkosi to meet Ruth in Newcastle over the Christmas holiday when they were driving down to Pennington, and they could perhaps all visit the grave then.

She said to Nkosi: 'When you commit yourself to something, you commit. You don't back out of it afterwards. When they get this fax, they're going to blame me for the whole thing.'

Dudu telephoned and spoke to Nkosi. Gail heard him say: 'It wasn't Mommy – it was me.'

She took the phone from him and said: 'You know, Dudu, I would never stop him from visiting his family or his mother's grave. It was his decision.'

It was a special ritual in Newcastle that they were planning. Known as a 'cleansing', it involved the slaughter of a goat and the use of certain parts of it to ritually cleanse the deceased's children and other members of the family. Maybe Nkosi had agreed to go in the first place just to please his township family, knowing that he didn't really want to. Maybe he really did want to while he was with them, but when he got home and realised that he would be missing the holiday at the sea and other Christmas excitements, he changed his mind. Whatever the reason for his change of heart, he felt he had let them down, and caused a lot of ill-feeling between them and Gail, too. Again, he was caught in the middle.

It was from then on that his physical condition began markedly to deteriorate. Infected people are always made much worse by mental stress, and from that time onwards Nkosi began to experience the chronic diarrhoea and tiredness that were never to leave him.

Gail said: 'You've got to sort this out in your mind, 'Kos, because I reckon 50% of your diarrhoea is your guilt pulling you down. When you are stressed, darling, it always makes the sickness worse.'

Warwick Allan suggested that it might help if he were to visualise what would happen if he visited his mother's grave.

'Just think of yourself holding Granny's hand, 'Kos, and going up the little koppie – what would you see?'

But he didn't seem able to reconstruct the scene in his mind. He didn't have that sort of imagination.

In a video film called *Nkosi's Mission,* which Inigo Gilmore started making of the Johnsons at the end of 1999, Gail narrates a commentary that includes the following: 'He's lost his black culture, but he's a hell of a lot more comfortable in a white culture. Maybe he misses his black culture, but he's never asked for it. To me, it's more of an issue that he's clothed and fed and given proper medication.'

And in the same film, Nkosi says: 'I would like to be able to speak Zulu so I could talk to my friends. Sometimes black people speak to me on the street in a black language and I don't know how to talk back to them. I have to say: "No, I only talk English." I feel embarrassed with myself.'

'Look at this!' says Gail. 'President Mbeki's[34] questioning the link between HIV and AIDS. That's going to cause shit.'

'How do you mean, Mom?' says Nicci.

'They're all using condoms to prevent the spread of HIV because they've been told it causes AIDS. Now, if they're told there's doubt, they're going to stop using the condoms. It's already hard enough to persuade people to use them.'

'Maybe they won't listen.'

'Like fuck! It's what a lot of people want to hear. If the president says it – you believe him.'

'Mom – can we have our own separate rooms now? It's a horrible thing to say, but I can't handle it when 'Kos messes his bed.'

Gail puts the newspaper down.

'Sure, babes, Nkosi can move into Brett's old room.'

When Nkosi was told about this, he wanted to know why.

'Basically, 'Kos,' said Nicci, 'you're getting older and I'm getting older and it's nice to have our own rooms, don't you think? Ja. And you can spread out your racing track, there's lots of room – it'll be much better.'

'Is it because you don't like it when I have diarrhoea?'

Nicci puts her arm round him and sits him down on the bed. 'You mustn't be embarrassed about the diarrhoea, 'Kos. Everybody knows you can't help it.'

'But I am embarrassed.'

'We're family, 'Kos. In the family nobody has to be embarrassed. It's like talking to Mom when she's in the bath. Everybody does that. We're family.'

'What's that about Mom's bath?' asks Gail, appearing in the doorway.

'I'm telling him he doesn't have to be embarrassed about the diarrhoea,' says Nicci.

'I think you'll be cross with me because of the mess.'

' 'Kos, you get up, you strip your bed down – you know how to do that – and you take the sheets through to the bathroom and you put them in the bucket,' says Gail.

'Don't ever worry about it, 'Kos,' says Nicci. 'Just clean up every time like it's a normal thing.'

It wasn't so bad when it happened at home, but at school it was the pits, even though Badie was so nice to him about it. And he had to wear nappies like he was a stupid baby.

Melpark Primary School had always taken care to allow Nkosi to be 'just one of the children'. Once the media excitement surrounding his arrival at school had died down, no further fuss was made until the National Policy on HIV/AIDS for Learners and Educators was finally launched by the Minister of Education. This was the result of several years of consultation between NGOs, the South African Law Commission and the Department of Education. The media, of course, remembered that it had been sparked off in the first place by the controversy surrounding Nkosi's attempts to go to school two years earlier, at the beginning of 1997.

So it was cameras all over the place again and Nkosi Johnson's name was back in the news, particularly around World AIDS Day on 1 December. This was a problem for him, for his teacher, and for the other children in his class. Although he was the centre of attention, he was probably the least thrown by all this as he had never been camera shy, nor was he the sort of child who liked showing off. A serious, calm, relaxed little boy, is how his teachers remember him, someone who could interact with other people but who never imposed himself on them.

Now, suddenly, all the children wanted to be his 'best friend'. Here was a chance to be on TV, photographed standing next to the famous Nkosi Johnson. It was very difficult for Mrs Pitchers to maintain discipline when this was happening, and it seemed to be happening nearly every week: SABC TV, ITV from London, other TV companies from Holland and as far afield as Japan.

All this had the further result that other children became quite protective towards Nkosi. 'Shall I help you down the steps, Nkosi?' 'Shall I carry your bag?' 'Do you want me to get you something from the tuckshop?' Some of this was genuine, but a lot was to do with the media hype.

On the way home one day, a car draws up beside him.

'Uh-oh,' he thinks, and stops.

A man puts his head out. 'Am I speaking to the famous Nkosi Johnson?'

Nkosi admits cautiously that he is.

'Can I give you a lift home? That bag looks heavy.'

Now here is the situation that Gail has been warning about since for ever. Nkosi wonders how to say no politely.

'It's all right,' says the man. 'I'm Paul's uncle.'

Paul in the Grade above. He's talked about an uncle. And the guy looks friendly. You have to take chances sometimes. He gets in and puts his bag on the floor between his feet.

There's not much time for more conversation as it's such a short distance, but when he stops the car Paul's uncle holds out his hand. 'You're a nice boy, Nkosi, and I'm very pleased to have met you.'

Nkosi gets out and waves as the car pulls away. Lucky Gail didn't see him arrive. If she caught him taking lifts from strangers she'd go ballistic, as Nicci would say.

In July 1999, the Minister of Health had announced the development of a strategic HIV/AIDS plan to cope with the epidemic, which was now estimated to have risen to 4.2 million infections in South Africa.[35] The plan would be developed in consultation with other political parties, organisations and institutions concerned with the problem, and was in response to President Mbeki's challenge to all sectors of society to become actively involved. Task teams were set up, and in November a draft HIV/AIDS Strategic AIDS Plan for 2000–2005 was presented. The final document was completed the following January.[36]

President Mbeki suggested at the National Council of Provinces held in October 1999 that the theory that HIV causes AIDS should be revisited. He had come across the ideas of Peter Duesberg, a California-based scientist, who said that AIDS is not caused by the HI-virus, that the drugs used to counteract the disease are toxic, and that poverty causes AIDS rather than being a contributing factor.

In parliament in November, he also stated: 'There exists a large volume of scientific literature alleging that the toxicity of this drug (AZT) is such that it is a danger to health.' The government would therefore not be providing it to prevent transmission through rape or needlestick injury. (During the previous year, 1998, the Health Ministry had announced that the government would not be giving AZT to pregnant women, on the grounds of toxicity and cost. AZT, the most widely used anti-AIDS drug, was known to reduce the risk that babies would be born with HIV.)[37]

On World AIDS Day, 1 December, President Mbeki addressed the nation, exhorting them to protect themselves by being faithful to their partners or using condoms and also to be open about the disease. He said that there could be no talk of an African Renaissance if AIDS was at the door of the continent and urged everyone to join hands in a partnership against AIDS. He made no mention, however, of what the government might be doing to combat the epidemic.

According to an open letter addressed to 'Dear Everyone,' appearing in the Virusmyth homepage the following March, Dr David Rasnick, another American AIDS 'dissident' (those whose views conflict with orthodox medical opinion) said that President Mbeki had telephoned him in January and asked for his support in his efforts regarding AZT and AIDS. This led to a detailed correspondence between him and the President, in which he brought a number of arguments to prove that it was socio-economic conditions, not AIDS, that were killing so many in South Africa. He doubted the existence of HIV/AIDS, and said that 'highly toxic, anti-HIV drugs' had 'killed many thousands, perhaps tens of thousands of Americans'.[38]

Criticism of President Mbeki for his apparent determination to 'revisit' orthodox medical questions that had been assumed to be settled back in the 1980s was rife at home and overseas.

On 3 April 2000, he wrote a letter to United Nations Secretary-General Kofi Annan, President Bill Clinton, Prime Minister Tony Blair and other world leaders, emphasising his concern on the subject of AIDS. He wrote that since the epidemic manifested in a more virulent way on the continent of Africa than in the rest of the world, and since in the West AIDS was 'said to be largely homosexually transmitted', which was not the case in Africa, this was 'a uniquely African catastrophe', and he therefore requested their support in his search for a specifically African way of dealing with it. 'A simple superimposition of Western experience on African reality would be absurd and illogical,' he wrote. 'We will not, ourselves, condemn our own people to death by giving up the search for specific and targeted responses to the specifically African incidence of HIV/AIDS.' He spoke of an 'orchestrated campaign of condemnation' and likened opposition to the dissident view to the erstwhile 'racist apartheid tyranny... because, it is said, there exists a scientific view that is supported by the majority, against which dissent is prohibited.'[39]

On 4 May 2000, he appointed a presidential panel on HIV/AIDS, some of whom were orthodox medical scientists, and some of whom were AIDS dissidents. Orthodox medical opinion and the AIDS dissidents' view met head-on. The debate widened and was taken up by the public and aired on radio and TV programmes. It formed the content of several sessions of the popular phone-in radio programme *The Tim Modise Show* on SAfm. Tim spoke on air to Peter Duesberg who gave his views and was sharply challenged by many orthodox medical callers. More people called in during the following weeks and months, some on one side and some on the other. Listeners became more confused than ever. What *was* the truth about AIDS?

It was against this background that the 13th World AIDS Conference was to take place in Durban in July 2000.

Chapter
Eight

IN THE YEAR 2000, Nkosi was promoted to Grade Four – Mrs Bateman's class.

By then, he was feeling unwell a lot of the time, but since he had such a good command of language and could talk easily in most situations, his mental deterioration was not apparent even though he was looking more and more frail. At school his contemporaries were leaving him alone much of the time. They would talk to him, but he had neither the stamina nor the inclination to play with them. More and more during the year, he was left to himself, or to seek refuge in Badie's office.

Badie, in fact, allowed him to come and go more or less as he pleased, to attend Mrs Bateman's class or wander into other classes.

''Kos,' says Gail, 'the events manager of the World AIDS Conference has been to see me. It's going to be held in Durban this year. They want you to speak at it.'

'Oh, ja? Can I have some Coke?'

'It's a huge international conference, and the theme is Breaking the Silence. Think what you could do, 'Kosi, to publicise the plight of AIDS children. It's a wonderful opportunity. Yes, there's some

Coke in the fridge. But it's all going to be a lot bigger than the school hall.'

Nkosi goes into the kitchen and takes a glass off the draining-board.

'And it's a great honour, sweetheart – you're the only child ever to be asked to talk about such a thing. They are asking people who are infected to speak out.'

'What would I have to say?'

'Just tell them your life story. You are a child with AIDS and everybody is asking everybody to be open about it. You've always been open about it, so it's easy for you.'

Nkosi sits on the bench at the kitchen table and looks at his mother over the rim of the glass. 'What did you tell them?'

'I told them you've always spoken out, but I wasn't going to accept for you – you'd have to decide.'

'How many people will be there?'

'Only about ten thousand in the auditorium, but they estimate sixty million television viewers worldwide.'

'Quite a lot.'

'Ja. It's like when you watch soccer. It's a wonderful chance.'

Nkosi heaves a sigh. 'All right, I'll do it,' he says.

Nothing more was heard about the Durban conference for some months, and meanwhile the work at Nkosi's Haven was going forward. Gail thought that it would be good for the mothers to do some pottery or other art, and asked Sharon's son, Ross Jamieson, whether he would like to teach them at weekends.

Ross had known Gail most of his life. He was a year younger than Nicci, and they had played together as children most of the time they were growing up. Now he had become an art director with a communications company. He suggested that, as well as being a form of therapy, some of the work done by the mothers could be exhibited at the Durban AIDS Conference. He began going to Nkosi's Haven every Sunday and teaching them to make pottery, paper, and then their own illustrated books. In them they wrote or drew whatever they would like to communicate – their own stories that they would like to pass on to their children.

Other people joined from the Thandanani project and from the informal settlement at Orange Farm, a little to the south of Johannesburg. Some wrote about their childhood and their parents, some wrote about their lives at Nkosi's Haven, some wrote about how they saw the future.

Ross got them to participate in communication exercises in which they could act out their feelings of victimisation and aggression. On another occasion, he brought photographers from the Market Theatre Workshop to teach the mothers about photography. A photographic company sponsored some disposable cameras. They hung a studio sheet in the lounge and the mothers dressed up in whatever they thought would best express their identities. Nkosi himself became involved in this one, posing enthusiastically in some of the pictures.

Although he didn't join in many of the activities, he often told Ross how much he appreciated what he was doing for the mothers and what a difference it was making in their lives. Many of the books and photographs and other art work were subsequently exhibited at the Durban World AIDS Conference.

'You know,' says Gail one day, drawing in a long pull of nicotine and blowing it out at the ceiling, 'it's not working so well with me and AIDSLINK.'

'Oh?' says her friend Laurette. 'Have one of these Syrian biscuits – my Mom makes them.'

'Thanks. I need to get away from them and do Nkosi's Haven all on my own. They think too much money and effort are going into this one project. But I want to be in there personally on a day-to-day basis.'

'But you can't break away easily, Gail – that house is very expensive.'

'But their vision for it isn't the same as mine. It's a completely different management style. And they allocate funds here and they allocate funds there – I want to concentrate all my effort and all Nkosi's effort into Nkosi's Haven only. I know we can do it.'

'Mom,' says Julia, coming in with Nkosi, 'Nkosi's tired. I'm going to let him lie down – okay?'

'Yes, darling,' says Laurette, 'give him some juice first.'

'So will you help me?' Gail's eyes are as big as roulette counters.

'Me? What can I do? I work twelve, fourteen hours a day.'

'You'd just have to be a director and a signatory on the cheques because we can't have only one person running a non-profit organisation. We have to have a constitution and we have to have directors.'

'And I'm working weekends and I'm not one of those hands-on people who can keep going there.'

'Laurette, you run an efficient business. All I need is for somebody to help me draw up the constitution and sign a few cheques.'

'Oh, well,' says Laurette, 'if that's all it is, then I'll help you.'

Laurette Scheffer and Gail had met through the Guild of Motoring Journalists back in the early 1990s. They were very different personalities – Laurette being, as she describes herself, rather shy and conservative – but they became good friends over time. One day there was a Guild function and Gail wasn't there. Laurette said to Alan: 'Where's Gail?'

'Oh, she's looking after her black baby.'

'Gail? A black baby?'

'Yes, she's got a care centre for HIV people in Houghton, and she's got this infected baby whose mother is down with AIDS and can't look after it.'

Laurette was amazed. Glamorous, party-going Gail – she was surely not the sort of person who cared about terminally ill people, about sick babies?

But next time she and Gail got together, little Nkosi was there too. It was at a Guild weekend at the Elangeni Hotel in Durban, and Gail had brought him along, as she took him everywhere with her, unless it was an entirely inappropriate occasion for a child.

In the subsequent years, the two women became very close. At first, Laurette was nervous about even touching Nkosi, and when her daughter Julia was hugging him and carrying him around and putting him in her bed she thought it was really not a good idea. However, through contact with Gail, she became more and more knowledgeable about HIV/AIDS and more and more attached to Nkosi himself. She came to understand that Gail wanted to be down there with the actual sufferers, caring and giving. Gail would relate everything she was doing and Laurette would be deeply interested and sympathetic, but not personally involved. Until now.

Gary Roscoe had an office not far from Nkosi's Haven. His advertising agency had done quite a bit of work with Cotlands Baby Sanctuary, giving them free advertising space. Through them, he heard about Gail's initiative and went to see the house at 23 Mitchell Street, Berea. The outcome of this was that he became a major donor, following on the kitchen tea and the opening of Nkosi's Haven. Gail asked Gary to become the third director she needed if she was to 'go it alone.'

Gail and Laurette got hold of a copy of a sample constitution from the Department of Social Services and they sat round Laurette's dining-room table and amended it to be appropriate for Nkosi's Haven. They had it properly drawn up by an attorney.

Laurette couldn't believe that she'd got herself so involved so quickly. In the past, Gail would tell her about some new terrible case she'd discovered in Tembisa and Laurette would say – 'Shame, poor people, do you want a bag of vegetables?' – but really she'd only been half listening because it didn't affect her directly. Now it was going to be different.

Gail went through to the registration office in Pretoria, and within two weeks, on 1 May 2000, Nkosi's Haven was registered as a non-profit organisation.

Oscar, still an employee of AIDSLINK, and therefore obliged to cease working for Nkosi's Haven when they broke away, was unhappy. After a while he left them and did freelance consultancy work. He went on visiting the house at 23 Mitchell Street, however.

'This is the first time I've had a real family,' he told Gail.

So when she felt able to offer him a full-time job, he re-joined as the official Administration Manager. He recruited Jane Mwazi, a

volunteer worker and counsellor, and she moved in as Residential
Superintendent to assist in running the house.

And then the owner of 23 Mitchell Street disappeared. The bank
wanted to repossess the house because he had stopped paying the
bond.

The first inkling they had of this was when a man from First
National Bank arrived at Nkosi's Haven one day. He gave Gail his
card.

'Don't tell me!' she said.

'What?'

'That the bond hasn't been paid.'

'I'm afraid that's right. But who are all these people? What's
happening here?' The man from the bank looked rather dazed.

'You can see what's happening. It's a care centre for people with
AIDS. If you kick me out I shall come and sit on First National's
front stoep with all my children.'

The bank was sympathetic, but because of legal requirements to
do with sequestration, the house had to go on public auction.
However, they generously agreed that there would be no reserve
price, so in theory Gail could have got it for R1. (This was a
considerable gesture, since the current owner had a bond
outstanding of about R90 000.)

But an estate agent came around to take a look as soon as the
auction was advertised.

'Please,' said Gail, 'don't bid for it. It's a care centre for people
with AIDS. We need it.'

The estate agent said it was out of his hands. 'My bosses have
instructed me...'

The Rev. Linda Tarry-Chart was a director of Iris House, a care
centre for people with AIDS in New York. She had made several
visits to South Africa and wanted to link up with a similar South
African enterprise to start a craft project that would eventually
benefit both. She had initiated a scheme in the township of

Guguletu, near Cape Town, whereby a group of women started making black dolls for export, and as an extension of that, was planning a beaded AIDS ribbon project. Through Diane Stevens, she made contact with AIDSLINK and Gail.

She talked to Gail about the beaded AIDS ribbons project – they were to be mounted on cards bearing photographs of people with AIDS. Nkosi became one of the models for these. When she returned to New York, she said to Diane Stevens: 'You know, Nkosi is looking terrible. Wouldn't it be a wonderful idea to get him over here for a visit to Disneyworld?'

Diane in her turn talked to the Francois Xavier Bagnou Foundation, which raised funds to help AIDS orphans in Africa, and to American Airlines, and succeeded in getting sponsorship for the trip. She telephoned Gail.

'Get your passports ready – you and Nkosi are coming to Disneyworld!'

The trip was fixed for later in May.

'Are you sure you want to go?' Gail asked Nkosi.

'Yes, Mommy, I want to go.'

'Well, as long as you're sure. It means I've got to go without a fucking cigarette for twenty-two hours.'

(And, in one of the lighter moments of Inigo Gilmore's film, Gail is inhaling her first cigarette after arriving on American soil and saying: 'Aahhhh! Multiple orgasm!')

In the meanwhile, however, Nkosi was off to Cape Town to visit Anso and Gerda. A journalist specialising in health matters, Anso had covered the story of Nkosi for the newspapers over several years and also the opening of Nkosi's Haven. She and Gerda Kruger and their adopted child Siyabonga had become friends of the family, and when she and Gerda moved down to Cape Town in 1999, she had asked whether Nkosi could spend a holiday with them.

'Of course,' replied Gail when they asked her, 'but don't fucking spoil him!'

Nkosi felt quite okay about going on his own, and a pharmaceutical company generously sponsored his air ticket. It was arranged for the Easter holidays.

Anso and Gerda went to fetch him at the airport. They stood at the window watching the plane come in and the passengers disembarking. When Nkosi came out, he was not the child they remembered. He was wearing his yellow windbreaker with a big red AIDS ribbon, and underneath it he looked so small, so shrunken. They were desperate not to let him know what a shock his appearance was to them.

He came with a huge smile and his pockets full of sweets and biscuits he had collected on the flight.

On the drive home, he said: 'I gotta new joke.'

'Tell us, 'Kos.'

'Well, there's a blue fish and a red fish swimming in the sea. What did the blue fish say to the red fish?'

'I don't know. What?' said Gerda.

'How are you today?' said Nkosi and dissolved into cackles of laughter.

'But 'Kos, that's not even a joke!'

'All right, I'll tell you another one...'

He seemed tired so they put him to bed early that night, but he was up in the early hours, waking Anso and saying he had had a bad dream. When she got up to settle him again she found he had messed his bed. And again the following morning. And all through that day and the next day. He was taking in scarcely any food. They took him to their doctor, who immediately put him on a drip because he was so dehydrated.

They had planned all kinds of activities to do with him – going up Table Mountain, swimming in the sea, surfing, but it was obvious that he didn't have the energy or inclination for such things. He wanted to go to the Waterfront for shopping, however, and when they went there he was recognised by several people who wanted to chat and shake his hand. They went to see *Toy Story Two*, and both he and Siya fell fast asleep.

They let him do a lot of sleeping while he was there – just left him to rest or not, as he felt like it. In retrospect, Anso thinks that might have been why he was so ill there. By sheer force of will, Gail got him up and busy and fighting his illness, whereas she and Gerda gave him the space to give up. Eventually, he went home earlier than had been planned.

The filming of *Nkosi's Mission* by Inigo Gilmore meant that, from December 1999 until mid-2001, on and off, Gail and Nkosi had an 'eye' and an 'ear' watching and listening in their lives, sitting in their house, following them around when they went to the townships – even to America and back. Inigo was an AIDS activist, very much involved in AIDS awareness programmes. He was a self-taught video film director and cameraman. Initially, the SABC commissioned a film on Nkosi with minimal funding, and then the BBC gave him a budget to do more. From all that raw footage, he put together a compelling story.

Much of it was narrated by Nkosi himself, and by Gail. In the course of it, she says: 'I get very cross with God – not that I'm religious – to me no child on earth should die, no babies should be born sick. Us oldies who've had experience of life should die. But you shouldn't say that to a child.

'I don't want him (Nkosi) to be angry or to distrust God – not that we're religious in this house, but he's got a little Bible he wants me to read and God is supposed to be peace and forgiving and all that – and how do I say that God decided he should only live eleven years or whatever? Can't say that. I'm going to have to zoom in on what he's achieved and is going to achieve. But he needs to think a lot more positively or aggressively for himself against the virus and I don't know how to instil that in the child.'

Inigo was very keen to involve Nkosi's biological family in this film – to show 'the other side' of Nkosi's world, so after nearly a year of very little contact, they came on 3 June to Nkosi's Haven.

Nkosi is excited. Today his Granny Ruth and his sister Mbali are coming to Nkosi's Haven to be part of the film that Inigo is making all about him.

At Nkosi's Haven all the mothers know they are coming: they have been busy tidying and making the place nice from early morning. One of them suddenly shouts from the gate: 'Nkosi! They are coming!'

In the road, there's a blue Toyota Conquest. Uncle Fika is busy locking its doors, and Granny Ruth and Mbali are coming along the pavement. Mbali is wearing a smart blue tracksuit with gold stripes.

Suddenly he feels shy. He hasn't seen them for a long time, not since the wedding last year in Diepkloof. Now they are coming through the gate. Mbali looks taller than he remembers. She hugs him. Then he looks at Granny Ruth. She's the same, except she's wearing big glasses. She picks him up and presses him against her and kisses his cheek. He smells the warm brown township smell, feels her big cosy jersey against his face.

He takes them inside the house, and they say *Sawubona* to the mothers who are in the kitchen, waiting to see them. Mbali is very shy. She doesn't say anything, just murmurs and ducks her head.

After a while, they all sit round the coffee table in the lounge, Uncle Fika and Mbali on one sofa, Gail and himself and Jane, the new residential superintendent, on the other one opposite, and Granny Ruth on the chair between. Inigo's camera is there watching as usual, but Nkosi forgets about it quite soon because everybody is talking – well, Gail is talking about how they are soon going to America and Disneyworld and all that. He looks across at Mbali. She doesn't understand – at least he hopes she doesn't because it's a shame he gets all these treats like going overseas and she has to stay home in Daveyton. Uncle Fika is saying something about going to Mommy Daphne's grave, and Gail is saying that he, Nkosi, can go if he wants to and if he's well enough, and then she puts her arm round him and says: 'Do you want to go to Mommy's grave, Nkosi?'

They are all looking at him and waiting for his answer, so he nods and says 'Ja,' and Gail says well, then, they'll plan for him to go. And then they talk to each other in isiZulu and look at him and it's probably about how he didn't go last Christmas and he tries to make himself as small as possible, sitting there on the sofa beside Gail. He can't see Granny Ruth's eyes behind those big glasses so he can't tell what she's thinking.

Then Uncle Fika starts talking about 'access' and how he feels it's their right to come at any time to see him.

'You must telephone first,' says Gail, 'to find out whether it's convenient.'

Fika says that this is insulting to him as a close family member.

'Even my sister telephones first,' says Gail.

She suggests every third Saturday here at Nkosi's Haven. Then Nkosi's family could also have a closer connection with what was happening here.

Granny Ruth says something in isiZulu, and then Uncle Fika is talking about phoning and how whenever he telephones Nkosi tries to cut the conversation short, always says he has to go now because Gail wants to use the phone, and how Gail used to say 'you don't have to phone so often, you are confusing the boy'. And Fika says he doesn't feel welcome at her house when he comes to visit and he's getting quite upset and angry and Gail starts getting angry too. Nkosi looks across at Mbali and she looks frightened.

It's really bad when grown-ups fight, especially now when this is his black family visiting Nkosi's Haven for the first time. Then Uncle Fika jumps to his feet and goes out and Granny says something else in isiZulu and gets up and goes out and Gail says to Jane 'What did she say?' and Jane says something about Ruth thinking she's been tricked, and Gail goes out after them and Nkosi can hear the argument carrying on outside, much louder.

He feels horrible. When they've gone, he can't help crying.

Gail sits down with him in the lounge. She holds his hands and looks into his face. 'You get upset and confused when they come, don't you?' she says.

Somehow, it's all his fault. It's because of him that they are angry with Gail. And now she's angry with them again because he's upset. If it wasn't for him, there wouldn't be any fighting at all.

Ruth's cousin Billy was to comment later: 'He wanted to satisfy both of them – Gail and his Uncle Fika. Xolani means "peace". He always wanted peace.'

Such differences were to culminate in an overt split between Nkosi's biological and foster families. Later, Granny Ruth and Fika were to vent their suspicion of Gail's motives. They were convinced that she was making money out of Nkosi, and that she had planned right from the beginning to use him to make herself famous. 'He worked for Gail for twelve years,' said one family member.

It is perhaps not surprising that they had this impression. In Inigo's film, Gail says: 'I realise today how he could be working for children's rights... he could do a lot in schools. He must continue working his ass off for HIV/AIDS.' But that was said in the year 2000. When she took him into her family as a small child, there was little likelihood of him surviving to work for any cause, let alone to make Gail famous.

He did survive, and that he did work for the cause of infected people seems to have been his own decision. Judge Edwin Cameron was later to say: 'This whole thing about whether Nkosi was used – of course he was used. All of our lives are instruments in the service of something, whether it is material gain or spiritual fulfilment or bringing up a family. The fact that he survived for longer than five years was the consequence of Gail taking him in, and the fact that she took him in was a political statement about the fact that other kids were being abandoned. I don't think you could separate Nkosi from the cause.'

In another scene in the film, Nkosi declares that he 'must not live in a shack with dirty toilets.' Such a remark made in a film that was subsequently shown on national television was hardly palatable for his black family. To them it was evidence of the kind of talk he must be hearing at home. And when she saw the film on TV, Gail was upset on several counts. In the first place, it was all very gloomy – 'We do laugh in this house, you know' she commented; and secondly, she did not like the emphasis on the white life versus black life issue.

Nkosi had not been brought up to see a social difference between blacks and whites, but he could not help seeing the difference in comfort between Gail's life in the suburbs and his Granny's life in the informal settlement, and he was an outspoken person.

Twenty per cent of the feedback from viewers after the film was negative, mainly because what he had said seemed to have a racial bias.

Nicci is puzzled. It's the mid-morning break at college and she's taken out her purse to pay for coffee at the canteen. Surely last time she looked there were two hundred-rand notes in it, not one? She thinks back. The purse has been in her pocket since she took it from the dining-room table at home this morning. It was probably lying around on the table since she got home from the movies with Vince last night. Hmm. There's just time to make a phone call before the next class.

'Melpark Primary School, can I help you?'

'Please may I speak to Lyn at the tuckshop? ... Lyn, this is Nicci Johnson. Look, if Nkosi or his friend Aubrey come to you today with a R100 note and want a hot dog or whatever, please give it to them, but don't give them the change.'

'Why?'

'Well, there's a hundred rand gone from my purse, and I think it's Nkosi. If my Mom wants to borrow money, she asks me.'

'All right, Nicci, give me your cellphone number and I'll call you.'

It's not long before she calls.

'Nicci, one of the girls selling hot chocolate says Nkosi went to her with a hundred-rand note.'

'Okay,' says Nicci. 'Please get hold of Nkosi and give him a hot dog and a cold drink at lunchtime, but tell him the rest of the money must be put in my drawer at home, and that will be the end of it.'

Later in the afternoon Nicci received a phone call from Oscar, working that day in the office in Melville. 'Nkosi's come home and told me that he took a hundred rand out of your purse.'

'Ja, Oscar, I know. There's no point in me getting angry about it now. He must just put the money back.'

When she got home, Nkosi was waiting for her, looking very small and scared.

'I'm very sorry, Nicci.'

'But why did you take it, 'Kos? Why didn't you just ask me? I'm not stingy with money, am I?'

'No.'

'And what do you need a hundred rand for?'

'I'm very sorry.'

'Look, Nkosi, I was angry with you this morning – that's why I telephoned the school and made Lyn keep my change for me. But I'm not angry now. You must see that you can't do this sort of thing, 'Kosi – it's wrong.'

'Sorry, Nicci.'

On his way back to class after break, Nkosi has to stop for a moment and lean against the railings. His legs don't seem to want to work, neither does his head, and it feels like he might mess his pants again any minute. In any case, what's the point? Whatever he tries, it's all going to end the same way. He's going to America. He's going to the AIDS Conference in Durban and making a speech. Everyone else is so excited for him, but right now it makes him tired to even think about it.

All the other children have disappeared now, but here comes Mrs Pitchers, his class teacher last year in Grade Three. He likes the way she talks, not too soft and sympathetic like some people, but like she understands how you feel and tries to give you a matter-of-fact answer.

'Hello, Nkosi – why aren't you in class?'

'I was waiting for you.'

She stops and really looks at him.

'You want to talk to me?'

He nods. He wants to say, yes that's exactly what I need to do, but he doesn't want to start crying so he just nods.

'Come on, then, my class can look after itself for five minutes. You talk. What's wrong?'

He looks at the ground between his feet, not at her, and says: 'I hate this stupid disease. I hate taking my medicine.' He looks at her and then quickly down at his feet again. And then, almost whispering: 'I want to die.'

For a long time, she doesn't say anything, and then: 'You're talking from the bottom of your heart, Nkosi, so I'll talk from the bottom of mine. When we all first heard about AIDS, you know what? I was terrified. I wouldn't even go to the public loo. That's how scared I was. But you showed me I could hold your hand, I could hug you, I could even take you on my lap and I wouldn't catch it. If it hadn't been for me and you being involved together, I'd still have been walking round saying "Don't come near me!" It's true, isn't it?'

He nods. Already, he's feeling a little better. She doesn't seem to be shocked and horrified at what he said.

''Kosi, it's not an adult, not a book that's changed my attitude, it's an eleven-year-old called Nkosi Johnson. I'm a teacher. I'm supposed to have all the answers. But this is one answer you know better than I do. You've taught me that I don't have to be frightened.'

She's looking so serious – so anxious for him to understand. He can feel himself beginning to smile at her. 'Okay,' he whispers.

'You've still got a lot of work to do, Nkosi. You can't just give up now. You've got this wonderful trip to America coming up and you're going to be teaching people in a different part of the world just what you've taught me. And you've got your speech coming up at the conference. And that's an honour. Not everybody gets asked to make a speech.'

He does feel better, definitely. Not nearly as tired as he did half an hour ago. It's good, leaning back on the railings and talking.

'And by now my Grade Threes will be killing each other in the classroom, so I'd better go.' Indeed, the noise from inside is awesome.

He catches at her arm. 'Can I come back to Grade Three?'

'Yes, if that's going to make you feel happier. You'll have to discuss it with Mr Badenhorst, but if it's okay with him, you're welcome to come back.'

In any case, Nkosi hardly ever goes to the Grade Four lessons. He spends much of his time in Badie's office, sitting on the upturned wastepaper basket and chatting, whenever Badie will let him.

But when he did eventually come back to her class towards the end of the year, Mrs Pitchers was shocked and saddened to find how much he had deteriorated. There was no doubt that he could no longer do the work, even of Grade Three.

How much Nkosi was aware of his mental deterioration is not certain. It's very likely that the virus was already damaging his brain by the end of his year in Grade Two, since Mrs Serrao remembered that he coped well at first, but less well towards the end of 1998.

The telephone rings. Nkosi happens to be passing. He picks it up. 'Hello?'

'Hello – please may I speak to Gail?'

'May I ask who's speaking?'

'Michael Jackson.'

'Who?'

'Michael Jackson.'

Nkosi sighs and shakes his head. 'You've got to be joking,' he says.

'No, Nkosi, it's me.'

'Michael Jackson is American,' says Nkosi, and hangs up.

'Who was that?' calls Gail from the kitchen.

'Some fool pretending to be Michael Jackson,' says Nkosi.

''Kosi! That really was Michael Jackson.'

'No, it wasn't. He didn't even sound American.'

'Not THE Michael Jackson. The man from the Rotarians. Now I've got to phone back and apologise.'

'Well, how was I to know?' says Nkosi.

'You know, Nkosi,' says Oscar, 'I'm in love with Janet Jackson. If you see her when you're over there, just tell her about me, will you?'

'Okay,' says Nkosi.

(When he got back after the trip he told Oscar: 'America's too big, I couldn't find her. I'll do it next time I go there.')

The telephone rings again. This time it's Diane, phoning from America.

'Only take what Nkosi needs for overnight,' she says. 'As soon as you get to New York, we're going to take him shopping!'

She was as good as her word. Among all the other bewildering events that tumbled over each other when they arrived in America, there was a visit to Bloomingdales, where Nkosi acquired a stunning navy blue jacket and trousers, shorts and T-shirts – a generous donation from Linda Tarry-Chart's Project People Foundation.

Diane arranged for Gail and Nkosi to do a radio interview – at six o'clock in the morning, to Gail's dismay – on a station with a large African-American listenership. They gave a talk at a school, which was arranged through Global Friends. This is an international network of school children, created by a Swedish NGO called 'Children's World'. It tries to help less fortunate children throughout the world, those who are starving, abused, or mistreated in any way. Every year since 2000 they award a prize to the child or children's group which they feel has done the most to uplift the lives of other children. They communicate with each other through the Internet.

Gail and Diane attended a fund-raising breakfast given by Hillary Clinton, who was running for Senator at the time. She made a very articulate and hard-hitting speech on the abuse of women.

They also, with Nkosi, went to the offices of DDB, a big advertising agency, where the launch of Linda Tarry-Chart's Beaded AIDS Ribbon Project was taking place. The agency had adopted

Linda and her work with AIDS, and organised the launch for her at a cocktail party in the boardroom/reception area of their offices in Manhattan. Linda talked about the work she was doing with Iris House, and Nkosi told the guests all about Nkosi's Haven.

This was a major fund-raising occasion for both the care centres, and by the end of it, the agency had offered to adopt Nkosi's Haven too, through their local South African branch.

Gail comes back to the hotel after having supper with Inigo Gilmore the following evening to find Nkosi lying back in bed, propped up on pillows, watching television. On the coffee table is a tray with a tall glass on it with prawns hanging all round the edge, their tails sticking up in the middle and curling over to look like a fountain, all covered in pink sauce.

'And now?' she says, having bidden goodbye and closed the door on the babysitter. 'What is that?'

'It's a prawn cocktail,' says Nkosi. 'Only they call it a shrimp cocktail here. I ordered it from Room Service.'

'So why aren't you eating it?'

'I don't feel like it any more.'

'Oh, excuse *me*.' She switches off the television. 'Nkosi, we are on a sponsored trip. Do you know what that means?'

'Someone else is paying?'

'Someone else is paying. And when someone else is paying for everything you eat, you don't order the most expensive thing on the menu and then not eat it. You try to save the donor as much money as you can.'

'Can we send it back?'

'Not after you've eaten one of the prawns – of course we can't.'

'Sorry, Mommy.'

'Yes, Nkosi, but "Sorry, Mommy" is too late. You've got to think for yourself. You are eleven years old. You ought to be responsible.'

Nkosi sinks down into the bed.

Gail settles him for the night and then undresses herself and cleans off her make-up. The glass with its pink fishy fountain still sits in the middle of the room. Her eye keeps going to it. After a while she takes a prawn, chews its tough, tasty flesh slowly. She doesn't have much room after that supper. But it's really a pity to waste it.

She sits down in the armchair, turns on the TV with the volume very soft and watches the late-night news. Very soon the prawn cocktail glass is empty.

On the Friday they went through to Orlando, to Disneyworld. While they were there, some ladies from a local church got to know about their visit and asked them to speak to their congregation. This they did, briefly, as Nkosi was not feeling at all well.

Disneyworld was hot and humid, and although they borrowed a wheelchair for him to ride in, Nkosi quickly became exhausted. The crowds, the noise, the movement – above all the heat – seemed too much for him to cope with. They went through a black tunnel to see a science-fiction show, they watched the action presentation of *Indiana Jones,* and they went into the Jungle Pavilion. They did not attempt the Funfair. They watched the Disney characters, Mickey Mouse and so on, parading in the street. On film, Nkosi complained that he was having to do too many interviews.

However, everything changed once they arrived at the 'Give Kids the World' village. He loved it. This is a place where terminally ill children and their families can spend up to a week enjoying a free holiday. Everything, even the food, is free. They stayed in a semidetached, three-bedroomed cottage, furnished and equipped by sponsors. All the furniture is child-size, so Gail felt as though her knees were round her ears when she sat on the veranda. There was a magic castle and a mini-Disneyworld of things to see and do. Nkosi could walk around at his own pace, go to the dining room for breakfast on his own, and it was tranquil and beautiful, surrounded by wide green spaces. He told Inigo that he'd like to spend the rest of his life there.

He also confided on camera how tired he was of the constant diarrhoea.

'I feel like I'm going to die quickly, like my mother died, very soon. But at least she got to be a grown-up. I can't feel happy. I hate having this disease... I wish I could be well like my sister is. It makes me think of my mother. But my second mother says "Don't think about it. Think of what's ahead of us. You've still got a long life and lots more things to do." '

Towards the end of the film, Gail says: 'I love him and he drives me to drink. He's a special little boy and I admire his courage. I get very angry with him often. I've never lost a child, but I'm going to – I don't know when. I want him to have peace – inner peace. Acceptance of whatever comes in life – and I will deal with whatever that brings.'

After that weekend, they flew back to New York and on home, on the Monday afternoon, to Johannesburg.

The trip to America had opened Nkosi's eyes to a different sort of life, so much so that on the flight home Gail felt obliged to say: 'Don't think this is carrying on when we get home, babyshoes. At home it's back to feeding the cats and doing your homework.'

Later, when he sees Oscar for the first time, he says: 'Oscar, everybody in America goes like: "Oh Nkosi, you're so different, you're so special." Why?'

Oscar looks at him and shakes his head. 'Don't fool yourself. It's just how they talk there. What makes you different is what you did for a whole lot of other HIV kids when you got admitted to Melpark Primary. You're still a normal child. Don't go round thinking "I am special." '

He looks so downcast that Oscar takes him by the shoulders and gives him a little shake.

'People love you, Nkosi. Just fix your mind on that. That's far more important than all these strangers thinking you're special.'

Chapter Nine

AT THE END of 1998, Dr Ashraf Coovadia had reopened the specialist paediatric (IC2) clinic at Coronation Hospital, which had been temporarily closed since Dr Alan Kelly emigrated to Australia in 1996. In June, on their return from America, Gail took Nkosi for his routine check-up. They saw one of the other doctors, not Ashraf Coovadia, but as soon as he knew they were there, he came to have a word.

'I'm going to the AIDS conference in Durban,' Nkosi tells him.

'You are?'

'He's been asked to make a speech,' says Gail. 'It's a tremendous honour. We've only just had it confirmed, although they first approached us months ago.'

Ashraf sits down and takes Nkosi between his knees. 'What are you going to say?'

The child's face is shining with pride, but solemn, in spite of the smile.

'I'm going to tell them about myself and – and how it is to have AIDS.'

'And a bit about Nkosi's Haven,' says Gail.

'I'm going to be the first speaker,' says Nkosi, 'before the President.'

'We're all very excited,' says Gail, 'but very nervous.'

Ashraf says: 'Nkosi, this is wonderful. This is your one-off chance to say what you like on a world stage.'

'I know,' says Nkosi.

'I'm sure you've thought about this anyway, but please talk about the plight of infected children and how it can be prevented.'

'Okay, I will,' says Nkosi earnestly. 'I'll say everything about that.'

'It's very dear to our hearts as paediatricians.'

'It's dear to my heart as well,' says Nkosi. 'I want to tell them about Mickey.'

'Who's Mickey?'

'He was a little baby who came to us. He was very sick. He died very soon.'

'Well, there are thousands of Mickeys out there, Nkosi, and they could be helped.'

'Yes, I know. The government has the money – it just has to be organised.'

Ashraf is taken aback. This child who is eleven but looks as though he is only six is talking like an adult. He looks up at Gail.

'Oh, yes,' she says, 'we've always discussed the wider issues with Nkosi.'

'Well, this is very important,' says Ashraf, 'because, as we all know, there's a huge silence about this in South Africa. As a paediatrician, I fully support the Treatment Action Campaign's efforts to prevent mother-to-child transmission. But we need people who will speak out.'

'I'm going to speak out,' says Nkosi.

'What about treatment once they've tested positive?' asks Gail. 'Until a month ago, when a private donor in America came forward, Nkosi has been only on vitamin supplements and Bactrim. Are you having success with the anti-retrovirals?'

'Well, we had one child who had a viral load of more than 500,000, which is not unusual for children with HIV, and within two months of treatment with anti-retrovirals it was down to less than 500.'

'What's a viral load?' asks Nkosi.

'It's the count of viruses in the blood, which we can measure and monitor. The problem is that after a while the viruses start getting resistant. So what we do is to try to give two drugs early on so that we reduce the viral load fast, and the chances of developing resistance are much smaller. As the virus multiplies, it mutates – sometimes to forms that are resistant. But the government is not providing anti-retroviral therapy anywhere. It's only being taken by those who can afford it. Here we prescribe the drugs, but people have to pay for them.'

'Is it very expensive if you're only a baby?' asks Nkosi.

'Yes, I'm afraid it is. But we are hoping that the drug companies will start dropping their prices to have minimal profit margins. Or that we can get generics. There's a lot of pressure on them worldwide to agree. There's been a court case pending about it since 1997. At the moment, it probably costs between R350 and R400 a month, say, for a one-year-old child. For the middle class it's just possible, but most of our patients are from squatter camps.'

Ashraf has to get back to his other patients. He stands up. 'I am very pleased to have met you, Nkosi,' he says, 'and I look forward to hearing your speech. I'm going to be there too.' They shake hands. Nkosi's hand is like a bundle of little sticks. 'Goodbye, Gail. Look after him.'

'Always.'

'Darling,' says Gail, 'you're going to have to work out what you want to say at the Durban conference. You can't just talk off the cuff to forty thousand people or whatever.'

'Yes, Mommy.'

'Well, have you thought about it?'

'I'm going to tell them about how I've got AIDS. I'm going to tell them about Feroza and the others at Nkosi's Haven and Mommy Daphne, and maybe...'

'Whoa – hold on, 'Kos. First of all, you must introduce yourself, you know, like you usually do. And then start at the beginning.'

'Like how I was born?'

'Well, ja, but don't take up the whole evening, 'Kos. Give President Mbeki a chance.'

'Can I tell them about Mickey?'

'Ja, but just remember why they've asked you. You are an infected person. You're not afraid to disclose your status. You're speaking on behalf of all infected people. This is what it's all about. The theme is "Breaking the Silence".'

'Ja, but we must tell them about letting the children stay with their mothers. Like at Nkosi's Haven.'

'Okay, 'Kos, go for it. Get your tape recorder and talk into it. Then learn it off by heart. Then you won't have to worry.'

A couple of days later she asks: 'Okay, 'Kos, what are you going to say?' He starts, but almost at once he gets stuck. 'All right, let's listen to it.'

He gets the recorder and plays it back.

'But 'Kosi, it's all a bit of a muddle. You've obviously thought about it, but you're jumping from things that happened when you were nine to things that happened when you were two. Look, you stand and dictate, I'll put it on the computer and then get everything in the right order, and you can record it over again.'

When he's finished dictating she says: 'It's a good speech. I just hope to God you remember it all.'

Every day he would come home from school, have his lunch and then have a sleep. He was losing weight quickly now and he was exhausted from all the diarrhoea. It didn't seem as though the triple therapy was having the hoped-for effect. A generous private donor in America had offered to pay for it, and Gail had taken Nkosi to Dr Leon Levin, one of the foremost specialists on the treatment of AIDS in the country. He had put Nkosi onto triple retroviral therapy in May.

When he woke up, Gail would say: 'Come on, babes, work on your speech. Go and sit outside with it. It's lovely out there under the bignonia.'

She'd be cooking in the kitchen and she would watch him through the window. There he would be, eyes closed, dreaming away...

'Nkosi!'

'Yes, Mommy?'

'Don't dream. Talk, babes. If you dry up, it will look as though it's a forced scenario. If you are fluent, you'll come across as a very confident little boy, which you are. Darling, you're not doing it for me, you're doing it for women like Feroza and their children – you are speaking for every infected person in the country.'

One night, Ross Jamieson comes to dinner to talk about the artwork made by the Nkosi's Haven mothers that should go down to the conference. After they have eaten, Gail says: 'Why don't you go through your speech with Ross, Nkosi? Get some tips on how to do it. He's studied drama and knows all about how to stand up in front of a big audience.'

So off they go upstairs. Ross hears the speech and they talk about it and talk about how Nkosi feels about his mother and his life and what he is trying to achieve. He tells Ross how proud he is of being the first boy with AIDS to go to school, and how proud he is that because of him the mothers are being housed and fed at Nkosi's Haven. Suddenly, Ross sees that he is crying. He puts his arm round him, sitting there on the sofa.

'What's wrong, 'Kos? Do you want to tell me about it?'

Nkosi nods and hiccups but he is sobbing too much to speak. He seems to be on the edge of complete fear and complete collapse. Ross pulls him onto his lap and goes on rocking.

At last, Nkosi sits up and scrubs at his face. He says: 'What's – what's really scary is when I go to sleep.'

'What happens, 'Kos?'

'I... I close my eyes, and I... I...' Another sob comes up unexpectedly but he deals with it and goes on: 'I see myself all sick and weak and I can't do anything. And there's this army that's coming to kill me and I don't know what to do.'

Ross tightens his arms around him.

'And I know I have to fight but I don't know how.'

There is nothing Ross can say. After a bit, he turns Nkosi round to face him and says:

'Nkosi, you are the softest, gentlest little human being I have ever met. You are like a little butterfly, but what is so amazing is that you are also this huge fighting activist who can stand up with such strength and determination to get the message across. If I had AIDS, I don't think I could do that.'

They don't talk much after that and eventually Ross says: 'Come on, 'Kos, let's get you to bed. You must be tired out.'

Gail's suitcase is open on the bed. She is taking down things from the cupboard and putting them in. Here comes the dark suit with the white edges. She packs fast, buttoning the jacket, turning it over, bending back the sleeves, folding it in half, one, two, three. Nkosi is sitting on the bed. His packing is finished.

'Nkosi, go for it, my darling. Stand in front of the mirror over there and show Mommy what you're going to say and how you're going to say it.'

Well, the first part is easy. He's said it many times before. Maybe if he opens his mouth the rest will all come out like magic. After all, he knows it, really.

'Hi. My name is Nkosi Johnson and I live in Melville, Johannesburg. I am eleven years old. I have AIDS. I was born HIV-positive. When I was two years old my Mommy couldn't keep me and I... she visited me... she...' He sticks.

'Go on.'

'I can't.'

Gail bangs down the lid of the suitcase.

'What the fuck have you been doing? It's your words, baby. I just wrote them down. We are in shit.'

'Yes, Mommy.'

'Christ, 'Kos, you are speaking to sixteen million people and you don't know it. In twenty-four hours you'll be on that stage. Don't look at me like that. This is the big one, babes.'

On the flight, Nkosi rolls himself up small on the seat. He tries to say his speech in his head. Hi, my name is Nkosi Johnson. Hi, my name is Nkosi Johnson. He can't seem to get past that phrase now.

They arrive in Durban and are greeted as though they are VIPs. A hire car has been organised for them, as they are staying with Colleen in Pennington. On the way, they stop off and look at the cricket stadium, which is the venue for the Opening Ceremony. There's a grandstand and a stage that goes on for miles, and millions and millions of chairs.

'This is quite big, Mommy, isn't it?'

'What did I tell you?'

'I am going to shits myself.'

'Yes, you are, and so am I going to shits myself. We are going home to Col, and you are going to fucking learn the thing.'

'Yes, Mommy.'

They were told about the rehearsal the following day, and that there had been a change of programme. President Mbeki was now going to speak first, and Nkosi immediately afterwards. Then they set off down the coast road to Colleen's, where indeed they sat on the lawn and went over and over the speech.

Colleen kept running in and out. 'Shame, Gail, you're going to kill the child.'

'No, I'm not. He's got to do it.'

And then he got a break, because a BBC team came to interview him.

Next day there's a rehearsal at the stadium. When it comes to Nkosi's turn, they give him a hand microphone to hold. He gets going on the speech and it's weird because although at first he thought he wasn't going to remember it, the words slip nicely into his head one by one and he begins to enjoy himself. In fact, with the mike in his hand, he feels almost as though he's like Michael Jackson. He can see himself up there, holding the mike, casting his spell over millions and millions of people...

Gail is standing at the side with a group of UNAIDS people, and they're all laughing. 'Nkosi,' she says, 'talk, babes, don't sing. Who do you think you are, a pop star?'

They arrive at the venue at the appointed time. They are placed right in the middle of the front row. It is going to be broadcast live, so they have to start exactly on time, there's no waiting. The evening opens with some people dancing and singing and drumming on the stage. Then Professor Jerry Coovadia, Chairman of the Conference, Peter Busse of NAPWA and Peter Piot of UNAIDS welcome everybody and talk about the conference. While this is going on, President and Mrs Mbeki arrive with their entourage, and sit down next to Nkosi, where the people now on the stage had been sitting. There aren't enough seats for them, so some other people have to move and there is quite a disturbance.

Then President Mbeki gets up and makes his speech. Nkosi tries to listen, but there's something thumping away in his chest that stops him from concentrating on what the President is saying. Right now, he can't remember his own first opening sentence. The sweat is trickling down his back although he also feels cold. Thank goodness he's wearing a nappy – just for safety. And thank goodness nobody knows. He looks down at his tackies, dangling at the end of his legs. If he claps them together – quietly, of course – in time to the thumping, maybe he'll feel calmer. President Mbeki seems to have finished at last. Everybody is clapping.

'Come on, sweetheart,' says Gail, 'this is it.'

She takes his hand and he gets down off his chair and walks with her, miles and miles round and to the side of the stage. Another man has the mike and is saying something that ends in the words: 'NKOSI – JOHNSON!'

Gail gives him a little push, and he's walking across to the man who is holding out the mike and smiling. Nkosi takes it, and turns to see where Gail is. She's sitting on the steps, there at the side. He turns back to face the crowd. Funny, he can't see them very well, the lights are so bright. He coughs a bit to clear his throat. Here goes.

'Hi. My name is Nkosi Johnson. I live in Melville, Johannesburg, South Africa. I am eleven years old and I have full-blown AIDS. I was born HIV-positive.'

The millions of faces out there are just pale blobs, but the one or two he can see seem to be smiling. This is okay. He grasps the mike a bit more firmly and carries on.

'When I was two years old, I was living in a care centre for HIV/AIDS-infected people. My Mommy was obviously also infected and could not afford to keep me because she was very scared that the community she lived in would find out that we were both infected and chase us away.

'I know she loved me very much and would visit me when she could. And then the care centre had to close down because they didn't have any funds. So my foster-mother, Gail Johnson, who was a director of the care centre and had taken me home for weekends, said at a board meeting she would take me home.'

He looks round at Gail and she is nodding at him, so it must be okay so far.

'She took me home with her and I have been living with her for eight years now. She taught me all about being infected and how I must be careful with my blood. If I fall and cut myself and bleed, then I must make sure I cover my own wound and go to an adult to help me clean it and put a plaster on it. I know that my blood is only dangerous to other people if they also have an open wound and my blood goes into it. That is the only time that people need to be careful when touching me.'

Something seems to be happening out there. There's some sort of a disturbance there right in front of him. People are getting up out of their seats and walking away. It's all the people who were sitting next to them. Has he done something wrong? He looks at the microphone man standing at the side, but he's nodding and making 'carry on' signs. Now, where was he? Oh, yes...

'In 1997 Mommy Gail went to the school, Melpark Primary, and she had to fill in a form for my admission and it said does your child suffer from anything, so she said yes, AIDS. My Mommy Gail and I have always been open about me having AIDS. And then my Mommy Gail was waiting to hear if I was admitted to school. Then she phoned the school who said we will call you, and then they had a meeting about me. Of the parents and the teachers at the meeting, 50% said yes and 50% said no. And then on the day of my big brother's wedding, the media found out that there was a problem about me going to school. My Mommy Gail and I did a whole lot of interviews about me going to school. No one seemed to know what to do with me because I am infected. Then AIDS workshops were done at the school for the parents and teachers to teach them not to be scared of a child with AIDS.

'I am very proud to say that there is now a policy for all HIV-infected children to be allowed to go into school and not be discriminated against.'

Suddenly, they are all clapping. But it isn't the end. Gail is signalling – Wait, Wait... But what's next? What's next? Mommy Daphne.

'And in the same year, just before I started school, my Mommy Daphne died. She went on holiday to Newcastle – she died in her sleep. And Mommy Gail got a phone call and I answered and my auntie said please can I speak to Gail? Mommy Gail told me almost immediately my Mommy had died and I burst into tears. My Mommy Gail took me to my Mommy's funeral. I saw my Mommy in the coffin and I saw her eyes were closed and then I saw them lowering it into the ground and then they covered her up. My Granny was very sad that her daughter had died.

'Then I saw my father for the first time and I never knew I had a father. He was very upset but I thought to myself, why did he leave my mother and me? And then the other people asked my Mommy Gail about my sister and who would look after her, and then my Mommy Gail said "Ask the father".'

'Ever since the funeral, I have been missing my Mommy lots and I wish she was with me, but I know she is in heaven. And she is on my shoulder watching over me and in my heart.

'I hate having AIDS because I get very sick and I get very sad when I think of all the other children and babies that are sick with AIDS. I just wish that the government can start giving AZT to pregnant HIV mothers to help stop the virus being passed on to their babies.'

The audience is suddenly clapping again and shouting. He can't hear what they're shouting, but there are whistles as well, so he knows they are pleased. As soon as it dies down, he begins again. This is the piece he specially cares about.

'Babies are dying very quickly and I know one little abandoned baby who came to stay with us and his name was Mickey. He couldn't breathe, he couldn't eat and he was so sick and Mommy Gail had to phone Welfare to have him admitted to a hospital and he died. But he was such a cute little baby and I think the government must start doing it because I don't want babies to die.

'Because I was separated from my mother at an early age, because we were both HIV-positive, my Mommy Gail and I have always wanted to start a care centre for HIV/AIDS mothers and their children. I am very happy and proud to say that the first Nkosi's Haven was opened last year. And we look after ten mommies and fifteen children.'

It's getting easier the nearer he is to the end.

'My Mommy Gail and I want to open five Nkosi's Havens by the end of next year because I want more infected mothers to stay together with their children – they mustn't be separated from their children so they can be together and live longer with the love that they need.

'When I grow up, I want to lecture to more and more people about AIDS – and if Mommy Gail will let me, around the whole country. I want people to understand about AIDS – to be careful and respect AIDS – you can't get AIDS if you touch, hug, kiss, hold hands with someone who is infected.'

Some people start clapping but there are only a few sentences to go, so he carries straight on:

'Care for us and accept us – we are all human beings. We are normal. We have hands. We have feet. We can walk, we can·talk, we have needs just like everyone else. Don't be afraid of us – we are all the same!'

That's it. And then he remembers to say 'Thank you!'

There is a huge noise from the audience. There is Gail, with her thumb stuck triumphantly in the air. He walks back to her and she hugs him so tight he can't breathe. There are tears on her face.

And then there's a whole lot of people crowding round and wanting to say something and hug him and a lot of them look as though they've been crying. A Japanese journalist takes off his watch and hands it to him, saying 'This is with love from me!'

'Why did the President leave in the middle of my speech?' he asks Gail when at last he is going to bed that night.

'I don't know, babes. Perhaps he had another appointment. Someone said he was scheduled to fly to Ghana.'

'Doesn't he have his own plane?'

'Sweetheart, who knows? He probably thought you were going to go on for another two hours.'

'He didn't wait to hear what I said about the babies.'

'Never mind – millions of other people did.'

'But will they do anything?'

'Let's hope. But according to his speech, they are calling poverty the number one killer in South Africa, not AIDS.'

The Tuesday night following the opening of the AIDS Conference Gail and Nkosi were invited to a curry dinner with Countess Albina du Boisrouvray, who had started the Francois Xavier Bagnou Foundation (named after her son, who was killed while on a mercy flight). During the evening, she suggested that they should stay for a press conference she was holding on the Thursday, when Nkosi and Gail could perhaps say a few words. It was decided that they could fit this in on their way to the airport with Colleen for the journey home.

Another speaker at the conference was Danny Glover, the American actor, who was there in his capacity as Goodwill Ambassador for UN Development Programme. He was also at the press conference, and Gail sat next to him with Nkosi on her lap. When it was his turn to speak, Nkosi said:

'This is about orphans. When my mother and father died, I was an orphan and infected. But I am really a lucky little boy because I'm living with a foster family and I'm strong and healthy. That's what I want all other orphans to have. I think all orphans need that because they are rejected. The community does not want to have anything to do with orphans.'

After the press conference, Gail, Nkosi and Colleen were invited into the VIP suite. Nkosi chatted to Danny, who told him about his films. Gail suddenly had a brilliant idea. She asked Danny whether he would be prepared to help establish Nkosi's Haven. He wanted to know more about it, and she and Nkosi were only too happy to describe it and the mothers and children who lived there and how they were being cared for, and how they were hoping to be able to expand to take in more.

Danny said: 'May I take a while to think about this?'

'Of course,' said Gail, 'and if you're ever in Johannesburg I'd love to show you what we're doing.'

Almost immediately after that, Colleen said that they must go if they were to catch their flight, so they said goodbye to everyone and drove out to the airport. By suppertime they were home in Melville.

The next day, Friday, Gail got a phone call. Danny Glover. 'I'm in Johannesburg – I'd like to come and see your project tomorrow.'

'How about a curry supper?'

'Can't make that I'm afraid, but we'll be at Nkosi's Haven for tea at about ten o'clock.'

Gail phoned Laurette and Gary Roscoe, and they were all there the next morning at ten to welcome Danny Glover. They showed him around, and he talked to several of the mothers and children. He walked round the garden and looked at the boys' dormitory (tidier than usual). He sat in the lounge drinking tea, and the three directors told him all about the running of the house and then about the man from the bank and the upcoming notice to auction.

Danny said: 'Well, let's see if we can do something about that.'

And the result was that he facilitated financing which would help them to bid for the house at the auction.

Gail wrote and asked him whether they could call it 'Danny Glover Nkosi's Haven.' He replied: 'Why not "Nkosi's Haven and Friends"?'

Danny came back to South Africa later in the year to attend a

AIDS benefit concert at Sun City, and Nkosi's Haven put on a thank-you gathering for him in the form of a press conference on 11 November.

It is during one of Nkosi's visits to Nkosi's Haven that he and Oscar have an important conversation.

'Oscar, what is it like to die?'

'Nkosi, for me that's the wrong question. Try again.'

'No, I really want to know.'

'All right, let me tell you a story. When I was still young, many years ago, I used to be so naughty. I used to steal money, I used to tell lies.'

Nkosi sits very still on the sofa beside him.

'One day I made the mistake of stealing the coins from my mother's purse instead of a note. Now, if I had taken a note she might not have noticed, but the coins were heavy and she could see that something was missing. She said she was going to kill me.'

Nkosi looks quickly at him to see if he's joking, but his face isn't smiling at all.

'She sent one of my sisters for a bottle of beer, saying she needed it to get up her courage to – you know – actually do it, but at that moment a visitor arrived so she locked me in my room to deal with me later.'

Nkosi knows that Oscar used to be a freedom fighter. Maybe he grew up in a family where the mother was a tough woman who really would kill her child. Where was this story going?

'Well, I was in the room all by myself and I started thinking. I thought – if I die now and go to heaven (I only thought of going to heaven; it never occurred to me it might be the other place) I'd have to start all over again and make new friends. I really couldn't stand that idea so I decided that I wanted to live and I'd better tell my mother I was sorry and maybe she wouldn't kill me. So I did and she didn't, because here I am. So, to come back to your first question, that's what I thought it would be like, when I thought I was going to die. But it's really up to you. What do you want to do?'

Nkosi's eyes feel all watery and stupid. 'I feel so tired. I want to go to heaven.'

Oscar gets up. 'Come on. What you want is to go and lie down and sleep for a while.'

Nkosi goes very slowly upstairs and lies on the bed. Within seconds, he's asleep.

Oscar gets on with his paperwork, makes phone calls, talks to Jane, shouts at three of the bigger children who are having a yelling argument down at the swings. An hour or so passes and Nkosi's face appears round the office door.

'Hello, Nkosi. Had a good sleep?'

'Yes. Oscar?'

'Mmm?'

'You know what we were talking about? About dying and having to make new friends and all that?'

'Yes. What have you decided?'

'I think I've decided to live.'

'That's right. I think that was the right decision there, 'Kosi.'

'You want to come to church with me, 'Kosi?' asks Grace, as they are settling down to sleep.

'Mmm.'

'You sure?'

'Mmm.'

'Because we've got to get up early in the morning. We have to be there six o'clock. Every morning I am going.'

'Where's the church?'

'In town. In Plein Street. It's the Universal Church. Everybody can go there.'

'Ja. I do want to go,' decides Nkosi.

It's still dark when Grace wakes him next morning. They make tea and eat bread and jam in the kitchen, and Nkosi has Weetbix, too.

'Who else is coming?'

'Just me and you.'

It's a long way to walk. Very soon Grace takes Nkosi up on her back. Through Hillbrow they go, now quiet after the night's sporadic outbursts of street fights, loud music, police raids. Some people are huddled round a fire in a tin bucket, doorways are dark with the shapes of sleepers. Grace hurries on past. 'God will look after us. Nkosi is going to be healed. God won't let anything happen to us on the way.'

They start on the long hill down into the city centre. 'It's just down to the bottom, and then we turn right and go along two, three blocks,' she says.

When they get there, Nkosi sees a big building like a movie house, with steps up to the front door. Already they can hear a big noise coming from inside.

'What's that?'

'It's the people. They're praising. You will see.'

Inside there are more steps leading up. At the top they find themselves inside a big hall – much bigger than the hall at Melpark, and it's full of people singing.

'Come on,' says Grace, 'we'll go and sit in the front and you can see all what happens.'

On the platform there's a lady holding a microphone and singing very loudly. Every so often everybody joins in. Beside him, Grace sings too, but Nkosi doesn't know the words, so he turns around and looks at everything. Up there in the ceiling there's a window, blue and green and yellow in little squares in the shape of a cross. All round the sides are small balconies with people sitting and looking down at the crowd.

His attention comes back to the platform. A man in a white shirt has the microphone now and is striding up and down saying: '... and Our Lord Jesus Christ went around among the people, healing the sick and feeding the weary and casting out devils. There's a devil waiting to enter every one of us, my brothers and sisters, and we need Jesus Christ to help us cast him out. I want all of you who have manifested the devil to come right here up to the front. Maybe he manifested yesterday, maybe last week, last month – doesn't matter. If he manifested in you – come up to the front.'

In ones and twos they come at first and then there's a small crowd there and the man is bending down and talking to this one and that one.

'Do you see what's written up there?' says Grace.

On the wall behind the platform there are words in fancy gold lettering. 'What is it?' asks Nkosi.

'It says 'Jesus Christ is the Lord' in isiZulu, in siSwati, in seSotho and in English. Do you know that Jesus is the Lord?'

'Oh yes, they talk about it often at school.'

'That's right,' says Grace.

A lot of the women around them have taken off their scarves and are fanning themselves. There are five or six people on the platform now, each of them being looked after by a helper. Somebody is moaning and crying very loudly. Nkosi sees that it is a woman in a bright yellow skirt with red flowers and the chief man has his hand on her head. Under his hand her body is bending forwards and backwards, turning and writhing under it like she wants to get away but is stuck to it.

'How long,' shouts the man down the mike at her, 'how long have you been manifesting?'

'Why does he have to shout?' says Nkosi. 'Why doesn't he just talk, seeing she's right next to him? She's frightened.'

'He's talking to the devil in her,' says Grace. 'He has to be powerful to scare the devil.'

All the carers have their hands on the heads of the sufferers. One or two are writhing and wriggling, just like the first lady. Most of them are crying. One boy is throwing out his arms from side to side.

'But it's not good for people –' begins Nkosi and then suddenly...'

'OUT!' shouts the man with the mike, 'SATAN, DEMON, TOKOLOSH – IN THE NAME OF THE LORD JESUS – OUT – NOW!' He has his hand on the back of her neck and she is screaming and throwing herself on the ground and the crowd is waving their hands above their heads and shouting 'Bless the Lord!'

And then it's all quiet and the man says: 'All of you! Close your eyes. And pray. In the name of the Lord Jesus – pray that the demons will leave – now.' And they all start murmuring and praying.

All along the row on the floor in front of them are the handbags of the women. Something inside Nkosi is telling him – 'Crouch down, Nkosi, open their bags. No one will see, no one will know. Take some money, Nkosi, just a little, just enough for a taxi home and maybe some sweets. Not even for yourself, Nkosi – for the children. Go on, quick, before they open their eyes.'

Before he knows it he is down, crouching on the floor. It is easy – nobody is watching.

Then Grace has got him by the shoulders, is whispering furiously. 'What are you doing, Nkosi? How could you steal in my church?'

She has got him up in her arms, she is pushing her way back up the aisle, out of the hall, down the steps, into the street.

'I didn't – I didn't – I was just looking...' he is whimpering. 'I'm hungry, Grace, I just wanted to get money for a taxi...'

She is marching along, with him bumping uncomfortably on her back.

'I'm sorry, Grace,' he says, at last.

She is walking doggedly back up the hill and she is beginning to wonder. Was it Nkosi, her sweet, good boy, all by himself, who decided to steal that money? There were a lot of demons being called out in that church during the strong prayer – a lot of demons.

Sharon was to say later: 'Maybe there was a piece of Nkosi that just wanted to be left alone and maybe that was his way of expressing his anger. There was no malicious side to him. If there was one thing Gail taught him it was the difference between right and wrong. How could a child with such a clear understanding of what's right and wrong live his life up to a certain point in one way and then suddenly change? Either his brain was being invaded by the virus or, if he was conscious of what he was doing, he was sending a message.'

Chapter
Ten

BY THE MIDDLE of 2000, it was estimated that the number of HIV/AIDS infections in South Africa had risen to 4.7 million[40], close to 10% of the population. The presidential AIDS panel of experts, some taking the orthodox medical view and some taking the dissident view, drew up a draft report in August 2000, which recommended that, inter alia, '... *a series of immediately doable epidemiological studies be undertaken to prove or disprove once and for all that HIV causes AIDS.*'[41] Some members of the panel refused to sign the draft, however, and a final report was deferred until December of 2000.

On 11 September, *Time* magazine published an interview with President Mbeki, which dwelt at length on the problem of AIDS in Africa. The following is an extract:

TIME: You've been criticised for playing down the link between HIV and AIDS. Where do you now stand on this very controversial issue?

MBEKI: Clearly there is such a thing as Acquired Immune Deficiency. The question you have to ask is what produces this deficiency. A whole variety of things can cause the immune system to collapse. Now it is perfectly possible that among those things is a particular virus. But the notion that immune deficiency is only acquired from a single virus cannot be sustained. Once you say immune deficiency is acquired from that virus your response will be antiviral drugs. But if you accept that there can be a variety of reasons, including poverty and the many diseases that afflict Africans, then you can have a more comprehensive treatment response.

TIME: Are you prepared to acknowledge that there is a link between HIV and AIDS?

MBEKI: No, I am saying that you cannot attribute immune deficiency solely and exclusively to a virus. There may very well be a virus. But TB, for example, destroys the immune system and at a certain point if you have TB you will test HIV-positive because the immune system is fighting the TB which is destroying it. Then you will go further to say TB is an opportunistic disease of AIDS, whereas in fact TB is the thing that destroyed the immune system in the first place. But if you come to the conclusion that the only thing that destroys immune systems is HIV then your only response is to give them anti-retroviral drugs. There's no point in attending to this TB business because that's just an opportunistic disease. If the scientists say... this virus is part of a variety of things from which people acquire immune deficiency, I have no problem with that.

This article provoked such criticism both at home and abroad that the government felt obliged, on 29 September, to publish a statement that appeared in many South African newspapers, saying that it had been an edited version of the interview and that President Mbeki had in the full transcript made it clear that he was prepared to accept that HIV might very well be a causal factor.

The statement went on to say that the government was putting money into research for a vaccine, that it had a five-year strategic plan, that it was continuing research on MTCT drugs, and that it had set up a panel of experts that included three cabinet members (Health, Presidency and Arts, Culture, Science and Technology).

Nkosi's jacket seemed to be getting bigger and bigger. When Laurette hugged him, she could feel only bones under it. But his voice on the telephone was as cheerful as ever.

'He always knows at once who it is before I identify myself,' she told Gail. 'He always says straight away "Hi, Laurette! How are you? How's Julia? How are the cats?"'

Gail said: 'I don't think he's going to live long. He keeps talking about dying. I ask him whether he wants to opt out and he says no, but he doesn't want to take the medication. So I've said to him, let's go to America and if he wants to opt out after that, if he's had enough, then he must stop taking it.'

'How long has he been on it?'

'Well, he's been on the triple therapy since May, but it's not making him feel any better. Edwin Cameron reckons it's too late. I don't know whether we should embark on this second trip to America. I don't know whether he's up to it.'

'When are you supposed to be going?'

'End of September. The AIDS Minority Council has invited us over for their conference in Atlanta. It's a great opportunity to get funds for Nkosi's Haven. And I thought perhaps while we're there I could go to San Francisco and thank those people who motivated the donation of forty thousand dollars for Nkosi's Haven: you know, Jerry and Judy Laughlin. But how I'm going to stand up to all those extra hours on the plane without a fucking cigarette I don't know.'

Two residents of Rossmoor, a wealthy suburb of San Francisco, had watched Nkosi making his speech in Durban on ABC Television. The programme went on to describe Nkosi's Haven and to tell the viewers a little about the conditions in South Africa and the struggle against AIDS there.

Jerry and Judy Laughlin were moved by this story and in particular by Nkosi who, they felt, 'put a face' on the problem. On the off-chance, they searched the Internet and found Gail's telephone number. Jerry gave her a call, and an association began that culminated in the Laughlins raising forty thousand dollars for Nkosi's Haven.

When the trip to Atlanta was planned, the money from Rossmoor was still in America, so Gail contacted the Laughlins to suggest that a little of it might be spent on a trip across to San Francisco. She and Nkosi could then thank the donors in person. Jerry and Judy were delighted, and set about arranging a seminar for local residents at which the Johnsons could speak. Past President of the American Medical Association, Lonnie Bristow, also agreed to speak. They managed to get the venue and the entertainment donated, as well as Gail and Nkosi's hotel accommodation.

Before they left on their trip, they heard from Diane Stevens that ABC Television wanted them to do a live talk show in New York in the morning on their way through, so they had to leave a night earlier than had originally been planned. But when they got to New York, the story all over the news was that a Portuguese ferry had run aground, allegedly because the captain was busy watching soccer, and ABC decided to cover that instead of Nkosi's arriving in America, so their broadcast was cancelled.

However, Diane managed to get tickets for them to the Amnesty Awards dinner that evening, where Danny Glover was to receive an award. They were invited to sit at Danny's table. Unexpectedly, he was on crutches, having just had a hip replacement. ('You have a beautiful crutch,' quipped Gail.) Also at their table, to Gail's pleasure ('*Hold me back!*'), was Harrison Ford.

Jerry and Judy Laughlin met them on their arrival in San Francisco and took them to their hotel. They were able to rest for that afternoon and evening, but the following day was the seminar for local residents and then a visit to a school that boasted the top school football team in America. Nkosi spoke to the children and they all loved him, and were much moved by what he said. Very few of them had ever seen an infected person. They gave him a football jersey with their logo on it, which fitted him like a generous ballgown.

Gail spoke to the children about trans-racial adoption, which is quite rare in America. One of them approached her afterwards and said reprovingly: 'You know it's very bad to smoke!'

A local journalist on the *Rossmoor News*, Wilma Murray, picked up the story of Nkosi and Gail's visit, and organised a trip in a cable car above the city and then a meeting for them with the Mayor of San Francisco, Willie L Brown Jnr. They visited him in his parlour, and he proclaimed that it was 'Nkosi Johnson Day in San Francisco,' and gave them a specially printed certificate to that effect.

Wilma Murray also had the idea of writing to Robin Williams, who was a local resident. Robin responded with warmth and invited them to lunch at a nearby Italian restaurant.

So Gail, Nkosi, Diane, Jerry, Wilma and her son were fetched in a stretch limo, and they all met Robin and his personal assistant over pasta. It was a hilarious lunch.

Diane slips her jacket half off her shoulders and fans herself.

'What's wrong?' asks Gail.

'Oh, I'm having a hot flash,' says Diane.

'O, Mamma!' says Robin, 'O, Sweet Jesus!' and it's off with his jacket and fanning himself too, 'O, Mamma, am I hot!'

He presents Nkosi with a signed copy of the script of his film *Jumanji*. Gail keeps disappearing onto the pavement outside to have a cigarette. Robin teases her about it: 'I can see you at home, Nkosi, sitting on your Momma's lap, and she says, "Hey 'Kosi," she says, "turn the pages darling, Momma's smoking." '

Nkosi admires Robin's luminous sneakers, and in a trice his PA gets sent out to find a pair for Nkosi. She's not successful, but comes back with the news that there's a toyshop round the corner. Off they all go as soon as lunch is over and Nkosi gets given a stunning aluminium scooter. Robin picks up a Trailer Trash doll. She's the equivalent of a Barbie doll, complete with cigarette and stiletto heels, a pig under her arm, wearing shorts, and her boobs are nearly bursting out. On the back it says 'My daddy says I'm the nicest kisser in the county.' Robin packs up laughing. 'Hey, Gail, this is for you!' he says, and buys it for her.

After two days in San Francisco, Nkosi and Gail and Diane flew on to Atlanta for the AIDS conference there. They stayed at the Sheraton Hotel. The conference was taking place in conjunction with an AIDS exhibition, and Diane had organised for them to help at the Project People Foundation's stand, run by Linda Tarry-Chart. At the stand they were selling Linda's beaded AIDS ribbons, which had been launched the last time Gail and Nkosi were in America.

At lunchtime Nkosi spoke to the delegates – about five hundred people in all – in the banqueting ballroom of the hotel. He told them how he had always thought of himself as a lucky little boy compared with other children, because he had three meals a day and running hot water, and he wanted to speak out on behalf of those who couldn't speak for themselves. He knew what many poor people had to go through in terms of rejection and abuse. He felt responsible, he said, to stand up and be counted as an infected child.

Gail comes into the bedroom of the suite they share with Diane at the Sheraton.

'What have you got there, Nkosi?'

'Just some Imodium.'

'Show me.'

Reluctantly, he opens his hand. It is full of small white pills.

'And just what the fuck do you think you are doing?'

'I want to be sure I don't get diarrhoea on the plane.'

'Give them to me.' She counts them. 'Do you know what nine Imodium tablets would do to you? Cement you up for good. What are you? A fucking idiot? And don't start crying at me. I'm not impressed.'

Nkosi slides down off the bed and disappears into the lounge. Gail gets on with her packing. Soon there are voices. Nkosi talking to Diane.

The door bursts open.

'How can you shout at the child, Gail? He's not well, he's exhausted; he's done a magnificent job on this trip, and all you can do is shout at him. It's time you thought about how he feels...' She has her arm round Nkosi and with her other hand is wiping his tears.

'Did you tell her why I *kakked* you out?' demands Gail.

'He doesn't have to tell me. You always...'

'I was just in time to stop him swallowing nine Imodium tablets. And you!' – she says to Nkosi, 'are a manipulating little shit! If you are going to tell someone a story – tell them the whole story.'

People were much nicer to children in America than they were at home, Nkosi decided. They were always giving him things and telling him how wonderful he was. But he could see Gail rolling her eyes every time it happened. Better make the most of it while it lasted.

Gail and Laurette attended the auction for 23 Mitchell Street on 12 October at the municipal auction rooms in Braamfontein. A big grey room in a big grey building.

True to the bank's promise, the bidding started at R1. But the estate agent who had visited the premises was there. Again Gail said to him: 'Please don't bid for it – we're running a care centre for people with AIDS.'

Again he shrugged regretfully. His bosses had instructed him...

The bidding rose higher and higher. When it reached R30 000, Laurette lost her cool.

'THIS HOUSE IS FOR HIV-INFECTED PEOPLE! WE NEED IT!'

Surprisingly, the bidding stopped almost immediately, and the house went to Nkosi's Haven for the relatively low sum of R35 000.

On Sunday, 22 October, the Rev. Brian Oosthuizen of the Methodist Church in Mondeor receives two unusual visitors.

One of the women in his congregation, Mrs Ursula Miles, has had the idea of inviting Gail and Nkosi Johnson to speak to them all. She is involved with the church AIDS task group and does AIDS networking with the pharmaceutical company Roche.

There are three services every Sunday at Mondeor, one at 7.45, one at 9.45 and one more relaxed and informal, with drums and guitars, in the evening. Gail and Nkosi have agreed to speak at all three, although they will go home for a rest after the second one. Also, this Sunday they have decided to have a Celebration of Song, and the children's choir from Dale Mondeor School is coming to sing for them.

The congregation has launched into *Onward Christian Soldiers* as the visitors appear at the door. Very appropriate, thinks Brian, as he hurries to greet them. He leads them up to the front, and everyone sits down in high expectation.

The trouble is, Nkosi is so small, no one except those in the front row can see him.

'Tell you what,' says Brian, 'you stand up on the communion rail, and I'll hold you steady.'

He scoops the child up – he's so light, it's as though he's a four-year-old – and perches him on the railing. Everybody laughs.

'All right, Nkosi, what have you got to say to us?'

Nkosi doesn't speak for long, but he tells them how he himself has AIDS, how Gail has looked after him, and how important it is to care for HIV children, to give them proper food and a safe place to stay, just as they have in Nkosi's Haven.

The congregation is visibly moved at the sight of this frail child, clearly in the last stages of the disease, talking to them so earnestly of the plight of other children.

Brian feels tears pricking behind his eyes. He lifts him down and gives him a hug.

When it is Gail's turn, she says: 'What'll I do with my broomstick?'

'Come on, Gail,' he says, 'you'll be fine. We've polished up her halo,' he adds to the congregation, 'so that she can stand in the pulpit.'

She tells them about the need to accept those with AIDS, about the need to care for orphans, and about how important it is to keep mothers and children together.

There was something about the warmth of Brian and his congregation that impressed Gail very much, so it seemed natural when Nkosi became really ill the following year, that she should telephone Brian. He visited the house a number of times, and his big, warm presence was just what she needed in the way of help and support.

Badie Badenhorst is troubled. There is no doubt that his boy, his Nkosi, is declining. He is taking leaps and bounds in maturity. Everybody who talks to him is amazed by his adult grasp of his situation and the way he can talk about it. But at the same time he doesn't seem able to cope with his school work any more. In fact, scholastically, he has gone right back to the level of a Grade Two child.

Gail has been to see him and they had quite a talk. Okay, as a mother she has high expectations and it's only natural she should want him to be able to read and write properly now that he's mixing with all sorts of important people. She said if he can't read a welcoming letter from a child in America, it's a disgrace. She's insisting that at the end of the year he should go right back and do Grade Three again. She says it isn't fair to the other kids. She has a point, but Badie doesn't want to fail him.

And then they got on to the subject of pizzas. Oh boy, that was a bad moment. Gail even said to him that there were probably other children at the school who hadn't had proper food in two days – why was he buying pizza for Nkosi? He tried to tell her that it was because Nkosi was such a special child, but she wasn't impressed. What he didn't know before was that Nkosi isn't supposed to have pizza because it makes his diarrhoea worse. And there's Nkosi coaxing him – and every other Tom, Dick and Harry, probably – into getting it for him.

Anyway, that's a side issue, the main one being that perhaps he ought to give Nkosi the choice as to what he does in the following year. The teachers think he's spending too much time out of class, too much time in his, Badie's, office. Well, maybe so, but Badie has a gut feeling that that's what's necessary now. No more pressure. They have been talking a lot lately, Nkosi sitting on the upturned wastepaper bin behind Badie's desk, and he has given quite a few hints that he knows he doesn't have long. It's as though he's been trying to cram a whole lifetime into his eleven years. Not sorry for himself – never that, but there have been times lately when his eyes have been, not tearful perhaps, but certainly having the look of recent tears and this is new.

There has been something else, too, about Nkosi's life that has been worrying him more and more, especially now. While Gail has, of course, done a truly Good Samaritan act in caring for Nkosi all these years, there is no actual practice of religion in that home – not as far as Badie knows. This child has no habit of daily prayer, no familiarity with a Heavenly Father as a reality – someone he can turn to in times of distress as Badie himself does. He puts his elbows on the desk and folds his hands. He puts his forehead down on his hands and doesn't say a prayer precisely, doesn't address his God in so many words, but the calling out for help and advice is there nevertheless.

After a while, he lifts his head, leans back in his chair and picks up his pen. It's tied by a piece of string to another pen, and even has a bit of Prestik to hold it down to his desk. But they still manage to walk off with it. 'Borrow me your pen, Badie,' they say, and it's gone. He twizzles the string back and forth between his fingers. Tomorrow is Thursday, the day when Jan Grobbelaar is booked to see one or two of the children. He will lay the problem before him, he will tell him that his boy Nkosi is busy dying and needs to be given – not a dose of religion, but some sort of an assurance that everything is not going to stop when he dies, that he will be going on to something better and that God has it all in hand and is moreover holding Nkosi in His hands and will not be letting him go. Better it should come from Jan: he is a man of deep faith and is trained in counselling.

Badie smiles to himself when he remembers how they first met. Bumped into each other, in fact. Quite a few years ago, it was. He'd been in his car, going from east to west, and he stopped at a traffic light, and this other car had also stopped, going from north to south, and they both drove off and collided. The other guy introduced himself as Jan Grobbelaar, and he introduced himself as Badie Badenhorst, and they became friends, big friends, and they had been friends ever since. It wasn't long before he discovered that Jan was, among other things, a counsellor at the Discovery Hospital Rape Clinic, and he had the thought that perhaps he could help some of the distressed children at his school too. Many of them came from very difficult homes, and had problems that Badie himself didn't feel equal to tackling. Furthermore, as the headmaster, he felt it necessary to keep a certain distance, not to get too involved. He leans forward and picks up the telephone.

'Well now,' says the man, holding out his hand. 'My name is Jan Grobbelaar. Most of the children call me *Oom*[42] Jan. I'm very pleased to meet you, Nkosi. I've heard a lot about you from Mr Badenhorst. I've even seen you and your mother on TV.'

Nkosi shakes his hand and settles himself down on the chair opposite. This man who Badie wanted him to see looks okay. He's seen him a couple of times around the school. Now, close up, he's got a voice and a smile that are round and warm, like his face.

'I'm a counsellor,' he is saying. 'Do you know what that is? I try to help people who are maybe worried or in some sort of trouble. I don't always succeed, but that's what I try to do. Sometimes I talk to people who are very unhappy – children who are unhappy perhaps – and we just have a little chat and I try to make them feel better about themselves. You've seen me around, haven't you?'

Nkosi acknowledges that he has.

'What makes people more unhappy than anything else is when they feel that they are no good, that people don't like them, or whatever. Mr Badenhorst thinks that perhaps you've got something that's worrying you, Nkosi?'

Nkosi is quiet for a while. What should he answer? This big man in his denim jacket and jeans, he really does look like somebody one could talk to. Maybe he should mention something to do with school.

'I do have a problem,' he says.

Mr Grobbelaar leans forward. 'Do you want to tell me about it? Don't be shy. Whatever it is, let's talk about it.'

Nkosi gnaws his lip. 'Um... it's... they don't want to play with me. Because I've got AIDS.' He's been staring at his feet, but now he ventures to glance up, to see how the man is looking. He's not looking at all. He's got his eyes shut. Squeezed tight shut, in fact. Nkosi's own eyes begin to wander around the room. Suddenly, the man is talking again.

'Nkosi, you aren't the only one who is sick. I'm going to tell you something. Every single person on this planet has got some type of "AIDS". This one's sick because he's hasn't got food for the day. And that one's sick because his parents beat him up. And you will see that children with the same sort of problem usually play together. You have a different problem and perhaps they feel you are different.'

It's not the sort of answer Nkosi expected to get. He'll take it home with him and he'll think about it.

Afterwards, in Badie's office, Jan says: 'I think, you know, they don't play with him because he's so much older in his mind than they are. They talk to him but they don't play with him. And maybe it's because they see him spending so much time with you. I don't know. But, you know, to answer such a question from a child of that age is very difficult. You can do so much damage. So I said, "God, please give me the answer to this one. A child can't die with such a question on his mind".'

The next time Jan sees him, the question is more difficult. It's the one so many people ask in so many situations. 'Why me?'

And again, before answering, Jan says a prayer and an answer comes to him. They are sitting close beside one another this time, and he lays one hand over Nkosi's small one.

'Nkosi, did it ever occur to you that you've got something I haven't got? Look at it this way. You know all about AIDS, don't you? You and your mother, you talk to other children with AIDS; you try to help them and give them somewhere safe to live, you try to make them feel a bit happier. You've even got it in your own body, you know what it feels like, you know how to deal with it. Now, you see, you can be the teacher. And Mr Badenhorst and I, we are the pupils. Because of what you teach us, we can help others. You are strong, Nkosi. You aren't like some of the others who give up. You can talk about your problem to people and show them how it is and what they could do to help.'

Nkosi is swinging his legs. He looks doubtful, but he doesn't take his hand away.

Jan gets up. 'Come. We're going to go to Mr Badenhorst's office and you're going to ask him the same question.'

They go, and Nkosi asks. Mr Badenhorst comes from behind his desk and puts his arm around him. 'Nkosi, I don't know what Oom Jan has told you, but I think it's so that we can all learn from you. The more you talk, the more people will listen.' He turns the child round so that he can look into his face. 'How's that? Are you perhaps feeling a bit better now?' Nkosi nods. 'Off you go then, and you think about what Oom Jan has said.'

The third time they talk, Nkosi is looking really down. Jan knows about this. There are times when you feel you just can't go on. He himself is struggling with a heart problem that makes him very tired. And when you do counselling, especially with children, you have to listen very hard because perhaps they will say one thing and mean something quite different. You have to be quick to read between the lines. He feels, today, that he must give up. He just doesn't have the energy to go on with it. But Nkosi is in front of him and Nkosi, he can see, is in trouble.

He gets down on the floor and he beckons Nkosi to sit down with him. It will be better if they can look at each other on the same level.

'Now then, Nkosi, what's the matter? You're not looking so good today.'

Nkosi shakes his head.

'You want to talk about it?'
'I want to see my mother.'
'Has she gone away?'
'Not Mommy Gail.'
'You are talking about your real mother?'
Nkosi nods. 'She died.'
'Well, that's very sad for you. When was this?'
'1997. Just before I started school.'
'Did you go to the funeral?'
Nkosi nods.

Jan leans forward and scoops the child onto his lap. 'What do you think it means, Nkosi, to die?'

He is quiet for a bit and then he says: 'Maybe you see your mother again?'

'I think so,' says Jan. 'That's one thing it means.'

'But maybe I'll go somewhere else and I won't see her,' says Nkosi.

'Oh no,' says Jan.

'How do you know?'

'Because your mother has gone to God, Nkosi, and that's where we all go when we die. It's not like going to sleep and never waking up. We go to sleep and then we wake up and there we are with God. All of us.'

'Is that heaven?'

'That's heaven. And the Bible tells us that the streets are all paved with gold. That's quite something, isn't it? But the best thing is that your mother is there waiting for you.'

'Can I go to church with you?' asks Nkosi.

Jan is surprised. 'Why do you want to do that?'

'Mommy Gail isn't keen to take me. She says it's not her scene.'

'But my church is all in Afrikaans; you wouldn't understand any of it.'

'No, but I'd like to go there.'

'Well, we'll have to talk about it. How about you coming one day with me to talk to some children at another school? I want to stand you up in front of them and say – "You see this guy? He's sick, very sick, but he never misses a day of school!" '

Nkosi laughs.

In the end, he went neither to Oom Jan's Afrikaans church, nor to the other school with him, because there never seemed to be an opportunity. But every time Oom Jan came to the school, Nkosi would go and greet him and have a little conversation. But the talks became shorter and shorter because Jan could see that Nkosi was tired.

Nkosi took his position as chief motivator for Nkosi's Haven very seriously.

'This is my house,' he would say, 'and I must know everything that happens here. Is everything all right, Grace?'

And Grace would tell him that in a houseful of women there would always be this or that, a little bit of jealousy and this one is fighting with that one...

'Right,' he would say, 'call a meeting. I want all the mothers here in the lounge.'

And the mothers would come and they would all try to talk at once.

'No, I will talk to Eunice first – you others wait.'

And Eunice would give her side, and Sibongile, and then Samantha...

'You don't want to wash the dishes?' Nkosi would say, 'but it's your turn. You go and do it now. You don't want her to discipline your child? Then you must discipline him yourself.'

No one argued. In Nkosi's Haven, Nkosi was king.

The mothers and children loved him. They respected him and spoiled him and laughed at his terrible jokes. He tickled one of the children until she shrieked and Oscar said: '*Ufletiza amabetri!*' Nkosi liked the sound of this and went around saying it proudly.

'Do you know what it means?' asked Jane one day.

'No.'

'It means you are wasting that person's strength because they laugh until they die.'

One day Sibongile is not looking good.

'What's the matter, Sibongile?'

Sibongile blows her nose and tries to pretend everything's fine, but Nkosi has her by the hand and he's bringing her to a little corner in the lounge.

'Come and sit down. I saw you crying. Are you sad?'

'Yes, I'm sad.'

'Aren't you feeling well? I want to know how you are feeling.'

'I'm scared for my baby.'

The small hand holding hers tightens warmly. 'Is she sick?'

'Yes, she's sick. She's got diarrhoea.'

'Well, you know what to do about that. Take her off milk and give her weak bush tea – lots to drink all the time. How are *you* feeling, Sibongile? Do you like being here?'

'Yes, I like it. Maybe I'd be dead if I'm not here. But I'm sick.'

'Are you frightened of what might happen to your baby if you die, Sibongile?'

She doesn't answer.

'It happened to me. I never got to stay with my real mother. And then she died and left me. We're all going to die sometime. But you know that Gail will always look after her, don't you? And she's got lots of other mothers here.'

'Yes, I know.'

'Come. Don't you want to make me some tea and toast? Or maybe I'll ask Eunice.'

'I'll do it. You don't have to ask her. She's busy. I want to do it.'

In the kitchen, Eunice is standing over the stove, making an omelette.

'Can I have a little piece, Eunice? I'll put it on my toast.'

'You want toast? I'll make you toast.'

'No,' says Sibongile, '*I'm* making his toast. He wants me to make it, don't you, Nkosi? He loves me best.'

'No, he loves all of us.'

Nkosi is looking from one to the other and smiling, but he doesn't say anything. Eunice waves the egg lifter. 'We have a competition once, me and two others. We ask him – Nkosi, who do you love best? And one said I'll buy you a car and one said I'll give you chips, I'll give you bread, and he sit down and say – "Let me decide." And he say "I love you all, but I love Eunice!" '

Sibongile takes out the bread and says, 'Well, I'm making his toast.'

'That's right,' says Nkosi. 'Little bit brown, not too much; and I'll have some of Eunice's egg on it. And maybe Samantha can make the tea.'

'Samantha!' yells Sibongile, 'Nkosi wants tea!'

'And we can all sit in the lounge and have a good talk,' says Nkosi, 'while the children are all still playing outside. I want to know everything you've been doing since I was here last weekend.'

'Sweetie-Pie, her mother died. She went home to her Gran. And there's a new mother.'

'A new mother? Why didn't Gail tell me? And I want to talk to Feroza. Where's Feroza?'

'She's in bed. She's not so well.'

'What's wrong?'

'She doesn't want to eat. She's too sick. She's sleeping all the time.'

'Ismail!' Nkosi calls to a small boy who is watching from the doorway. 'Go and see if your mother is awake. Come and tell me.' The child disappears.

Two toddlers stagger through the door he has left open, one trying to beat the other over the head with a plastic mug. She starts roaring, nose and eyes streaming. Nkosi crouches down beside her. He says to the new mother who has come to see what's the trouble: 'Pick her up. Wipe her nose. She's not hurt.'

The new mother looks in surprise at Eunice, who laughs. 'You must do as Nkosi says. He's the father here.'

Feroza Mohammed had been rejected by her family and community, and was taken in by Nkosi's Haven on 1 December 1999. She had a son Ismail, who came with her, but she did not tell Gail that she was pregnant at first, fearing that Nkosi's Haven might not accept her. Had they known, Feroza would have been given special care and extra supplements immediately to strengthen her and the coming child. In March 2000, Gail received an SOS call from Nkosi's Haven – Feroza was in labour and needed to go to the hospital. Gail and Nicci rushed over and loaded her into the back of the Uno. At full speed, Gail drove to the hospital, but they were only halfway there when it became apparent that the baby was about to arrive. Gail did her best, taking the snake bends of Empire Road like a racing driver, Nicci hanging out of the passenger window feeling sick, and Feroza in the final stage of childbirth. They were too late. The premature baby was born in the car, still in his caul, but only survived a couple of hours.

Feroza was on the point of death many times, but always managed to find the strength to pull herself back. She and Nkosi had a special relationship; they were able to support each other inwardly. They would talk together a lot, and although Nkosi was very short and she was tall, Feroza was to say later: 'When we talked together we were the same size.'

Gail sometimes said to her: 'Sweetheart, it's very important you should go to a hospice; this isn't the right environment. We can bring Ismail through at any time. I don't think your son should see you dying.'

'No,' said Feroza, 'I want to die here. This is my home.'

Several of the mothers had died since becoming residents of Nkosi's Haven, but never actually in the house; two had gone back to their home places and the others had had to be taken to hospital. It became Gail's dream to buy the house next door, and to open it as a hospice, so that those who died need never leave. Later, the dream was to be realised when Nashua Ltd donated the purchase money for the house next door.

At home time, Nkosi meets Eric at the school gate.

'Hi,' says Eric, 'I've been waiting for you. How are you feeling these days?'

'Okay,' says Nkosi. 'I get a bit tired sometimes. You know what? We went power-boating yesterday.'

'Cool,' says Eric. 'What's it like?'

'It makes waves this high, and it's kind of up and down all the time. There's a wheel you have to steer with and they said I must do it.'

'So did you?'

'No. I was too scared. So they turned round and took me back.'

Eric laughs. He bends down and picks a stalk of grass. 'Shame about Mr Stevenson, hey?'

'Ja.'

'Feels really strange when one of your teachers dies.'

'Ja.'

'Have you ever seen anyone dead?'

'Ja. I saw my Mommy Daphne in her coffin.'

'Were you scared?'

'No. But it made me sad. It makes me sad when I think about her. And Mr Stevenson dying reminded me.' Nkosi's eyes are tearful.

'Must be terrible if your mother dies.'

'Ja.' Nkosi heaves his bag onto his back.

'I'll carry your bag,' says Eric.

'Gee, thanks.'

They walk along in silence for a bit.

'Tell you what – I'm scared of dying,' says Nkosi.

'Ja. Me too. I bet everyone is.'

'Ja.'

They turn down the hill, towards his house. At the gate, he takes back his bag.

'Thanks, hey, Eric,' he says, 'See you tomorrow.'

'Tell me about death, Mommy, I don't want to die.'

She gathers him up into her arms. 'Sweetheart, all I know is you're going to have wonderful times and it's very peaceful with beautiful music. You're going to see your Mom and a whole lot of other friends. Look, I know you're scared, but you don't need to be.'

'I don't want to die.'

'Okay, then, 'Kosi, we've got to fight. And you fight with your medicine – you don't lie to me about your medicine, you don't have pizzas all the time. You can't say you don't want to die and not do anything about it. I can help you with physical things, but inside you've also got to fight. Look in the mirror every morning and say: FUCK YOU, VIRUS! Well, I know you won't say that, but that's what I'd like you to say.'

But Nkosi gave up on his triple therapy several times, and each time she would say: 'Kosi, do you really mean this – do you want to cop out?'

'No.'

'Look, 'Kosi. Every one of us has to die. Even me. Now why are you crying?'

'Because I don't want you to die. I'll miss you.'

'Well, I'm not quite ready yet so you mustn't worry.' She scoops him up onto her lap and hugs him. 'Come on, 'Kosi, stop crying. I'm not going to cry because my eyelashes will come off.' In spite of his tears, he has to laugh. 'You know, if you die before me, you can sit on my shoulder and tell me when I'm doing something bloody stupid. Which will be every bloody day, won't it? Don't think about it, 'Kos. Think about what's ahead of us. We've still got lots to do.'

But the diarrhoea didn't let up, and he was becoming exhausted.

In December, his CD4 count was very low again so Gail took him to the doctor, who persuaded him to go back onto two of the triple medications, leaving out the one that tasted really bad. He had had eleven and a half years of taking medicines and he had had enough. Maybe if the triple therapy had made him feel better, he would have persevered with it, but by that stage, nothing was helping. Nkosi knew what was going on in his body.

On World AIDS Day, 1 December, Gail and Nkosi took part in a discussion on AIDS on the Katie and Benedict Show on Radio 702. During the course of it, Nkosi appalled Gail by saying 'President

Mbeki better watch out!' This caused quite a sensation and Radio 702 decided to repeat the recording on World AIDS Day the following year.

In the year since November 1999, Nkosi and Gail had been invited to speak at Parkview Primary School, King David School, Coronationville School, Westbury Senior Secondary, Newclare Primary, Grantley College, Yeshiva College, Johannesburg Girls' Preparatory, Houghton School, and several others, as well as to give the trophy at an inter-schools drum competition at Helpmekaar Hoërskool, and take part in a workshop at a 'Living Openly' seminar. There had also been interviews on ABC television, Canadian Broadcasting, Finnish TV, BBC, the morning show on local television with Vuyo Mbuli, KTV, German TV, Radio 702, and Felicia Mabuza-Suttle's show. He was invited to attend 'Carols by Candlelight' at a shopping mall in Rivonia and to give a talk to the mineworkers at a local gold mine.

Also on World AIDS Day, Gail and Nkosi went to a food factory on the East Rand where they had been asked to participate in a programme on AIDS for the employees. Also giving a talk there was another child of eleven whose mother had recently died of an AIDS-related disease. This mother had started an AIDS action unit at the factory before she died, and the daughter had been brought up to be very concerned with the problems of infected people. She not only spoke at gatherings when asked, but took herself off to the St Francis Hospice and helped bath the patients on a regular basis.

At the end of the programme, both she and Gail were given donations in envelopes. When asked whether she charged a fee for giving talks, Gail always said no, but if the hosting institution had budgeted for a money allocation, then they should donate it to Nkosi's Haven. So, on this occasion, she got an envelope, the little girl got an envelope, but Nkosi got nothing.

The next time he was at Nkosi's Haven, he said to Grace: 'Grace, do you know how old I am?'

'How old are you, Nkosi?'

'I am eleven years old, nearly twelve. Do you think I should speak to Gail about paying me a salary?'

'A salary? What are you going to do with a salary?'

'Well, if I want a chocolate I must go and ask Gail for it. A teenager like me. Gail must work out a salary for me.'

'But how are you earning a salary?'

'Because I'm the one that's giving the talks at the schools and so on. I really think it's time I ask her for a salary.'

'And if she says no?'

'Well, then I'm not going to do the talks. And I need money for when I'm going to Cape Town.'

'Well 'Kosi, you must ask her.'

So after his conversation with Grace, in the car on the way home, he says: 'Mommy – I want to earn money.'

'What for? You've got everything.'

'To take you out to dinner.'

Gail nearly turns the car over. 'Don't bullshit me! You want to spend it on sweets and pizzas and ice cream. But okay, 'Kos, I hear what you're saying. In future, any talk that you give, I'll speak to the board and ask them to give you a hundred rand out of whatever donation is given.'

But very soon Nkosi himself is handed an envelope, on an occasion when he stands up on a chair and hands out certificates of completion for AIDS-counselling courses to Lancet staff. When he opens it, he shows Gail that he has been enriched by R200.

'Wow!' says Gail, 'now you can take me out to dinner! Tonight you can take me to The Fishmonger and we'll get sushi. How's that?'

Nkosi agrees, but with somewhat restrained enthusiasm.

When they get to the restaurant, a waiter shows them to a table, pulls out Gail's chair for her, flourishes two menus.

Nkosi is looking nervous. 'How much is this going to cost, Mommy?'

'I don't know. Doesn't matter. You've got money.'

'But I didn't bring it all!'

When a waitress comes to take their order, Nkosi tells her which plate of sushi Gail wants, and what they want to drink. For himself, he orders fish and chips.

While they are eating, Gail says: 'Now you remember how Daddy asked for the bill? When it comes, you check it to make sure it's okay, you put the money down – and, sweetheart, you must leave a tip.'

At once, Nkosi is beckoning the waitress.

'No-no-no-no,' says Gail. 'Let Mommy finish. Am I not allowed a second drink?'

Nkosi decides that is okay, but is evidently anxious to get on with the business side of things.

'Do I *have* to leave a tip?'

'Sweetheart, the service has been good. It's your way of telling the waitress that you appreciate how well she's done her job. Normally it's 10% of the bill.' She shows him how to make the decimal point jump back one figure.

Nkosi counts the money out into the saucer with a long face.

'Don't look so gloomy, sweetheart, that was a delicious dinner. Thank you very much.'

When he did have money in his pocket, however, it didn't stay there long. Especially if he was at Nkosi's Haven.

'Grace, I want you to go to the shops and buy me some litchis. A whole box of litchis. You must bring back the change, and don't forget the cash slip.'

When she returned, he'd call all the children and count them out – so many for Ella, and so many for Tshediso, so many for Ismail, so many for Mpho – where's Thabiso? – so many for Thabiso...

On 15 December, he flew down to Cape Town to stay with Anso and Gerda again. As soon as he got off the plane, people were clustering round at the airport wanting to meet him.

'We'll have to get you some sunglasses and a big hat so's you can be incognito,' said Anso.

Nkosi laughed. 'Ja, like I'm a film star. You know what? We went to visit Kaizer Chiefs. On Tuesday. It was so *lekker*. They're my best.

And you know what else? My Mom's got a new van. A four by four. One of the foreign embassies donated it for Nkosi's Haven. So now she's driving much faster.'

'Wow,' said Anso. 'Heaven help all the other traffic!'

There was no diarrhoea this time, but he struggled to eat because of thrush and a sore throat. He and Siya made a deal whereby they swopped plates and Siya finished up what Nkosi couldn't manage. They made plans – Nkosi wanted to go to the Waterfront to get Christmas presents for the family and some sandals for himself because his *tackies* were too hot.

Although his diarrhoea seemed better, they put nappies on him at night, just to be on the safe side. He was very embarrassed about this and would put his hand over his face and pretend it wasn't happening. But he was proud to be able to tell them the next morning that there had been no accidents.

The Sunday after he arrived, they went to 'Carols by Candlelight' at the Kirstenbosch Botanical Gardens. They arranged for a wheelchair for him and took blankets to sit on and a picnic in cooler bags. Nkosi loved it. He sat, holding his candle and singing completely out of tune. At the end, everyone raised their candles high and they lifted him up so that he could see all the thousands of lights waving in the warm darkness. He was thrilled, and couldn't stop talking about it all the way home.

Anso and Gerda noticed, however, that he often lost track of what he was saying. He'd tell the same story over and over, or he'd repeat the same questions. He would also, uncharacteristically, be irritated with Siya who wanted to play. 'Don't sit so close!' 'Don't touch me!' 'Go away – you're so naughty!'

Towards the end of his stay they all drove out to Cape Point. At a little restaurant some foreign tourists recognised him and wanted him to pose for a photograph with their children. He did so with grace and good humour.

They found a quiet little beach and carried him down to it. They perched him on a rock and made a video of him talking and singing. They got him to paddle a bit in the surf and they all fooled around with the seaweed. They picked up little white stones and said they would always keep them as mementoes of him and this moment down by the sea.

'How deep is the sea?' he said. 'How far does it go?'

When they got home, he began to talk about dying, and it became clear that there was a part of him that was very scared.

'My Mom died recently,' Gerda told him. 'She was very ill, but now I know she's completely better. When you get to heaven, will you go and look for her?'

'Can you look for people in heaven?' he wanted to know.

'Of course. And the good thing is you'll be quite better too. You'll be a strong, handsome guy with big muscles and you must go and ask her for a dance. And when I get there I'm going to look for you – I'm going to look for the handsomest guy in the place and that'll be you, 'Kosi. And you'll take me in your arms and we'll dance and dance.'

'But won't I miss all the people here?'

'We'll all get there in the end, 'Kosi, Gail as well, and she and your own Mom will be able to sit and talk together. That's the good thing about heaven.'

Just before he went home they went to the Waterfront and at the entrance there was a man selling newspapers. He started talking to Nkosi about his mother and sister who had recently died of AIDS.

'He saw something in Nkosi,' says Gerda, 'that was not just a famous TV star. And 'Kosi talked to him so calmly and gently and you could see that he understood the meeting was really meaningful for the man. You could see, you know, that he was very touched.'

While they were there he got his brown leather sandals and a little diary for Nicci, and he looked at CDs for Gail but found them very expensive.

When they got back from shopping they put on music and danced, and picked up Nkosi and whirled him around, and he laughed and laughed.

They took him and Siya out on the last evening for a prawn supper, but he managed to eat only two. In bed that night he seemed to become very anxious. His eyes began rolling around and they feared he might be going into a fit. They sat and held him, soothing him and telling him to calm down and breathe slowly. The next morning they put him on the plane home and he seemed dazed and as though something had shifted in his mind.

Afterwards, they found a whole lot of his pills under the bed where he had hidden them – under the bed and all over the house. Anso phoned Gail and told her, and said she had a sense that he was now very ill and really wanted to go. Gail said she also had that feeling, and that night in the bath with him she said: 'Look, sweetheart, it's really okay if you want to go now.'

'Who's going to feed the cats if I die?'

'Somebody else will, I promise you.'

'And what about the fight against AIDS?'

'Well, 'Kos, what's our goal? How many people must we save?'

'Fifteen thousand.'

'Well, darling, you've got my work cut out for me, haven't you?'

Nkosi had arrived back from his holiday in Cape Town on 22 December. The plan had been that, over Christmas, Gail would be on the yacht with Rob, and Nkosi would be at Pennington with Colleen, but when he came home Gail took one look at him and realised that he was too sick to go anywhere. She phoned Rob, who was already down at the coast, and Colleen, and cancelled the arrangement.

Instead, they spent Christmas Day at Nkosi's Haven. They were busy in the morning, packing presents and getting the turkey ready, when the gate buzzer went. Waiting outside was a woman with her arms full of toys for the children. Her name was Eleanor, and she had telephoned the day before, saying she had contacts in Switzerland who would like to help Nkosi's Haven.

'Come in,' said Gail, 'we're just packing all the presents.'

'And I've got this for you,' said Eleanor, handing Gail a scroll, tied with red ribbon.

'What's this?' She took it, undid the ribbon and unrolled it. She began reading.

'I didn't write it,' said the lady. 'It's by Lyn, a friend of mine.'

'Oh,' said Gail, 'oh, this is stunning.'

And she took it into the lounge, sat down, and said: ' 'Kosi, listen to this:'

NKOSI'S SOUL

Nkosi was a soul when he first met God.

He was amongst many other souls when he listened to what God had to say.

God spoke of the suffering of His children on earth

And that He wanted to send Angels to teach people

To be kind and loving to one another.

Eager to help, Nkosi asked if he could go along as well.

It was then that God asked Nkosi if he would be willing to go back to earth

And be born to a mother that was ill and could pass this illness to him.

Nkosi's smile froze, and puzzled, he asked God how he could help people

If he himself was ill.

When God smiled, Nkosi felt loved and safe.

'My child,' He replied, 'suffering is the greatest teacher.

Most people don't know how to love, so they are afraid of people that are different, and then they become cruel. You, my child, will help to open many hearts.

You will bring tears to some and laughter to others.

You will show strength and courage to all who meet you, my child.'

God paused at Nkosi and looked at him with such love. He then went on:

'You will have the brightest soul and the biggest heart. You are my special Angel.'

Nkosi broke into a beautiful smile and said to God:

'If I can help five people and open their hearts so that they can see others clearly,

Then I would have done my work well. But, just one more question.

Who will take care of me if I am ill and my mother is ill?'
God gave a wink and then replied:
'Do not worry, Nkosi, it is all arranged. There is a soul who
already knows all about
Love and kindness, and she will find you and raise you as her own.
Together you will teach the lesson of love and courage.
You will begin to touch many lives and change many hearts.
Nkosi, because of you, thousands of people will reach out and give.
They will learn the power of love, and you will speak for all
those that are too ill
To speak for themselves.
You are both my precious Angels,
So together you will shine and make a difference.'
It was then that Nkosi asked how he would know this soul who
would so readily
Become his mother. God paused, then spoke:
'Each letter in her name will remind you of your life here and
who you really are.'
'How?' Nkosi exclaimed. God chuckled, then spoke:
'The words 'God always is Love' will give you her name.
Take the first letter of each word and spell it out.' And on that
note, God winked at Nkosi and smiled.
And so it was that Nkosi's legacy began.

'Where did that come from?' asked Nkosi.

'Darling, I don't know. A lady called, Lyn whom we don't know, wrote it. Isn't it beautiful?'

'It's beautiful. Read it again.'

In the days that were to come, Gail read it again, to herself and aloud to Nkosi many times. It became a source of comfort to both of them.

On Boxing Day, the police brought a new baby to Gail's safe house. They had found him abandoned in a flat in the suburb of Yeoville. Neighbours had called them when they heard him crying. He was about four days old, they estimated.

'I've got a new baby,' Gail said to Laurette, over the phone.

'Gail, Nkosi's not at all well. You've got enough on your plate without taking in another abandoned child.'

'How can I let a little boy like that go into one of those institutions where he's just dumped into a cot or on the floor and nobody looks at him?'

Laurette says: 'There are hundreds and hundreds of kids like him.'

'No, I can't let him go.'

They decided to call him Thabo.

On Friday, 29 December, Rob arrives back in Johannesburg. It was the first available flight he could get.

'Let's go out for dinner,' he suggests.

'What about you, Nkosi?' asks Gail, 'Do you want to go with me to Nkosi's Haven this afternoon and then stay over, or do you want to stay home with Nicci and Thabo?'

Nkosi decides he would like to go to Nkosi's Haven. So Gail gathers together the groceries she wanted to deliver and off they go in the late afternoon.

'I've got to go out this evening,' she tells them all, 'and 'Kos has decided he'd like to stay over. But if he's tired, Grace, he must go to bed early, no nonsense. Goodbye, sweetheart, I'll see you tomorrow.' And off she goes, rushing as usual, to change into her going-out caftan (which nevertheless has a few holes in it), leaving Nkosi sitting on the sofa in the lounge.

Grace takes a good look at him. He doesn't look at all well. Since he's been back from Cape Town, he's looking like a little old man, not a child.

'I want a cup of tea,' he says, and she goes to put the kettle on. When she brings the tea he says: 'I want a boiled egg.'

One of the mothers goes and puts two eggs on to boil.

A little while later, he decides he'd like some roast chicken, and then it's a bowl of Weetbix and then it's bread with jam.

And all these things sit there on the coffee table, and Nkosi sits there also. And then he says: 'Call all the mothers,' and they come and sit around him, and he says: 'I've got some money in my pocket and I want you all to have a party.' He brings out a fifty-rand note and gives it to Grace. 'Grace, you must go and get cake and ice cream and Coke.'

Grace takes the note and puts it in her pocket, but she doesn't go anywhere because she can see that all is not right with Nkosi. His eyes are showing too much white and jumping, jumping.

Feroza says: 'Why did Gail bring this child here?'

'What do you mean?' asks Grace.

'Can't you see he's going to die tonight?'

'Why? You're also sick – you've got AIDS – when are *you* going to die?'

'I'm just telling you – can't you see he can just die at any moment?'

Grace is angry at this assumption of special knowledge on Feroza's part. She picks Nkosi up and takes him upstairs to her room and sits him on the bed.

He says: 'I'm cold. Grace, my legs are very cold. I need a nice hot bath.'

Grace runs to turn on the hot water, and because she knows he likes it, she gets into the bath with him. She sits behind him and starts washing his back.

'Wash my head, Grace,' he says.

So she tips warm water on his head and begins to massage it with her fingers, across and across.

'God,' she says, 'there's no place in the Bible where you don't heal someone when they pray. And I'm asking you now – don't let the devil take this child, not while he's in my hands. You took my husband, don't take this child too.'

Over and over again she says the same prayer: 'God, heal this child, God, heal this child...' And she goes on stroking his head.

But when she looks at his eyes they've gone up in his head and suddenly she knows that something very bad is happening because he is rigid in the circle of her arms and he can't seem to breathe properly. She screams for help, scrambles herself out of the bath, and when Feroza comes running, they lift him out and wrap him in a blanket.

Grace sits rocking him while Feroza runs to phone Gail.

'God,' says Grace, 'no one need tell me about God any more. There is no God.'

At the house in Melville, the phone rings. Nicci gets up to answer it. Gail has just returned from her supper out with Rob, and has taken off her shoes and picked up Thabo.

'It's Feroza,' calls Nicci, 'She says there's something wrong with Nkosi.'

Gail comes. 'Here,' she says, 'you hold Thabo,' and she takes the phone. 'What's the matter, Feroza? What do you mean, Nkosi's not talking? Well, bring him to the phone, let me talk to him.'

She waits, while Thabo grizzles a bit, he doesn't want to go to sleep. Nicci puts him up against her shoulder and rubs his back.

'Hello? Hello? Nkosi? What's the matter, my baby? Can't you breathe? Nkosi! Feroza? Feroza, hang in there, I'm on my way.'

And barefoot, wearing her fancy caftan, she grabs up her smokes and the car keys and is off, wrenching the van out of the driveway and through the gate, twisting through the suburbs, belting down the main roads where she can, leaving Rob to follow in his own car.

At Nkosi's Haven, she blasts the hooter outside the gate. 'Come on... come ON!' Someone opens up and she leaps out of the car, leaving the door swinging, and rushes into the house.

Grace has Nkosi with her on the sofa in the lounge, wrapped in a duvet. Feroza is hovering nearby.

He is rigid, shaking in every limb. Grace begins to tell what happened, but Gail stops her.

'Get in the van. We have to get him to Coronation.'

At that time on a Friday night the streets are full of late-night revellers going home. Gail weaves in and out of them, fuming at red lights, sometimes going through them when it is safe, her foot hovering between brake and accelerator. Beside her, Nkosi is snuffling and breathing heavily. Every so often, he arches back in another seizure, and Grace cries out and tries to protect him from hurting himself. Then she resorts to muttering prayers. On they go, twisting and turning through the traffic, causing other drivers to swerve and hoot. Gail curses them and keeps driving.

At Coronation Hospital the Casualty gates are closed. Gail leans on the hooter, and a young man leaps to open. She drives down the slope and stops at the entrance. 'You run in with him – get someone to help – I've got to park the car.'

Grace already has the door open. Gail helps her down, slams the door. Grace runs inside, Nkosi in her arms.

Gail gets back in the van, turns, drives back up to the gates and into the car park. She slows to thank the young man who had opened up so fast.

In Casualty, Nkosi is already being examined. As Gail gets there, he goes into yet another seizure. 'We'll have to admit him to Ward Three,' says the attending doctor.

'Can't you give him some valium?' asks Gail, 'Calm him down?'

The young doctor administers the injection, and slowly the shaking stops, the rigidity relaxes.

Nkosi is transferred to a trolley and taken up to the ward, Gail and Grace following behind. In the ward, he has another three convulsions and more valium. They wait, helplessly, at his bedside.

At about four in the morning, the doctor attending to him says to Gail: 'We've stabilised him for the time being. You go, get some sleep. Tomorrow we'll do a brain scan to assess the damage.'

Dr Ashraf Coovadia describes Nkosi's condition when he saw him in the ward the following day:

'An emaciated child who was really now not able to hear you; his eyes were open, but he wasn't communicating with anyone. What we would call an altered state, where you are not aware of what is happening around you. He had had several episodes of fits or seizures: that complicates the level of consciousness as it tends to starve the brain of oxygen.

'At that stage, he was already in full-blown AIDS and it was our impression that it was the AIDS virus and not a secondary complication causing this clinical presentation. Often children with AIDS present complications – fungal meningitis, bacterial meningitis, diarrhoea, which we can treat – but he presented none of these reversible complications. It was really now the AIDS virus itself that was causing direct degeneration of the brain.'

After seven days at Coronation, Dr Coovadia allowed Gail to bring Nkosi home. He would have to be carefully nursed: every two hours he would have to be turned to prevent bedsores. He would have to be fed through a naso-gastric tube. He would have to be permanently in nappies.

She brought him home for good on Friday, 5 January 2001, a month before his twelfth birthday.

Chapter Eleven

BEFORE GAIL HAS struggled up out of sleep, the mobile phone beside her bed is ringing. She drags herself up and fumbles for it.

'Gail Johnson.'

'Mrs Johnson, this is...'

The house telephone rings, and is answered by Mary. (Mary Hlatswayo is the new domestic worker who had replaced Emily a couple of months previously, when Emily did not reappear after a weekend 'off', having presumably decided that the job did not suit her).

'Gail, there is somebody...'

The other mobile rings; she puts the first on hold and answers it.

'Gail Johnson.'

Sometimes they ring simultaneously. Often she has to answer two at once. When she can get an assistant it will be better, but the callers always want to speak to her.

When she gets a chance, she pads through to Nkosi's bedside. Always that little hesitation, even if only a fraction of a second, at the door. What will she find?

''Kos? How are you, my baby?'

He's still lying as she last saw him. His eyes are open and they seem to be registering that she's there. She sits on the side of the bed and takes his hand. At least he's quiet. No sign of convulsions this morning.

'No, Gail, he have a good night,' says the nurse.

'Come, sweetheart, we're going to turn you over and rub your back with the stuff, and then we'll get some food into you. Pity it can't be sausage and eggs, hey?' There's a tiny pressure on her fingers. Nkosi is now existing on puréed and liquid food – everything strained and diluted.

The doorbell rings. Duke barks, dashes outside and continues barking. Mary goes to see and reports that waiting outside the gate is the day nurse and a man from the press.

'I'm going to get dressed. Tell him to wait in the lounge.'

Mary goes with the message, and in the meantime the telephones ring, all three of them. The journalist, accompanied by a cameraman, tramps through to the living room. They sit on the scuffed black leather sofa against the window, staring round at the poster of Nkosi in his baseball cap, the big vase of roses on the coffee table, the gap in the floorboards.

Gail arrives, pinning up her hair as she does so. They ask about Nkosi.

'I don't expect him to recover,' she says. 'I don't know whether I should be hoping. I just want him to go peacefully.'

Another ring at the doorbell. Another fury of barking. Granny Khumalo and her cousin Mavis. They go through and visit Nkosi briefly, return and sit opposite the journalists.

'I want God to relieve him,' says Mavis. 'We want him to go now. He doesn't know whether it's day or night.' Granny Ruth nods, and sheds tears.

'He responds to our voices,' says Gail, 'and sometimes he squeezes my hand, but he can't turn himself. We have a day nurse and a night nurse from the Berea Agency who do it every two hours.'

Telephone. Doorbell. Barking.

Outside is Dr Liz Floyd, Director of AIDS and Communicable Diseases at the Gauteng Department of Health, Pauline Molefe and Mandy, two colleagues. Another car has just pulled up and is disgorging more journalists. From inside the house the telephone can be heard ringing. Mary calls Duke in. Everyone troops through

to the living room. It is time for Nkosi to be turned. Gail goes
through to the bedroom to make sure the nurse is there. The
telephone. She runs back to answer it.

'You need help,' says Liz Floyd.

It is arranged that Liz and an assistant will stay as long as they are
needed. Telephone calls have to be fielded, appointments arranged,
VIP guests accommodated, press provided for. The foster family and
Nkosi's black relatives need privacy and time to come to terms with
what has happened; Nkosi needs peace and quiet. No phone calls
from the press, please, before 8.30 a.m. or after 5 p.m. The carers are
working out of the kitchen, visitors and the press must sit in the
living room, and Liz and her team will work with the telephones
around the dining-room table. The house is open-plan, so all this
activity takes place right in the middle. The only two rooms that are
quiet are the one where Nkosi lies and Gail's bedroom.

The family that in theory is trying to carry on a normal life and
look after a dying child is, in fact, unable to do so: he is not a
'normal' child, he is an international figure. Liz and her department
feel that people who go public on being HIV-positive do it at quite
significant personal cost, and the government's job is to support
them. It is through people such as Gail and Nkosi that barriers of
discrimination and prejudice can be broken down in the minds of
the public, so banning visitors and the press altogether is not really
an option, in terms of what they have been trying to do.

The first prominent visitor to arrive is South Africa's First Lady,
Mrs Zanele Mbeki. Her office is not far, and she is taking time off
to make a quick visit. Gail greets her with little Thabo in her arms.

'Who is this?' asks Mrs Mbeki.

'He's a baby who was abandoned at four days old. I've had him
ever since.'

'What's his name?'

'Thabo – but not named after anyone we know!'

Mrs Mbeki smiles and takes him in her arms and when he starts
crying, she comforts him. Press cameras flash from all sides in
Gail's living room. Gail becomes paranoid lest Mrs Mbeki should

trip on the broken floorboard. Granny Ruth Khumalo tells her that she watched her own daughter, Nkosi's mother, die of AIDS. But Mbali, Nkosi's sister, is healthy, she says. Mbali too is sad because he is dying.

Other early visitors are Judge Edwin Cameron, Dr Frank Chikane (Director General in the President's office), Gwen Ramokgopa (MEC for Health in Gauteng), Zackie Achmat[43] of the Treatment Action Campaign and Jack Bloom of the Democratic Alliance.

A visitor of a different kind is Tony Guinness, CEO of City Funerals. He arrives at an extremely busy moment.

Gail says to Laurette, who has also just arrived: 'Won't you please handle this? The phones are going mad and I think he's here on business anyway.'

Laurette takes Tony out into the garden and they sit together beside the pool. She has Gail's diary on her lap, and Tony takes it and writes out a list of what his company is prepared to offer in the way of eventual funeral services: hearse, limousines, gravesite, etc., and a free funeral service when anyone at Nkosi's Haven should die. He would be on call at any time during the day or night, he says.

Laurette says: 'Well, that's wonderful, but the child is not dead, why are we talking about it now?'

Tony stands up and looks compassionately at her. 'It's only a matter of time. It's as well to be prepared. Are we agreed, then?'

'I'm sure Gail will be very grateful,' says Laurette.

On 10 January, Mr Blade Nzimande, General Secretary of the South African Communist Party, comes. It is the occasion of the 80th anniversary of the Party, and he brings with him a large square floral arrangement – a hammer and sickle of red roses against a background of yellow and pink roses and green leaves. He talks for a while to Gail about Nkosi's condition and about the problem of AIDS in the country, and then goes in to stand by the unconscious child's bedside. Video cameras roll.

He speaks quietly to Nkosi and then presents him with a card of greeting, depicting the Red Flag.

'Put it beside the bunny on the bedside table,' says Gail, 'and the bunny will look after it.'

So on Nkosi's bedside table, the bunny, the Mickey Mouse mug and the yellow fluffy bee are joined by a handsome greeting card from the Communist Party.

Blade shakes hands with Gail and says: 'Thanks for all your commitment. We hope it will set an example to everybody in this country.'

'My commitment will carry on,' says Gail, 'but please bring me some tranquillisers and a couple of packets of cigarettes!'

To the journalists who have gathered Blade says: 'We need to pull together to show love and care for AIDS victims. We shouldn't treat them as outcasts... It's a shame that there are still some pharmaceutical companies that are fighting our government in court. This shows that they don't care about Africans.'[44] Outside, Granny Ruth has arrived, and Blade speaks to her for a few quiet moments, offering his sympathy, before he leaves.

In a hard-hitting column 'Talk Today' published in the *Pretoria News* on 15 January 2001, Mathatha Tsedu, Deputy Editor of *The Star* wrote:

'*What really galled me was the political mileage that some people were trying to make out of the lad's tragedy. On Wednesday, e-mails were sent out by the South African Communist Party advising that Secretary-General Blade Nzimande would be visiting Nkosi at a particular time. Why is there a need for media notices if indeed the intention is to see the boy and give the family support and solace? The obvious answer is that once First Lady Zanele Mbeki (whose husband's Presidency Office also issued invites to the media) went and got coverage, the propagandists went into full swing.*'

Other notable visitors during this time are Dr Manto Tshabalala-Msimang, Minister of Health, Mrs Winnie Madikizela-Mandela, Felicia Mabuza-Suttle, TV talk-show host, musician Mdu and the singer Yvonne Chaka Chaka.

Dr Tshabalala-Msimang is here, she says, in her personal capacity. She is unable to comment on behalf of the government –

she's here to offer personal support. Gail takes her to sit in a secluded corner. They talk about how it is to lose someone dear, and how there must be more emphasis on getting people to accept that AIDS exists.

On the wall outside, Liz Floyd's people have put up a big AIDS poster where anyone who wants to can write a personal message to Nkosi. Dr Tshabalala-Msimang adds her message: '*We love and care for you, Nkosi – Manto.*'

Others arrive who are visibly distressed. Many break down, many are comforted.

At this time of crisis, friction has been put aside, and Ruth Khumalo visits the Melville house every day. She is there on behalf of the family to show support. Gail gives her food every day, money for transport, and food parcels to take home. Sometimes, other members of the family are able to come with her.

One day, the phone rings and Liz answers it.

'Someone wants to reverse the charges,' she says to Gail.

Gail takes the phone. 'Hello?' An unknown person is calling. 'I'll accept the charges,' she says.

'I want to pray for your son over the telephone,' the caller says.

'You pray, I pay?' asks Gail.

'That's right,' says the man.

Another call from a charismatic church which wants to bring thirty-five members to pray at his bedside.

'Three or four,' says Gail, firmly.

More and more calls started to come in from people who wanted to pray during that first week Nkosi was home, and eventually it was decided to hold a prayer service in one of the main churches in Johannesburg. Oscar first contacted the big Methodist Mission in the centre of town, but the presiding bishop was absent overseas, and his staff did not feel able to take a decision, so Oscar then got in touch with Father Joseph of the Anglican Cathedral of St Mary the Virgin. The cathedral opened its doors and very generously provided flowers, candles and programmes, as well as the venue. The date was set for Friday, 13 January, at 12 noon.

Three hundred participants packed into the cathedral, many of them young people. Anyone who wanted to pray for Nkosi could come. Staff from the Gauteng Department of Health helped to get everything ready. Most of the people who came to the service had the feeling that Nkosi would not live more than another two or three days, so it was as much an expression of love and solidarity for him and his family as a service to pray for healing. Gail and the people from Nkosi's Haven were there, together with Ruth Khumalo, Mbali and other members of Nkosi's family.

A choir of young singers led the hymns and freedom songs, which seemed entirely appropriate in view of the fight against AIDS. The Anglican Dean of Johannesburg, the Very Revd Peter Lenkoe, spoke movingly on the theme 'Give a Living Chance to the Child' and said that Nkosi should become a reminder to everyone about the need to save our children. He said further: 'The time has come when government and drug companies must make a deal to make drugs available that will halt the spread of AIDS from mother to child. If ever there was a time, if ever there was a place, this is the time, because we are looking at a young, young life, and through no fault of his we're watching this life just being swept away.'

At the end of the service many pastors and others approached Gail and asked her whether they could come to her house to pray for Nkosi. To all of them she replied that now he needed above all peace and quiet, and this was precisely why the service had been organised, so that all who wanted to could come together and pray.

In the first week of Nkosi's return home, a meeting was held to discuss his inevitable funeral. Gail felt it best to be prepared, as no one knew how long he had to live. Present were Gail herself, Nicci, Oscar, Billy, Ruth, Fika, Mavis, and Zanele Mashinini and another colleague from the Department of Health.

Gail told them about the offer from City Funerals, and asked Nkosi's family whether they would like him to be buried back in

Newcastle, with his mother Daphne. Ruth said, and it was generally agreed, that he should be buried at West Park Cemetery in Johannesburg, and that Gail must make the arrangements. This decision was minuted by the Department of Health members. Ruth was to say afterwards that she did not feel it right to discuss these things before the child had died, and since it is un-African, according to an article published in the *Sowetan Sunday World* on 14 January 2001 in connection with Nkosi's condition, 'to write off a living soul and to prepare the epitaph' she may have decided at that stage to leave it all to Gail. In view of the public interest there was likely to be, Gail felt that it was impossible not to be prepared in advance.

4 February was Nkosi's twelfth birthday. The family and Oscar had discussed whether or not it would be appropriate, in view of his condition, to celebrate it. In the end, they decided to do so, and Oscar agreed to make the arrangements.

Firstly, he had to decide on the venue. It needed to be somewhere fairly central, and it would be good, he thought, if it were to reflect Nkosi's history in some way. He telephoned Badie Badenhorst.

'If you want my school,' said Badie, 'it's yours.'

Badie gave him carte blanche to use the school hall, the *lapha*, the kitchens.

The main problem would be the financing of this party. Oscar estimated that there would probably be about three hundred guests. He made two decisions. One was just to make press announcements about it and not send out any official invitations, and the other was to make it clear that anyone could come and celebrate together, but they should come under their own steam, and bring their own food.

The entertainment was a different matter. You could not call people together for a party and then not entertain them. He contacted YFM – a local youth radio station. They were eager to give their support. He contacted MTN Gladiators. They were delighted for some of their stars to attend. He called the cast of the musical *Umoja*, then playing in a local theatre. They said they would come and sing the popular South African hit of the 1970s, *Paradise Road*. A drama group from the East Rand showed interest, as did the Soweto Youth Drama Society. More and more people began telephoning and offering support. Nando's provided barbecued chicken, a butchery donated meat and *boerewors*, and an East Rand insurance company, Batho Batsho Bakopane (commonly known as B3), donated a birthday cake and commemorative T-shirts.

The Melpark school children set up the hall, and many local celebrities came just to be there and join in the fun – Miss South Africa and her two Princesses, Penny Lebyane from Metro FM, Felicia Mabuza-Suttle and many others. There was no set programme – performers just came and entertained the guests in a relaxed and happy fashion. It was a great success. The big oil portrait of Nkosi by Mike Frampton, specially painted to celebrate the birthday, was set up beside the stage. Gail and Granny Ruth cut the cake, and Oscar was offered the first slice. Oscar estimated that there were close on three hundred guests coming and going between twelve noon and half-past four that afternoon.

Afterwards, some people from the East Rand went and sang outside Nkosi's bedroom window, people gave him birthday cards, and the children from Nkosi's Haven also sang.

To further celebrate his birthday, a team of art students from a local design school came to the house and, as a special project taking only a few hours, designed and made a mobile of cut-out dangling 'heroes' such as Superman, Batman and Nkosi himself, a water bed made of balloons and a silver 'book' to commemorate his birthday. The mobile and the book have become permanent decorations in Gail's living room.

On 12 February, the Treatment Action Campaign organised a march through Cape Town, culminating in a service dedicated to Nkosi at St George's Cathedral. The leaders of the march then handed a memorandum, calling for the local production of generic medicines, to the chair of the parliamentary health committee.

One Sunday evening the gate bell rings and a woman's voice

over the intercom says she is a social worker. On investigation, they find standing outside a man with a walking stick who announces himself as Sonny Boy Mandela, and when Gail refuses him entry he goes on ringing and ringing the bell and shouting that Gail is a white bitch making money out of a black child. She wants to beat his head in but is restrained by the thought of tomorrow's headlines: *MANDELA SMASHED BY GAIL JOHNSON.*

The next morning, two girls appear at the gate. One has tears streaming down her face. 'I'm so happy,' she sobs, 'because Nkosi will be healed by lunchtime.'

Three people travel up from Port Elizabeth and stand in Gail's kitchen for hours, making special medicine for Nkosi on the stove.

A woman has walked all the way from Rustenburg, two or three days' journey, carrying a hibiscus flower. She has prayed over it as she walked. She doesn't want to disturb Gail, she doesn't want to see Nkosi, but asks her to put the flower next to his bed.

'Leeuwkop Prison on the line for you, Gail.'

'Huh?!' She takes the phone. 'Gail Johnson.'

'Good morning, Ma'am. We have a prisoner here who has created holy water and wants you to give it to Nkosi. He says it will heal him.'

'Holy water. How do you make that? Is it urine?'

'No. He's blessed it after fasting for a week. He wants you to come and fetch it.'

'Who is this? What's he in prison for?'

'He's a minister of religion who's been convicted of fraud.'

'Well, please tell him that's very nice, but I'm a bit busy just now.'

A little later the prisoner himself is on the phone. He says he's getting very hungry but is refusing to eat until Nkosi has had the holy water. He has managed to get permission from Social Services for Gail to go there and get it. Eventually, a social worker offers to bring it to her.

'Cool,' says Gail.

A man from Kokstad comes to the gate. He has a sure-fire cure, he says. He will cut himself, and Gail must pour some of Nkosi's blood into him. She tells him to go away.

'If you've got a cure, then go back to Kokstad – there's a high level of infection there.'

Next day, Clinton Nyirongo, the gardener, comes running. 'There's a white man trying to climb over the wall.'

When Gail goes out to see, it's the man from Kokstad. When he sees Gail, he takes out a knife.

'Don't threaten me!' she shouts.

'I want your son's blood.'

'Well, you can't have it.'

'I'm prepared to remove one of my own ribs – all you've got to do is wave it over Nkosi and he'll be cured.'

'Listen – Adam and Eve were quite a few years ago and if I want spare ribs I'll get takeaways.'

She goes back inside to phone the police. Suddenly, Mary and Grace are screaming outside. He has stabbed himself, and there is blood all over the pavement.

The police arrive and he is taken away. Afterwards, they hear he has been taken to Sterkfontein Hospital, a psychiatric facility.

So many telephoned to say they had cures. To all of them Gail explained that Nkosi had irreparable brain damage.

'We could get him to sit up again,' says one who wants to re-oxygenate his blood.

'Yes, but will he walk, talk and no longer be incontinent?'

'Well, we don't know about that, but there will definitely be an improvement.'

'If you can't promise me a 100% cure, I'm not interested. Whose need is this – your product's or my son's?'

A medical technologist came with an assistant editor of the *Sunday World*.

'I can reverse his brain damage.'

'Well, why aren't you in the paraplegic wards treating the car accidents and drownings? Go and do that and then come back with a journalist to write up the story.'

Someone telephones, offering to fly in a famous prophet-healer from Nigeria in a Lear Jet.

'You fly him in for six thousand AIDS children to be cured in the Ellis Park Stadium. On his way back to the airport he can come and cure Nkosi. But you don't bring him here just for one child.' Nothing more was heard about that.

One evening the night nurse calls Gail into Nkosi's room. His body is rigid, he is shaking with spasms, his breathing is very bad.

'I've given him some phenobarb,' she says, 'but it's had no effect.'

On and on goes the seizure: it seems as though it will shake him to pieces.

Nicci comes in to see what is happening. 'I'm phoning Netcare,' she says. 'We can't go on like this.'

(When Nkosi first came out of hospital in January, Netcare, a private hospital network, had made a media statement that they would cover any emergency treatment that Nkosi might need.) The operator says that their nearest vehicle is across in Edenvale, the other side of town, but they will do their best. In seven minutes they arrive.

The paramedics stay with him for about half an hour, trying to stabilise him. They telephone for an ambulance.

Nicci and Gail are standing by the bed. Through the window, Nicci sees across the road a white Toyota Cressida with someone inside it, apparently watching the house.

'Look, Mom,' she says, 'I think we've got a spy.'

'Close all the curtains,' says Gail. At that moment, the ambulance arrives. As they are putting him on the stretcher and taking him to the front door, the telephone rings. A journalist.

'What's wrong with Nkosi? There's an ambulance outside your house.'

'No, there isn't,' says Nicci.

'One of my colleagues has just driven past and says there's an ambulance there.'

'It's not for us,' says Nicci, 'it's for the house across the road.'

'Right,' says Gail, 'we'll book him into the hospital under an assumed name.'

So a child surnamed 'Pillay' was admitted to the Garden City Clinic, and taken at once into the Intensive Care Unit. After two days, he had recovered enough to be sent home.

Following his admission to hospital, Nkosi received special mention in parliament on 14 February, when there was an African National Congress notice of motion that stated that he had been readmitted to hospital, and sympathised with him, his family, and with all children who were living with HIV/AIDS or who had been made AIDS orphans. It called on the nation for *'prayerful attention to the plight of all children like Nkosi Johnson. We urge communities and extended family support networks and health workers to reach out to all such affected children. We salute all those people, networks and NGOs who are giving selflessly without regard to material gain. May a caring ethos forever shine on the dark places in the lives of all people.'*

A few weeks later, on 9 March, Nkosi went into another seizure, which they were unable to relieve. Again they telephoned the emergency service, and again the paramedics were on the scene almost immediately. They were unable to stabilise him, so again they took him through to the hospital. He was in intensive care overnight, but then he was stabilised and sent home again. The doctor in charge showed Gail how to administer valium via the rectum, so that in future she would be able to start emergency treatment herself. After he came home, members of his township family carried out a traditional cleansing ceremony (*ukugezwa*) on him, washing his body with goat's gall.

While Nkosi was ill, Gail's normal life came to a standstill. She became very tired. She also became worried about the expense of two agency nurses. Laurette pointed out crisply that if Gail herself got sick, Nkosi's Haven would collapse because she, Laurette, had no possibility of carrying it on without Gail. So Grace from Nkosi's Haven came to the house as Nkosi's day nurse, and they employed only a night nurse from the agency.

On 19 March, a gala dinner was held in Cape Town at the Cape Sun Intercontinental Hotel to raise funds for Nkosi's Haven. Guest of honour was Larry Hagman, better known as 'JR' Ewing in the 1980s television series *Dallas*. In real life, he is committed to human rights causes.

Another, very different visitor for Nkosi arrived on 10 April. This was nine-year-old professional DJ Llewellyn 'Welly' Owen from London. He was the youngest professional DJ in the world; he came, among other engagements, to spin the discs at an under-18 party to raise funds for Nkosi's Haven.

And then there was Lucas Radebe, number-one world-famous soccer player. Although then resident in England, he was on his way back to his birthplace. In South Africa, to play in a big match. He called in to see Nkosi en route from the airport and signed a pair of his soccer boots as a present for him.

Chapter
Twelve

NKOSI IS NOT quiet. Gail remembers that he spoke often of death and how it would be. And despite everything she could say to reassure him, he was still frightened of the actual moment. She had consulted her friend Carol, then living in Durban, who was a spiritualist. 'Acknowledge his fear,' Carol had advised, 'but keep telling him that everything will be all right.' Now that he is in a coma, she calls Carol again. Carol 'visits' Nkosi in spirit, and from then on, he seems to rest more peacefully.

Every day he slips further and further away. It is as though he cannot quite bring himself to leave, as though he feels there is something still for him to do.

Now that he is ill – 'sick unto death' in the telling biblical phrase – he is no longer able to function, but he has left behind the husk of himself. And this husk, this shell, still has a function. It goes on bringing home to the people what AIDS is. Nkosi's effort can carry on unabated because there he is as a constant reminder, every change in his condition reported in the national media.

He is kept in the public eye also because of those who come to pay their respects. The ones who come out of genuine love and concern are a source of strength to Gail and even to Nkosi himself, although on the surface he seems to be unaware of them. Children leave flowers at his gate, and many all over the world who have met him telephone their sympathy. Brian Oosthuizen of the Mondeor Methodist Church makes warm, caring pastoral visits.

Since Nkosi first went into his coma, there has been an outpouring of love and support and goodwill from all over the world – many of them people whom Gail does not know. Letters, e-mails, moving messages from people who have just seen Nkosi on television and been touched by his story.[45]

And what do these long months mean for Gail? What would they mean for any mother of a beloved child? On the many news clips she seems calm, matter-of-fact, very much in control. This is how she copes – how she has always coped. As she herself says, Nkosi began to die for her when he ceased to communicate. And there are practical things to be done: he must be turned every two hours to prevent bed sores, she must administer valium when he gets seizures, he must be kept alive through a feeding tube.

Nicci has now moved out of the house. She and Vincent have set up their own home in a townhouse in Windsor Park. So, apart from Thabo, Gail is alone. Although she spends as much time as possible with Nkosi, she has other activities that must carry on. There is Nkosi's Haven to be looked after, with its attendant crises, sometimes deaths. There is her commitment to a house in Tembisa where Flora Mogano tries valiantly as a home care-giver to do what little can be done for the dying in the surrounding township and comes home to a houseful of AIDS orphans. On several occasions, Nkosi had accompanied Gail there.

'Do you really want to come, Nkosi? It's not pleasant.'

'I really want to come. I want to see.'

Flora's patients are dying at a rate of up to twenty a week. For many of them, she is their only care-giver. Their families are too scared even to give them a drink of water.

When Gail gets home after each foray, Nkosi is still there for her to talk to and she does this every evening before he is settled for the night. Sometimes he squeezes her fingers when she takes his hand; sometimes he even makes eye contact. It is difficult to tell whether this is intentional or not. Mostly he is comatose. And there is the new bright spot in Gail's life – little Thabo. Her son

Nkosi may be leaving her, but Thabo is there, his life beginning to unfold under her wing, and she has him to come home to, to plan for. He is now testing negative for HIV. He may have a future.

While all this was happening in the house in Melville, the Pharmaceutical Manufacturers Association's case against the South African government over the Medicines and Related Substances Act No 90 of 1997 was finally coming to a head.

The Treatment Action Campaign described the issue as follows:

'At stake is the Medicines and Related Substances Act (90 of 1997). The drug companies are opposed to three aspects of the new Medicines Act:
- *the provision which allows for parallel importation, meaning that South Africa would be able to shop around internationally for the cheapest price from a particular company.*
- *the establishment of a price committee which would require drug companies to justify their prices and agree to a single price for each medicine.*
- *the generic substitution provision, which requires pharmacies to offer patients cheaper generic alternatives to patented medicines, even if these aren't mentioned by the doctor.'*[46]

In February, it was reported in the press that: *'some large pharmaceutical companies had made arrangements with UNAIDS to offer discounts and logistical support to developing countries. Pfizer offered to provide fluconazole, a drug to treat opportunistic HIV infections, free to poor people in South Africa. This will reach the public via hospitals once approved by the MCC. The TAC has imported a generic equivalent of Diflucan from Thailand.'*[47] Now the almost four years of delays were over and the case had come to the High Court in Pretoria.

There were worldwide demonstrations in support of the South African government, calling on the drug companies to drop the case. Thousands of people living with HIV/AIDS, together with people from unions, churches and NGOs, took to the streets in Cape Town, Durban and Pretoria.

The case had already been delayed for three years, since the original promulgation of the Medicines Act in 1997. Finally, on 21 April, there was an out-of-court settlement after Kofi Annan, United Nations Secretary-General, intervened. A joint statement was made, in which the industry withdrew their challenge to the 1997 law in return for which their help would be solicited in the development of a regulatory framework surrounding the as yet unimplemented law.

In May 2000, government announced that in two pilot sites per province (18 in all) Nevirapine would be made available for MTCT prevention as soon as it was approved by the MCC (Medicines Control Council). This project had originally been announced in September 1998, but had then been deferred. Nevirapine was registered on 18 April 2001. In these research sites a package of care was to be provided that included voluntary HIV counselling and testing, the provision of multivitamins to pregnant women, Nevirapine to mother and infant, formula feeding for mothers who could not exclusively breastfeed, and cotrimoxazole for infants. The Minister of Health said that Nevirapine would not be made freely available in all government hospitals until the government had completed certain studies and identified certain obstacles. This was disputed by the Treatment Action Campaign whose view was that the obstacles were self evident, and that the important thing was to prevent rather than have to treat the disease. Boehringer-Ingelheim (the manufacturers) had offered Nevirapine free of charge for five years to all SADEC (Southern African Development Community) countries.[48] The TAC pointed out in its subsequent newsletter that 18 pilot sites would only reach 10% of HIV-positive pregnant women.

On 6 June in the National Assembly, the Minister of Health, Dr Manto Tshabalala-Msimang, was to say: 'With regard to the use of anti-retrovirals in triple therapy for the long-term management of AIDS, our position remains the same. We have no plans to introduce the wholesale administration of these drugs in the public sector. Anti-retrovirals are not a cure for HIV/AIDS. In addition we remain concerned about aspects of toxicity, the availability of laboratory services, and infrastructural and educational constraints, particularly in the rural areas.'[49]

In the early hours of the morning of 23 April, Patricia the night nurse went as usual to turn Nkosi. When she stood up from doing this, there was a gun in her face. She could not see who was attacking her, but there were at least two men in the room. They hit her and shoved her onto the bed and covered her with a duvet.

'Keep quiet,' they said, 'we're going to be here for a long time. And you,' they said to the comatose Nkosi, 'shut your eyes.'

Gail, in bed in her room with baby Thabo beside her, woke to see lights under her door. The door was usually open, but somebody had shut it. Could Patricia still be watching television at one o'clock in the morning? Gail got up and marched through to Nkosi's room. In passing, she noticed that the big TV had gone from its usual place. Why had Patricia moved it? In Nkosi's room, a suitcase was lying on the spare bed with some of his clothes in it. His TV and his CD player were missing. A big bundle was on the bed, covered with a duvet.

She touched it, and discovered Patricia underneath, who started screaming.

'The guns!' she yelled, 'The guns!'

'What guns?'

'We've been robbed!'

Nkosi was lying quietly. Gail pulled Patricia into her bedroom with Thabo, set the alarm going and phoned the Flying Squad. It became evident that the burglars must have been loading their vehicle when Gail got up, as there was no sign of them when the Flying Squad arrived two minutes later.

Patricia was sitting on Gail's bed, her knees shaking violently.

'Here, drink some of this brandy,' said Gail. 'It tastes like shit, but you'll feel better.'

The burglars had tried to take the computer from the office upstairs. They had also taken the kettle from the kitchen, the sound systems, the video recorder and Lucas Radebe's soccer boots. These, however, were subsequently found thrown down outside the house. They appeared to have got in via the kitchen door by first opening the kitchen window, which could be done easily – if you knew how.

Gail installed a 24-hour security guard and Patricia had trauma counselling because she was absolutely terrified. Gail insisted that the guard should stay inside the house at night.

Two weeks later, there was another attempted burglary, but this time they tried to break in through the sliding door in Nkosi's bedroom. They were overheard, and the guard ran round the outside to intercept them. They fled, leaving behind a professional-looking toolkit full of spanners and saws.

During May, a delegation from the South African Council of Churches went to pray at Nkosi's bedside. Bishop Mvume Dandala, President of the Council, Dr Molefe Tsele, General Secretary, Ms Lindi Nyesa, Professor Masango and Father Gary Thompson, each of whom represented a different denomination, went together, so it was as though they were bringing the whole universal church with them to pray for Nkosi.

They were welcomed by the women of the household – Elizabeth (Gail's new secretary), Grace and Mary. Gail herself was away in Cape Town, but knew of the visit.

After talking a little, and enquiring after the wellbeing of the whole family, they were ushered into Nkosi's bedroom. Father Gary could see that although he was comatose – eyes closed and a tube in his nose – from time to time expressions would come and go on his face. There was still a soul inhabiting that frail body. Everyone, including the people of the house, knelt down, and Bishop Dandala laid his hand on Nkosi's head. The others stretched out their hands towards him – it was a small room, and they were kneeling wherever there was space; mostly they could not get near enough to touch.

The Bishop said a short prayer, asking God to bless and comfort
Nkosi in his pain, and to strengthen his family. Professor Masango
also said a prayer, and then they all got up to leave. But Father
Gary lingered a moment. He had seen, he was sure, that Nkosi's
face had become more peaceful during the prayer, and wasn't there
even the trace of a smile? It was a special moment for Father Gary.
In his mind was the image of the little boy who had so bravely
stood up at the international conference. This boy was now lying
in front of him in such helplessness. With it came another thought
– that unless we as a nation do something, we're going to see many
more such pictures of helplessness, sadness, hopelessness.

They stayed for a short while in the lounge, speaking to
Elizabeth, Grace and Mary, and then they left. Father Gary found
himself heavy-hearted; as they drove back to the city, it became
evident that it was a feeling shared by all of them.

In the second week of May, Mrs Ruth Bhengu, ANC Member of
Parliament, courageously raised the country's awareness by
standing up and telling the National Assembly that her 27-year-old
daughter Nozipho was HIV-positive.

The family had known about this since 1998, but Mrs Bhengu
felt that the time had come to 'open the wound of infection' so that
more people with high public profiles would be encouraged to
admit their HIV-positive status, and the atmosphere of shame and
secrecy pervading the disease could be dissipated.

She stressed the importance of a holistic approach to the
treatment of AIDS, including a healthy diet and extra supplements.
Nozipho, she said, was not at the stage of needing anti-retrovirals.
Mrs Bhengu had put her daughter on a special diet and 'alternative
herbal medication'.

She called on the government to set up a holistic programme to
treat AIDS – one that would not rely solely on drugs.

During April, Gary Scallan joined Gail's team. The previous year, when she was in New York, the advertising agency involved with Linda Tarry-Chart's initiative offered to assist Nkosi's Haven. It was eventually arranged that their South African division would look after Gail's needs from the publicity point of view. They offered clients a complete package: public relations, eventing, any ad hoc needs. Gary was the person in their PR division who was given responsibility for Gail and Nkosi's Haven.

Following the media frenzy when Nkosi first became comatose, it seemed necessary to have contingency plans in place to control the situation, to afford Gail as much privacy as possible and to allow Nkosi to go peacefully. His death would obviously attract attention from the media and the public worldwide.

Gary tried to look at the task from a holistic point of view. What was needed was: a venue for press conferences; a media list and accreditation (there had been at least 40 journalists who arrived on the scene when Nkosi first became ill); security around the area – maybe the police should block off one of two of the roads; arrangements for dignitaries who might want to pay their respects; at least six mobile phones to accommodate all the calls that would come in; somebody to monitor Gail's home telephone. All these things had to be coordinated. Then he thought: what happens to all the goodwill that may pour in when he dies – what about those people who want to donate large or small sums of money to Nkosi's Haven? There was no mechanism in place for international well-wishers and friends. Gail had already showed him the huge file of letters she had received from such people.

So it was decided that a Section 21 company should be created – the Nkosi Johnson Foundation – where such mechanisms could be put in place. iafrica.com in Cape Town agreed to host a website that would include a guestbook where people could sign in, and an electronic-banking company donated secure facilities. Other companies agreed to donate mobile phones, toll-free numbers, the services of switchboard operators, security guards – support from South African business was phenomenal. A group of people began to be formed who would sit on the Board.

Ideas for the Foundation grew and grew, beyond Nkosi's death and into the future, and Guardrisk Insurance Company came in and offered to administer it and draw up the legal documents. It was envisioned that the Foundation would become the umbrella body for Nkosi's Haven and for any other charitable projects that Gail would initiate in the future.

On 31 May, Gary had just climbed out of his morning shower and was watching the TV News in his bedroom, when the newspaper headlines were given. The *Sowetan: NKOSI ABUSED, CLAIMS DOCTOR.*

In shock, he telephoned Gail, and in fact woke her. 'Have you seen the *Sowetan*?'

'No, what does it say?'

He told her the news and said that he would shoot to his office and then be with her as soon as possible. On the way, he picked up a copy of the newspaper.

The front-page article was accompanied by photographs of Gail, a woman identified as Hilda Khoza, and Nkosi. The caption read: *HIV-positive youngster Nkosi Johnson is in the news again after Johannesburg reflexologist Hilda Khoza lodged a complaint with the South African Human Rights Commission to the effect that his foster mother Gail Johnson was committing child abuse on the bed-ridden child.* It appeared from the article by journalist Saint Molakeng that, after seeing Nkosi on TV back in January and diagnosing that he had constipation, Hilda Khoza had approached Ruth Khumalo, his grandmother, and dispensed medication for her to give to Nkosi without Gail's knowledge.

Khoza told the Sowetan *yesterday that Nkosi was 'fit to go to school' but his foster mother does not allow him to do so. 'Nkosi has become a bank to Gail. She does not want the public to know that the child is better because donations would no longer be forthcoming,' Khoza claimed.*[50]

The *Sowetan* had telephoned Gail the previous day, told her of Hilda Khoza's accusations and that they would be publishing them the following day. They had asked for her comment. Gail had denied the allegations and asked the journalist to come and see for himself that Nkosi was not fit to go to school. But neither Saint Molakeng nor anyone else from the *Sowetan* came to her house to verify the story.

While Gary was still at his office, Gail phoned to say that journalists were already starting to telephone and to knock at her door. They decided to issue a media alert through SAPA-Reuters to say that she would hold a press conference at her house that morning at 11 a.m.

When he got to the house, Gary found that Gail was deeply upset. Oscar and Laurette and Gary Roscoe, the other directors of Nkosi's Haven, arrived to give support, and Dr Ashraf Coovadia, who had been making monthly visits, was called in. They prepared a statement. They decided that Dr Coovadia should speak first and that Gail should then answer any questions. They would refute the allegations printed in the paper and then they would try to establish who Dr Hilda Khoza was. Gail said she was mystified as to who she could be. 'Who is this woman? I don't remember her at all.' People had come in and out of her house whom she didn't really know – perhaps Hilda Khoza had been one of those? And they contacted their lawyers to find out what their legal position was, as Gail wanted to sue for damages.

Hilda Khoza was later (February 2002) to state that she had spoken to Gail on the telephone when Nkosi had first become comatose and offered to treat him but that Gail had not taken up the offer. She had therefore, she confirmed, met with the grandmother, Ruth Khumalo, and arranged with her to give medication to Nkosi without Gail's knowledge. This resulted, she claimed, in a significant improvement in Nkosi's condition, which she deduced from a newspaper photograph showing Nkosi and Lucas Radebe printed on 2 February. (Whether Ruth Khumalo would have had the opportunity or the expertise to administer the medication by means of Nkosi's naso-gastric tube is open to question.) This was why, Hilda stated, she wrote a letter to the Human Rights Commission, accusing Gail of keeping Nkosi out of school unnecessarily, thereby continuing to benefit from people's donations, and making other vague accusations of 'abuse' by Gail. She had not, she said, kept a copy of the letter. Ms Charlotte McClain of the Human Rights Commission confirmed receiving such a letter on 15 May.

At the press conference, the media wanted to know whether Gail was denying the claim that Nkosi was fit to go to school, and wanted her to answer the charges about finance. They asked how many cars she had, how many houses, and what her bank balance was.

Laurette, as the financial director, was able to assure them that Gail had no personal access to donated funds, and as for enriching herself, they should perhaps look around them at her house, at the roof that was rusty, at the chipped paint, at the floorboards that needed renewing. Gail said that they were welcome to examine all her account books.

Then Saint Molakeng, writer of the *Sowetan* article, asked: 'What gives you the right to decide that Nkosi is dying?'

Gail realised at that point that her whole effort and integrity had been called in question.

She said: 'I want to let them come in and see Nkosi.'

Photographers were allowed into Nkosi's bedroom two at a time. At that stage his eyes were open; he seemed to be staring at the ceiling. When the first lot came in, his eyes did not move or indicate that he knew anyone else was there. He looked very, very frail, and was covered from the neck down by a blanket. Nicci came to stand beside him to give any help that might be needed.

At first he was treated with respect, but after a while some of the photographers insisted on the blanket being taken off so that they could see what the rest of his body looked like, and he was turned onto his side so that they could get a better picture. Gail came in and saw what was happening, saw Nicci standing there in tears.

'Can't my little boy have any dignity?' she shouted.

These were the photos that were distributed throughout the world the next day.

Afterwards, Nicci said: 'We knew Nkosi didn't like it. We could always sense when he didn't like things. He was constantly twitching that day. But some of the photographers said "We're so sorry you have to go through this – so sorry we have to take these photos." It meant a lot that they said that.'

Among the journalists who went into his bedroom was Saint Molakeng. He seemed reluctant at first but was encouraged by Laurette. He looked deeply shocked at seeing the reality of Nkosi's condition, so much so that Laurette felt she should offer him some tea. 'No,' he said, 'I want to go.'

Calls kept coming in – mostly from friends. As the news hit the international media, friends from overseas began phoning to ask whether Gail was all right. They all expressed concern and support.

No newspaper actually reported in so many words that Hilda Khoza's 'diagnosis' was incorrect – the photographs were allowed to speak for themselves. Also, it was reported by SAPA that Human Rights Commission spokesperson Phumla Mthala said that the Commission had met Hilda Khoza to discuss her accusations, found they could not be substantiated and recommended that she make a public apology to Gail. But the damage had been done. Had she been 'abusing' him? Did she enrich herself by means of him? No amount of denial could still those doubts in the minds of many people.

And with these questions came lesser, but none the less damaging ones. Did she go on pushing him to give talks and interviews when he was too ill? Did all that hasten his death?

'I never once asked him to do anything public he didn't want to do,' she says to Laurette when the journalists have finally left. 'He moaned in Inigo's film about having to give "thousands" of interviews in America. Actually, on that trip it was three. One in the school, one in the church and one on the radio. But he was never pushed into any of it. In fact, he sometimes did refuse, and I went along with that.'

'What worries me most,' says Laurette, 'is the money angle. The fact that people think we're raising funds immorally through Nkosi.'

'It's because I don't fit the image,' says Gail. 'They think because I have false eyelashes and long nails and all that shit I must be insincere. They think because I don't look like a fucking Vestal Virgin I must be exploiting the situation.'

'Yes,' says Laurette. 'It is as though people can't bring themselves to believe that someone can act out of simple kindness and concern.'

Gail takes a long drag at her cigarette and blows the smoke explosively at the ceiling. 'I see something that needs doing and I do it – that's all. Aren't I allowed to be glamorous because I'm looking after people dying of AIDS? It hurts. It really hurts.'

'Look – I've seen you wiping up his diarrhoea with your own hands. Most mothers would have put their children in hospital at this stage. And he isn't even your kid, legally.'

'Well, I'm going to continue what I'm doing, and fuck the rest.'

'Gail, everybody knows you're his mother – he knows, and that's what matters.'

'I was stopped by a street vendor yesterday wanting to sell me some fluffy toy and he saw the logo on the van and he said "Are you the mother of that little boy with AIDS?" And I said yes, and he said "I want to thank you as a black person." And I said "A lot of black people wouldn't agree with you." And he said "Thank you," again, and I drove off. He was a foreigner, a Nigerian I think. So, you know, sometimes it happens. But sometimes I get angry. Jesus Christ, Laurette, I get angry.'

Chapter Thirteen

THE NEXT MORNING, 1 June, Gail was woken very early by the night nurse (a new one, not Patricia – it was her night off).

'Come, Gail, quickly.'

Gail thought perhaps that Nkosi was having another seizure and that she would have to administer valium, as she'd been taught, but there was something different about him. He was just lying, his eyes staring, with no apparent sign of life except for a very faint pulse. Gail tried to close his eyes but they kept opening.

She leaned close.

'Nkosi? It's okay to go now, darling.'

He gave no sign that he had heard.

She sat with her hand in his for a while, and then got up to put on his music – Sarah Brightman singing *Time To Say Goodbye*.

She sat down again on the edge of the bed and watched his face. After a time she realised that all expression had gone. Nkosi had slipped peacefully away.

It was 5.40 a.m., and it was International Children's Day.

Now there were things to be done. She telephoned Dr Coovadia, who said he would come immediately. She also telephoned Nicci and Gary and Laurette and then the police, who have to be informed if there is a death in the house. Nicci and Vince arrived, the cops arrived. Dr Coovadia arrived and confirmed that Nkosi was dead. City Funerals was informed.

Laurette arrived, and together she and Gail went through to Nkosi's bedroom to put clothes out for him. The telephone rang. Laurette took the call.

'Gail, it's B3 on the line. They say they want to do the funeral.'

'What do you mean? B3 is an insurance company. They donated the cake and the T-shirts for Nkosi's birthday.'

'No, they've got a funeral division as well, apparently.'

'Well they can't – you know that. City Funerals is doing it.'

'They say they want to come through to the house anyway.'

'Maybe they want to pay their respects. All right, let them come.'

An international media alert was issued from Gary's office. Initially they thought to have the press conference at a nearby hotel, which had offered its facilities, but Gail decided they might as well have it at her house. The police were called to put extra security into the area, and to look at the possibility of closing off roads. Gail was concerned to disturb the neighbours as little as possible, after the media excitement of the previous day.

But the journalists were quicker than the police. The news of Nkosi's death had made the early newscasts. Within half an hour, the switchboard at Gary's office was jammed. The toll-free number went into operation, the Nkosi website was ready to host. On every available phone, mobiles and landlines, media were calling.

The moment Oscar arrived, Laurette asked him to phone all the board members of Nkosi's Haven and also Ruth. He had no success in getting through on Ruth's number, and she had to hear the news of Nkosi's death from a neighbour who had heard the early-morning radio broadcast.

When Gary arrived at Gail's, he found the street in front of her house parked solid, and two hearses outside, one belonging to City Funerals and one belonging to Batho Batsho Bakopane – B3. Three security guards were in front of the gate, which had come off its rails and had been padlocked. Inside, the house seemed full of people – friends, mostly, although Gail didn't know everybody there. (One of her friends, in fact, reported later that her purse with credit cards and cellphone had been stolen while she was there. Gail was appalled that such a thing could happen in her house and on such an occasion.) At first, no media representatives were allowed in, although some were already climbing onto the wall with cameras to try to see inside. Gary estimated there were probably about fifty people plus TV and press cameras outside by about nine o'clock that morning. He asked why there were two hearses, and was told that one had been arranged in advance by Gail, and the other, apparently, by Ruth.

It appeared that she had made arrangements with B3 to do Nkosi's funeral, which is why they had arrived, expecting to fetch the body. The fight was now on between them and City as to which should take him. Gail said that City Funerals should take him in the meanwhile, and if the family insisted on B3 and if it could be done amicably, then B3 could perhaps take over. By this time, Ruth and family had also arrived, and were sitting in the TV room.

A little marquee had been set up in the back garden, with borrowed chairs, a table, an urn and cups donated by a hire company, and coffee and tea for the people who kept arriving all through the day. On the surface, Gail and Nicci were calm, but somewhat taken aback by all the noise, especially the telephones. Instead of the house being kept still so that they could mourn in peace, all was chaos. At first they thought to switch the phones off, but Gail felt that friends might be trying to get through to her. After a while, she retreated with her cigarettes and her coffee to a couch in the lounge, and only took calls from family and very close friends. Someone else monitored all the calls and had a book in which all the names and numbers were noted.

Nkosi's body was still in his room, lying in the casket that City Funerals had brought. All but his face was covered, and it was surrounded by flowers. The bedroom door was closed. Nicci was the one who stayed with him now. She had been his faithful care-giver all her teenage years, now she did the only thing left for her to do: she sat quietly and played music for him. Much of the time she was in tears. Over and over she played the same song – *Time To Say*

Goodbye. After a while, Gail and Laurette brought in the Rev. Brian Oosthuizen, who had come to lend his support and counsel to the family and to pray beside Nkosi's body.

Gary said to Gail: 'Let's have the press conference – the journalists will come in, we'll put them in the back garden – then the hearse can come into the driveway and we can bring the coffin out and they can take it away while the conference is going on.'

So all the journalists were brought into the back garden. Ross Jamieson arrived, and stayed to guard the gate while the hearse came in.

The conference didn't last long; no questions were asked. Gail spoke, telling briefly of Nkosi's death, and hitting out, in passing, at the unprovoked attack in the *Sowetan* by Hilda Khoza. Nicci spoke briefly also. Many of the journalists requested interviews with Gail: CNN, ABC, BBC, Australian Broadcasting, SABC among others. These were all journalists whom she knew, who had interviewed her in the past and shown her respect and kindness. She said that she would accommodate them a little later – she wanted to speed Nkosi on his way without media presence.

When they realised that Nkosi's body was being taken away, the journalists rushed off hastily, to get a sight of the coffin being taken out to the hearse. Nicci and Ross and other friends held up sheets and blankets around it, but even so, cameras were poked through the blankets, aimed from trees and from the top of the wall – anything to get a picture of the child's coffin. Nicci badly needed moments of private comfort with her mother, but they were given no chance. One journalist even told Nicci to go away because they were busy with Gail.

The representatives of B3, together with Ruth and family, were very angry that City Funerals had taken the body. Gail asked Ruth why she hadn't told her in the first place that they wanted B3 to do it, since she knew as far back as January that City Funerals had offered. However, she said that if that was what the family wanted, she would ask Joe Sandows, the Chairman of Nkosi's Haven, to telephone City Funerals and ask them to release the body to B3. It was embarrassing because she had made the arrangement with City Funerals in good faith, but for the sake of peace she went along with it. Joe made the call, and came down to report that Tony Guinness, CEO of City Funerals, had agreed to come to a meeting to discuss it.

It was at this point that Father Gary Thompson of the South African Council of Churches arrived. He had heard on the radio that morning that Nkosi had died, and resolved to go to Gail's house to express his sympathy and ask whether there was anything he could do to assist. He was at once told about the controversy between the two funeral parlours, and remained to try to help resolve the matter.

When Tony Guinness arrived in the early afternoon, he stated that under no circumstances was he prepared to release the body. After considerable discussion, he eventually got angry, picked up his briefcase and left. Gail, who had stayed out of it so far, now became angry in her turn. She felt that she had given her word to Tony Guinness, but because the family had seemed so upset she had gone against her word. She also felt that Tony had appeared genuinely concerned: 'How are you, Gail, how are you coping?' Whereas the B3 representatives had just marched in and said 'Where's the body? We're here to take it.'

It had been planned in advance that there would be a memorial service as well as a funeral. Originally, it had been decided to hold the memorial service at the FNB (First National Bank) Stadium, and FNB had agreed to let them have the venue free of charge. However, there still remained the question of paying for security, cleaning, a stage for musicians and singers, and buses to get people in from the townships, so they now suggested that B3 should take over responsibility for all those items at the memorial service and leave the funeral to be done by City. It was pointed out to B3 that the exposure would be far greater at a huge venue such as the stadium – the funeral would be considerably smaller. The publicity it would afford them would be wider, it would be a great marketing opportunity, which was what B3 admitted they wanted. At first it seemed that B3 were going to accept this. Father Gary Thompson and the Rev. Brian Oosthuizen had also joined the discussion at this stage, and while taken aback by the intensity of feelings aroused by this tussle over who should get the publicity, did their best to keep the peace.

The matriarch of the family, Mirtha Mlambo, Ruth's aunt, had appointed her son Billy as the official family spokesperson at all negotiations surrounding the funeral arrangements. He and Nkosi's Uncle Fika were deeply unwilling to allow City Funerals to have any rights at all. They said that since all the arrangements had been made in advance between B3 and Ruth, B3 should conduct everything. They also said that there had not been sufficient consultation between the families about the funeral arrangements in the first place.

In the end, B3 decided against the offer of the memorial service, so at yet another meeting of everybody at about five o'clock, it was decided that Gary should go with the B3 hearse on the following morning to City Funerals' parlour, and ask them to release the body to B3. Food had been sent around from a local supermarket, so the people remaining at Gail's house were looked after.

One by one, almost everyone leaves. Nicci remains – she has decided to stay with her mother for the weekend, while Vince is in Warmbaths. Gail and Gary go upstairs to the office.

A little later, Nicci's friends Ross and Claire Jamieson, Mandy Sewell and Mark Dreyer arrive, bringing a big bunch of flowers for her. She sits down with them in the living room. They talk. She can even join in the laughter when someone makes a joke. Mark gets cross with Gary when there's an argument over a lost telephone number. Nicci begins to feel ordinary again.

And then there is a ring at the door. It is Sharon. Sharon, after such a long time.

'Mom! It's Sharon.'

Gail comes downstairs. Sharon is standing in the hallway, flowers in her arms. She says, 'Hi.'

'Hi.'

'These are for you.'

'They're beautiful. Thank you.'

They go into the TV room and sit by themselves.

'Would you like a glass of wine?'

'Thanks.'

Gail busies herself in the kitchen with glasses, smokes, lighter. In the old days, Sharon would have gone and helped herself.

They sit together, at first silent. Then Sharon says: 'Feels like a light has gone out.'

'Mmm. But he was gone really the day he stopped communicating. That's when I said goodbye to him. I've had five months to get used to the idea.'

'I'm not saying he was an angel. But he was such a peaceful child. And he connected. He looked right into you. He was a person. A beautiful person. I can't bear the way people are calling him an AIDS activist. I mean, you brought him up to be a normal little boy and then suddenly he's an instrument of the activists. He was a human being, for God's sake.'

'He wanted to do it, you know.' Gail lights up her hundredth cigarette of the day.

'I know he wanted to do it. He was born to change people's ideas – look at the way he changed my mother's attitude without even trying – she was a bit of a racist but she adored him. I think he was meant to do it. That was his job, but it was hard for him, Gail.' She gets up and pokes a fallen rose back into its vase. 'Look, maybe you're going to hate this and I know you're not religious and me neither, but when I saw him standing up there giving his speech in Durban it was like he picked up his cross and went on his last walk. Seeing him standing there and knowing it was his destiny. I cried on and off for days.'

'Jesus – sounds like I was the one carrying out the crucifixion.'

'No. Look, if he'd been my child I would have shut that door, I wouldn't have exposed him, I would have stopped his mission in life. But he chose the right person. You empowered him, but you also protected him. So many people have got the wrong impression. You were brave enough and bold enough to go where you had to go with him. Look, it's not about you – you didn't martyr him to

the cause. If anyone martyred him, it was the press and the public.
Maybe we all did. I don't know. Maybe I don't know what I'm
talking about.' She gets up and stands for a moment, looking at the
portrait of Nkosi. 'Good picture. The eyes are just right.'

'Yes.'

'Yes, well. I'd better go.'

'Well, thanks for coming. Regards to Dominic.'

'I'll tell him. Bye.'

'Bye. Take care.'

Gail goes into Nkosi's room and begins pulling the bedclothes off
his bed. Sheet, pillowcases, duvet cover. And then the bedspread
and a couple of extra blankets. She drags them through the house
and begins stuffing them into the washing machine. If there was
space she would be putting in the curtains as well. Bang the door
shut on all of it. Open drawer, shake in soap powder. Turn on tap.
Switch on. The sound of the water, flowing in. And the rhythmic
thump starting up, turning and turning the clothes, pushing the
water through them, carrying away, finally, the last vestiges of his
warmth, his smell.

The next morning, Saturday, Gary went to Gail's house and typed
a letter in her name, formally requesting City Funerals to release
the body of Nkosi Johnson. Gail decided not to sign it at this stage,
preferring to see whether they would release the body in response
to an amicable verbal request. The letter would be used as a last
resort. They discussed the possibility of bringing in the police or –
if the worst came to the worst, getting a court order. But the
lawyers told them it would cost in the region of R60 000, so they
hoped that none of that would be necessary.

Gary set off with Mr Matthews Mogafe, Managing Director of
B3, in his luxury limousine, their hearse following on behind. After
a frustrating morning in which he was refused entrance to the City
Funerals' premises, made an abortive attempt to enlist the

assistance of the police and yet another attempt to gain the cooperation on the telephone of Tony Guinness, Gary had to return to Gail and report failure.

On the way back there was a call on his mobile phone. *City Press*. 'What's this we hear about a wrangle between two funeral parlours over Nkosi's body?'

'Nothing to worry about, we're merely looking after certain logistics.'

Ten minutes later, another call. *Sowetan on Sunday*. The reporter who had aired Hilda Khoza's allegations. 'What's this we hear about there being a wrangle between two funeral parlours over Nkosi's body?'

'Nothing to worry about – there is some speculation that there might be a slight problem but we can assure you that everything is fine.'

At last he was back at Gail's, sitting with a glass of wine and a cigarette. They discussed the possibility of taking the matter to court, but realised that the public picture was going to alienate a great many people – a squabble over the dead body of a little boy. It seemed to be the only solution – that City Funerals should be left to organise everything as had originally been planned.

Gail by this time was so tired she couldn't hold back tears. 'I can't believe all this is happening.'

They called in Mr Mogafe and his assistant from B3, who were still waiting.

'Sorry, guys, we've tried our best but we cannot afford any more of this from the media point of view. We've offered you the memorial service.'

B3 went downstairs into the garden to discuss it in private all over again with Billy. In addition to their funeral services, they had offered the Khumalo family a full traditional funeral meal of meat, which they would cook and serve. The refusing of their offer was therefore also seen as an affront to black cultural practices. They came back after half an hour to say that the story was not over and that they were not interested in doing the memorial service. And they left.

So now new arrangements had to be found for the memorial service. There was no further funding for the FNB Stadium so they had to give up that idea. Then they remembered that Brian Oosthuizen had said that he thought the Central Methodist Mission would agree to having a memorial service there as well as the funeral. They telephoned him, and he said that he would find out, and get back to them. This he did and telephoned back to say that all was in order and the memorial service could go ahead at the Central Methodist Mission on the coming Wednesday. So that was one big problem solved.

Gary put through a call to Tony Guinness. 'Tony, I am phoning from Gail's house: with regard to what happened this morning, we are staying with the original agreement that you will continue with the funeral.'

Tony was delighted. He couldn't do enough.

'But be careful,' said Gary, 'B3 are not satisfied.'

'As a matter of fact,' said Tony, 'I've already had a call from someone threatening to kidnap Nkosi's body. But don't worry, we've put extra security around the premises.' It was not very satisfactory, but they had to trust that everything would be all right.

A call from the *Sowetan*: 'What's the story about fears that Nkosi's body might be kidnapped?'

Gary: 'We are certainly not under the impression that there's any danger to Nkosi's body. Why do you ask? City Funerals is organising everything and there will be absolutely no problem.'

On Sunday, *City Press* ran an article headed *BOGUS DOCTOR DIDN'T FOOL US*. The article stated: City Press *has established that Khoza is neither registered as a medical practitioner nor reflexologist with any recognised professional South African body. In one of her controversial letters – which we never published – Khoza told us government parliamentarians are among her patients. Khoza has gone on record as being able to cure breast cancer through her techniques which appear to be mere antics. She has also warned women to avoid contraceptive pills which she said 'blocked the body's systems and stopped circulation'.*

On Monday, 4 June, the *Sowetan* reported that Hilda Khoza had faxed them a public apology. It read: '*It is regrettable that the statement to the press hurt Gail Johnson. The aim was to help the child. The great pain that is going through us is the death of the child. This is a blow to all of us. May his soul rest in peace. I am sorry.*'

On Monday a meeting was held at Gail's house to talk about the funeral arrangements. Present were Laurette, on behalf of Nkosi's Haven, and Billy on behalf of the family. Liz Floyd acted as mediator. Billy, as custodian of traditional culture, said that it was necessary to hold a vigil, and he wanted to know who would provide the money for that. Also, who was going to get City Funerals to release the body for this purpose? Laurette said that Nkosi's Haven could not pay for the vigil, especially if the family wanted to slaughter a cow, for instance, as was the custom – such an expense could not possibly be borne by Nkosi's Haven. Billy felt that again, as with the controversy over the two funeral parlours, their culture was being ignored and the family slighted. Round and round went the argument and in the end nothing was resolved.

On Tuesday, a journalist from the *Sowetan* phoned. 'Are you aware that Grandma Ruth is holding a press conference today at one o'clock in Daveyton?' At the same time, a fax came through from an unnamed person also giving details of this press conference. Billy had not been informed of Ruth's intentions, and now tried to get her to cancel, but she refused. A report of this press conference was to be widely circulated in the *Sowetan*, *City Press* and other newspapers the following day.

Father Gary Thompson, who had witnessed the conflict between the various parties about the funeral arrangements, felt that in terms of their programme of peace and justice, the South African Council of Churches was the obvious body to become involved. The most urgent need was to try to mediate between the families. He contacted his colleague, staff member and Provincial Secretary of Churches, the Rev. Gift Moerane, who then communicated with

Father Steven Mbande, local pastor, chairperson and community leader in the Daveyton area. They agreed to speak to Ruth Khumalo and her family.

They felt that the world must not see a split, most especially a black/white split. If the feud were allowed to carry on, all the good work being done by Nkosi's Haven and other projects helping AIDS orphans could be jeopardised in terms of public opinion and outside funding.

So the SACC's first task was to try to get the families to agree on the funeral arrangements, especially as Ruth Khumalo had declared her intention of boycotting the memorial service. As the Rev. Gift Moerane saw it, on the one side there were the Johnsons: they had raised and cared for the child and therefore had the moral right to decide how and where he should be buried. On the other side there were the Khumalos who came with the issues of traditional practices and rituals, which were necessary if Nkosi were to rest peacefully and be accepted by his ancestors.

He and Father Steven Mbande soon found that there was a lot of negative feeling to overcome. The family said that the Johnsons had not consulted them, had not informed them of Nkosi's death, were not interested in the necessity of burying Nkosi according to their ancestral customs, and had ignored the claims of B3 undertakers as arranged through Ruth.

In African tradition, the first people you inform of a death are the elders of the family because they are the ones who will come and give direction as to how to wrap the body. On the morning of Nkosi's death, they had first heard about it on the radio. They felt that traditionally it was up to them to handle the burial of their child: when death occurs, the role of the foster parent is over. However, Father Mbande realised that within the family there were also those who sympathised with Gail and supported her, who thought there was nothing wrong with Nkosi's lifestyle, and that the role Gail had played qualified her to be the real mother. 'We believe that Gail is doing a good job,' they told him, 'and that she is entitled to bury the young man.'

But another source of anger complicating the issue was that

certain other members of the family had doubts as to what was happening to all the funds donated to the projects that bear Nkosi's name. They suspected that with such huge international recognition, he must have become a very rich child, while they, his family, were struggling. Tempers were high and things were said that made it evident that it was no longer a family affair but had spread into the surrounding community.

Perceptions there were very confused. Some even thought that Ruth and her family had become rich themselves through Nkosi. The whole question of entitlement suddenly became a huge issue, so much so that threats of murder were being bandied about, should any member of the Johnson family come to Daveyton. So a meeting was called in the community hall and Father Mbande went there to talk to the community leaders to try to deal with the negative attitudes. He appealed to them to let this young boy's soul rest in peace now by creating common ground with the Johnson family so that the funeral process could move forward.

He told them that the boy's body could not be buried at Daveyton but would merely lie in state there, and that the reputation of everybody would be at stake should anything happen to the body between Johannesburg and Daveyton. It was also necessary to try to resolve the feud between the undertakers – City Funerals, who perceived themselves to be a very powerful outfit, and B3, who were antagonised by their attitude – and to persuade them moreover not to use Nkosi's death as an opportunity for marketing.

So it was necessary to negotiate, to compromise, to remind the families that although their practices would be accommodated as far as was possible, this child belonged not only to his families but to the nation.

At a meeting on Tuesday evening at Gail's house, she, Billy, Rev. Brian Oosthuizen, Fika, Joe Sandows, Father Gary Thompson, Rev. Gift Moerane, Laurette and Oscar came together to try to resolve the situation.

Gail said: 'You know what? From day one, back in January, I told you that when Nkosi dies you can take his body to Newcastle and bury him with his mother. I gave you my word from the beginning. You came back to me and said you wanted him to be buried in West Park Cemetery, Johannesburg, and we also agreed on the Methodist Church. This is what your family decided. I really have tried to accommodate your wishes.'

Billy agreed that she had. He also realised that more harm than good could come from the continuing feud between the undertakers, so as the family's spokesman he said that they agreed that things vis-à-vis City Funerals should be left as they now were.

The question of holding a vigil was then raised again, and at first Gail did not want this to happen in Daveyton because of the anonymous phone call threatening that Nkosi's body would be kidnapped. On the other hand, she did not like the idea of certain of the rituals – slaughtering an animal, for instance – happening at her house.

Fika and Billy felt that what was important was that there should be a healing and cleansing process, and these rituals should be done personally by the family. The family should be able to touch the child in farewell at the vigil. This was, in fact, more important to them than a fancy casket and a big funeral with dignitaries present.

Fika said that decisions on the burial should wait until the elders of the family from KwaZulu-Natal should come and give their input. Others felt that as the elders had allowed the child to be adopted by Gail, they should have no say. Fika then voiced his dissatisfaction that everything was in the end going against the family's wishes. He reiterated that B3 should be doing the funeral and that no proper consultation had taken place. He said that as Gail had put her foot down about the undertakers, he was now insisting on the vigil in Daveyton.

Gail was still unhappy about this, since Daveyton was B3's territory. She also had to be reassured that in the traditional rituals there was no question of interfering in any way with the body. It has rather to do with speaking to the spirit of that person, and if certain rituals are not carried out involving the family members, then the legacy of that death would remain with them as a bad omen for the family in the future.

The Rev. Gift Moerane recalls: 'The whole issue of the rituals was very problematic. There are some issues so fundamental that you cannot negotiate, and the key to this was that Gail had either to allow the rituals to take place at her home where Nkosi died, or to allow his body to be taken for that purpose to Daveyton. There were times when she would just cry and say "My son, my son – I would like to see my son resting in peace. He doesn't deserve all this."'

The meeting ended with no real resolution, but with the priests appealing to everyone to go home and think and pray about the situation, because it was obvious there would have to be compromise on both sides if there were to be a peaceful, dignified funeral for Nkosi.

The next morning (Wednesday, 6 June), Father Mbande collected Ruth and family from Daveyton and brought them to the chapel at Khotso House, headquarters of the SACC, for a final attempt at reconciliation with the Johnsons. It was felt that Khotso House would be neutral ground, more conducive to a peaceful atmosphere. But that very morning, the statements Ruth and Dudu made at her press conference the day before were in the newspapers: *NKOSI'S FAMILY WANT TO BURY THEIR CHILD*, shouted the headline in the *Sowetan*. *Nkosi's family... had decided to bury their flesh and blood without any help from Johnson. The family said their decision to go it alone stemmed from the fact that Johnson had not been honest with them about the funeral arrangements... They claimed that Johnson had told them B3 Funeral Undertakers were conducting the burial and 'the next thing she went to the newspapers and said something else.'* Lower down on the same page was a report by Saint Molakeng headlined: *GAIL TREATED US LIKE DIRT – GRANDMA* *'Gail's harshness made Xolani tremble before her. It was like the boy was locked up in jail... I know people are going to think I am ungrateful and that now Xolani is dead I am saying Gail was a bad person. But that is not so... I have tried everything humanly possible to work hand in hand with her up to the last minute but my endeavours are not being reciprocated. Gail is treating me and my*

*family like dirt people who do not matter. That is why she even went
to the extent of making and changing funeral arrangements without
our knowledge,' Khumalo said... 'One time I (Dudu) phoned him and
he wondered what he had to do when, having fed Gail's dogs and
cats and the food was finished, Gail would ask sternly why the food
was finished so quickly.'*[51]*

And in the *Pretoria News*: NKOSI'S GRANDMOTHER SLAMS
JOHNSON: Nkosi's maternal grandmother Ruth Khumalo made
furious allegations against Ms Johnson yesterday, insisting that his
biological family was denied access to him while he was alive, has
not had a say in planning his funeral and that Ms Johnson
emotionally abused Nkosi... Her emotional tirade follows similar
allegations made by Johannesburg reflexologist Hilda Khoza in a
submission to the South African Commission for Human Rights,
published by the* Sowetan *last Thursday, on the eve of Nkosi's
death. Ms Khoza, who had met with Ms Khumalo, was quoted as
saying Ms Johnson used Nkosi to make money, was abusing him
and keeping him from attending school... Ms Khoza said yesterday
she had merely approached the Commission in a bid to help the
Johnson family mend the rift with Ms Khumalo, and that she
intended suing the* Sowetan *over the article.'[52]*

Journalist Saint Molakeng was later to state that Hilda had
approached the *Sowetan* and given him the story exactly as
reported in his article of 31 May, and that it was only after Nkosi's
death that she accused the newspaper of twisting her story.

It was against this background that the two families came
together at Khotso House for one more attempt at reconciliation.

It was at this meeting that it finally came out that B3 had
offered Ruth a house if she would promise that they could organise
the funeral arrangements. Emotions ran very high, and the
atmosphere of the meeting was extremely tense. It was finally
agreed that the night vigil should take place in Daveyton on the
following Friday, with the proviso that heavy security measures
should be in place. Strict orders would be given to the undertakers,
the police would be informed about the threats made by one
against the other, a police escort in unmarked cars would be

arranged for the body travelling between Johannesburg and Daveyton, and it would be ensured that the deployment around Nkosi's family would not interrupt their mourning process.

The family said that in their culture it was customary, when the body was brought from the mortuary to the vigil, to notify the deceased that he was now going home to meet his ancestors, and that from there his body would be taken straight to the church and cemetery for burial. However, since Gail wanted City Funerals to take him back to their parlour from the vigil, to dress him again and make sure that all was in order, the family were obliged to compromise.

The SACC took it upon themselves to let the undertakers know in no uncertain terms that if anything happened, they would be held responsible. They would inform them that security police would monitor the entire process. They would point out that their businesses would be destroyed if they were seen to be fighting over this young boy's body.

Again the meeting saw no real reconciliation, but Gail had to leave to attend the funeral of a family friend, Gladiator Christy 'Sahara' Skoglund, tragically dead of a burst blood vessel in the brain.

This whole experience brought home to the SACC representatives that there was a danger that people might shy away from adopting AIDS children because of the friction that could arise through differing cultural practices when the child dies.

They resolved that a programme of counselling must be worked out and put in place so that such problems would not suddenly arise. As the Rev. Gift Moerane puts it: 'We are living in a country that is quite unique, where things happen in a way that you don't expect in life. The adoption of Nkosi was just one case... One wouldn't imagine that Gail would take such a bold step. That's why we felt proud of her... We can't allow any ill feelings to taint the gesture that she projected to the nation – that we are a caring nation. Colour is not the determining factor... human suffering is what people are concerned about. That for us was the statement we read in this situation.'

And Father Gary Thompson comments further: 'It highlights the problem we are going to have in time: when we have cross-cultural fostering arrangements... Should we allow interaction? If the stories (of Nkosi sometimes asking to stay on with his biological family) are true, it reflects to a certain extent the pain he had to endure as a little boy... It appears he wasn't sure where he belonged. The policy makers will have to decide that if people are prepared to "give their child away" to be fostered or adopted by someone else – then I think it would be only proper for that child to be handed over completely.'

While the meeting at Khotso House has been taking place, Gary and his assistants have been busy at the Central Methodist Mission in Pritchard Street, getting everything ready for the memorial service, due to start at 2 p.m. A contingent of volunteers from the Gauteng Department of Health are there, and the Rev Brian and Father Gary also arrive as soon as the meeting is over. The sound system is put in place, floral arrangements arrive, a huge poster of Nkosi in his orange jersey is hung from the balcony, other photographs of him are placed all about, seating is arranged for the press and VIPs. The two ministers go around removing or obscuring City Funerals stickers that are on everything: they feel that a funeral should not be made an opportunity for advertising. A platform is in place for the singers. The media are beginning to arrive, and say that their view is obscured by an arrangement of candles in the shape of Africa. This is then moved to the other side of the podium. More flowers arrive. Everyone wonders what is happening to Gail and Ruth – whether Gail is coping and whether Ruth will come to the service.

The congregation then begin to arrive. Each person is given a red candle. A group of AIDS demonstrators with placards appear up in the gallery. The volunteers ask them to remove the placards, which they do without argument. Somebody says to Gary Scallan: 'Go and see who's outside.'

He goes, and finds Hilda Khoza, dressed in a red .cocktail outfit. A TV station has its camera trained on her, and she is talking to the media. She has changed her story and says that she now supports Gail, that is why she is attending the memorial service. Gary introduces himself and says that he has a special place for her, behind the VIPs. She asks to speak to Gail.

'Why, Hilda?'

'I really am sorry – I really have made a mistake.'

Gary knows that Gail has already spoken to her lawyers to start proceedings against Hilda for false accusations and defamation.

'Look, Hilda, this is the story. You have to retract what you've said, you have to publicly apologise to Gail, not just via a fax message in a newspaper.'

Hilda accepts this, and goes to sit in the place he indicates.

Almost two thousand people are now filling the church. The afternoon sun has moved round, and is shining directly through the stained glass windows. Nkosi's families have arrived and are seated; Gail and Ruth are here.

The Rev. Brian and Father Gary have together worked on the liturgy for this service and for the forthcoming funeral on Saturday. They wanted to include as many people as possible. Father Gary welcomes everyone in different languages. Many musicians have come and have offered to perform spontaneously. Among them are PJ Powers, Thandi Klaassen (who sang her version of the *Lord's Prayer*), Mercy Pakela, Pure Gold, David Isaacs and Yvonne Chaka Chaka. Craig Urbani and Clayton Stewart sing a song that was specially written for Nkosi – *Rainbow Child*. Tears are shed as *I believe I can Fly* is sung – Nkosi's favourite song.

Ruth the granny and Gail the mother come to the front with tapers and take light from the candle on the altar. Together they light all the candles making up the map of Africa. Hymns are sung: *O for a thousand tongues to sing* and *Ma Sibulela Kuyesu!*[53] and *Mazith' Linqcondo Zethu.*[54] Prayers are offered. The Rev. Brian gives a short homily. Nkosi became, he says, 'the face for all AIDS sufferers in South Africa. He was a brave man for his age. We all unite at this sad moment in memory of Nkosi, who personified the struggle of children living with HIV/AIDS. We must not forget that he was but a child, and yet because of his disease, he was a man.' The Lord's Prayer is spoken in isiZulu.

The lighting of candles represents peace and life in the Christian tradition. Gail and Ruth again take flame from the altar candle and pass it to all the members of congregation – candle to candle. Two thousand points of light for Nkosi, going out into the world from his memorial service, spreading hope that the pandemic will be overcome. Dr Donald Craig speaks the Blessing.

Slowly, people begin to disperse. The Rev. Brian comes to Gary.

'We have to do something about Gail and Ruth, people are speculating.'

'Hilda Khoza also wants to join the party. You keep Ruth and Gail together while they walk out of the door, and I will bring Hilda.'

Outside, Gary says to Gail: 'Hilda Khoza is here – she wants to speak to you. She wants to apologise.'

Brian is there with Ruth at his side, Gail is there with Hilda and Gary. The media home in on the sight of the three women together; Brian lights one of the candles and the three of them hold it, Ruth's hand touching Gail's beneath it, touching Hilda's at the bottom. Hilda turns to Gail and says: 'I'm sorry.'

So, at last, ended the day of the memorial service.

But there was to be one more twist in the funeral arrangements saga. Following Ruth's declaration in the *Sowetan* that she wanted to bury Nkosi herself, persons alleged to be representing the Pan-Africanist Congress also approached her with the offer of a house for herself, saying that they would take over the responsibility of burying Nkosi in the township. So she was being pressured not only by people with considerable commercial interests but by what appeared to be political opportunism as well. Billy, the family spokesman, stood firm by the existing arrangements, but not without cost. 'Amongst ourselves we look at each other like enemies,' he says.

The next day, Thursday, candles were lit in the township when about five hundred mourners gathered at the Victor Ndlazilwana

Community Hall in Daveyton for a simple memorial service. Nkosi's Uncle Fika pleaded for more tolerance from the community for people infected with AIDS. He cited the example of Nkosi's mother. 'My sister was not happy when she died because of the treatment she received after people learned she was dying from AIDS. I am pleading with you to accept that AIDS exists.' And the listeners were much moved by a poem recited by Nkosi's sister, Mbali:

To my brother Xolani

To the only brother I have
The only family I had
The only brother I had
You were a hero to others
A young brother to me

Poverty really separated us
Rich side had you
Poor side had me
But emotionally we were together
The family bond had us
I love you brother

Give my love to Mama
I would miss you both
Now I am stuck with you
Stuck with your memories

I would miss you
Now and always
As I am lonely in this world

Also on Thursday, at about lunchtime, Gary Scallan received a call from Saint Molakeng, saying that he had some questions he would like to put to Gail. They were: firstly, was Nkosi legally adopted by Gail? Secondly, was an autopsy carried out on Nkosi's body?

Gary consulted with Gail and then immediately telephoned Aggrey Klaaste, the editor of the *Sowetan.*

'These are the questions your journalist has asked Gail. Quite frankly, she has had enough.'

Aggrey Klaaste said that he would investigate and call back. He called back in less than half an hour.

'I have summoned the journalist into my office and taken him off the story. Please extend my sincere apologies to Gail.'

Gail accepted the apology. Saint Molakeng was to insist later that all he had wanted to do was to settle the question of who was the legal guardian of Nkosi and to find out the cause of death. He said that if Gail had not adopted Nkosi legally, then she had less legal right to him than the grandmother, and it was therefore important to hear what the grandmother had to say. He also said that while he was not against Gail, and in fact applauded what she had done for Nkosi, he felt that no one was giving enough attention to the pain of the grandmother.

During the week following Nkosi's death, Colleen and Judy arrived from Pennington, Nicci had to have a lumbar puncture, and Gail had yet more media interviews, this time with the Australian Broadcasting Corporation, the SABC, and a live crossing to Scottish radio.

In Cape Town on the Friday, a memorial service attended by a few hundred people took place at St. George's Cathedral. Among those present was Zackie Achmat, leader of the Treatment Action Campaign. He paid tribute to Nkosi and Gail for motivating the National AIDS Education Policy for Learners and Educators, which stated that no child or teacher could be discriminated against in schools.

In Melville, Friday was spent in last-minute arrangements for the funeral the following day, such as deciding who would read out the messages of condolence. Brett arrived from Israel, and in the evening the family sat down to a curry supper. They were receiving regular updates from the security people at the vigil, and all seemed to be going well. They began to relax, and remember incidents that had struck them during the week.

There had been Mr TP Daya who had telephoned from Durban, asking about Nkosi's dimensions, and offering to make a suit for him to be buried in. He also wanted to know the shoe size, whereupon Gail said: 'Absolutely not! Nkosi will be buried in his tackies. They were his favourite shoes.' The day Nkosi died, Gail had had him dressed in his best jeans and T-shirt. But when the suit arrived she did not feel able to dress him again herself. She offered Granny Ruth the opportunity to do so.

There had been the man who telephoned from the Johannesburg Parks and Recreation Department, the Director of West Park Cemetery, saying that they wanted to donate the plot for Nkosi's grave.

'We want to bury him in Hero's Acre. Where would you like the plot to be?' he asked.

'Where would you suggest?'

'Well, there is the plot right next to Mr Alfred Nzo, the late Minister of Foreign Affairs. Or you could have one near the children from the Westdene bus disaster.' This seemed much more appropriate. (Forty-two children, all aged between thirteen and eighteen, pupils of Hoërskool Vorentoe, drowned when their school bus plunged into Westdene Dam on 27 March 1985.)

There had been the call from someone at Kaizer Chiefs – Nkosi's favourite soccer team. They offered their under-13 team to act as pallbearers. Gail was thrilled – she knew how keen Nkosi had been on them.

But in all their minds was – what was happening in Daveyton? Were the security arrangements holding? Was everything going peacefully?

A tent has been set up outside Ruth's house and people have been gathering since the morning. Preparations are proceeding well – the goat has been brought and slaughtered. Along the roads leading into the squatter camp crowds are waiting expectantly, many of them schoolchildren. News of the vigil has spread and they are beginning to sing, even before the hearse bringing his body is in sight – the body of this child whose mother had been stigmatised by the community before she died.

The hearse comes, it draws up in front of Ruth's house, and the coffin is carried inside. Members of the family accompany it; the women sit beside it on the floor, wrapped in blankets.

Because Nkosi had not been through the 'cleansing' ritual after his mother died, it is now necessary that it should be done. The goat is the one that will lead Nkosi's soul to his ancestors – she is the bridge whereby he can reach them and be recognised. Although he had been brought up in a white foster family, he must go back, in the end, to his own people. They must be invited to meet him halfway, to welcome him, and it is through the mediation of the death of the goat that this can happen.

The blood of the sacrificed animal also speaks for the deeds of the one who has died, in expiation, so that he or she may be forgiven.

The gall and other internal parts of the goat, mixed with water and aloes, are used to wash Nkosi and his close family.

Nkosi and his mother are invoked: 'Here is the goat that is cleansing you because you are not cleansed. We are asking forgiveness that we did not do this at the proper time.' And then: 'Here is the goat that is cleansing your son, because during his life we could not do this. Please accept your son now that he has been cleansed.'

The following day the flesh of the goat will be eaten by the mourners after the funeral. At that time, water and aloes will be ready for them to cleanse their hands and faces, especially the children, to ward off any malicious spirits that might attack them after being at the cemetery.

In the tent, the vigil goes on from ten in the evening until four o'clock the following morning. Father Stephen Mbande is presiding. He gives a prayer of supplication that people will be enabled to accept what cannot be changed in the situation, and to admit that sometimes cultures must accept other cultures. He prays for calm and self-control, and that people may see this not as a crisis but as a victory.

People get up one by one and speak. Despite the presence of strong feelings, it is a disciplined gathering. Some say that the family has been made to compromise too much. Others say that Nkosi was an international figure and must have an appropriate funeral.

One says that he has made us aware of AIDS. He was not afraid to tell the world that he was HIV-positive. Another says that because of Nkosi, his behaviour will change. Others talk about how the family must revisit the situation of why he was brought up in Melville. 'How many of us would have come forward, even if we had a million dollars, and said: Here am I – I will adopt this young man?'

Another says that because of him everybody will be given houses, better roads and electricity. The next one crushes this view but says that the presence of this boy here tonight indicates that there is indeed light at the end of the tunnel.

After the ceremony, in the small hours of the morning, the cortege is made ready to take Nkosi back to Johannesburg. People follow it, singing. Only when it has travelled several kilometres do they begin to disperse.

The Khumalos said afterwards that they were disappointed that Gail had not attended either the memorial or the vigil at Daveyton. Gail felt, however, that in view of the friction, she did not feel happy about attending without an invitation.

Father Stephen Mbande sums up what happened between the families:

'It is not easy to compromise a culture's rituals... In the past, one would even lose one's life for compromising culture, (or) lose status in one's clan... The Nkosi family... really compromised to have their blood shared with the white woman. They opened their hearts and said – yes, you are his mother in adoption... you have given him a home, treatment and so on. It was not an easy one. Even Christianity has a problem when it comes to different cultures. But Gail has also compromised. I think she had a right to say – the child Nkosi belongs to me – I can invite you to the funeral. But she didn't do that, she said – let's go together. I think if it was me, I would have said – come or don't come, it's not my problem... She opened her heart and shared.'

And John Conyngham, editor of the *Natal Witness*, commented in his article 'Caught in a Whirlwind' on 8 June:

'...the rift between Nkosi's adoptive and biological families emphasises once again the seemingly unbridgeable cultural canyon that exists between many white and black South Africans. Quite what it is that has set the Khumalos against the Johnsons is hard to understand. Perhaps Frantz Fanon, that great guru of anti-colonialism and the psychological damage foreign occupation caused, could explain why the grandmother of Xolani Nkosi, an afflicted orphan with no prospects, should be so angry with someone whose care enabled her grandson to live far beyond the short lifespan of someone born HIV-positive. Did she see it as a patronising relationship? Did she regret Nkosi's loss of his culture? Did she resent him becoming a celebrity? Was she denied the right to care for him herself? Did she decline to do so?*

'...Only when South Africans evolve to a point where actions speak louder than race or culture or class, will we be finally free from bigotry. Until then, let us give thanks for the life of Nkosi. Let us also give thanks for the kindness of Johnson, who opened her house and heart to him. Let no one who hasn't done the same, cast the first stone.'

At the funeral on Saturday, 9 June, the mood is quieter. It is less of a celebration of Nkosi's life and more of a seeing him home to sleep at last. Before it begins, Bishop Dandala calls Gail and Ruth into the chapel and prays with them. They then enter the church together – an important sign of reconciliation for people to see.

Nkosi's white and gilded coffin is placed near the podium, and the families sit facing it in the front row. A banner stretches across the front of the steps saying: '*Lala kahle*,[55] Xolani Nkosi Johnson'.

Fresh flowers are there, and the Methodist Church choir, supported by other choirs, leads the singing. Dr Kenneth Kaunda, past-President of Zambia, has come down especially for the occasion. Hundreds of tributes have been received from all over the world, not only from celebrities such as Archbishop Desmond Tutu and from Deputy President Jacob Zuma, but also from ordinary people, both friends and strangers. Some are read out by Alan Johnson who has come up from his home in Hermanus. Desiree Thomas – 'Shadow' from *Gladiators* – reads Jesse Jackson's tribute.

When Alan Ford and Gareth Cliff sing *Time To Say Goodbye*, many are moved to tears. Prayers that people may be united and accepting of each other are offered up. Ruth Khumalo speaks in isiZulu, with Rev. Gift Moerane translating into English. She thanks Gail Johnson: 'I want to thank humbly this white lady, Gail Johnson, who was led by God on this road with a small boy following behind. I thank you, Gail, for what you have done.' She speaks of obstacles that they have encountered along the way and says that finally they have all been brought together here.

Gail asks that we should all care for the children who are infected or orphaned, so that their lives should not be empty. 'Nkosi taught me unconditional love and acceptance, and I ask South Africa to do the same.' She reads the poem: 'Nkosi's Soul'.

Dr Bongani Khumalo from the President's office pays a tribute. 'Nkosi,' he says, 'lived only a dozen years but the impact of his life is profound, is infinite. He stood tall like a warrior, and fought the fight on behalf of those affected by HIV/AIDS. He was a child of the world and of God.'

Two brother tenors from Pretoria sing, most beautifully, *I'll Walk with God*.

Bishop Mvume Dandala, presiding bishop of the Methodist Church of Southern Africa, gives his sermon. Reconciliation is his theme. 'I hear Nkosi Johnson saying to us in a land where our difficulties get complicated by our history of racial alienation, I hear him saying: "Overcome with love." ' Also in the course of his address, the bishop castigates certain undertakers who descend upon the families of deceased persons 'like vultures.'

Hymns are sung: *How Great Thou Art* and '*Mpele, pelo, le moea.*'[56] The mothers and children from Nkosi's Haven sing alone for Nkosi. Again, many are in tears.

And then the procession, headed by the enormous white limousine carrying Nkosi's coffin covered in flowers, drives at a walking pace through the city out towards West Park Cemetery. There is one disappointment: Kaizer Chiefs Under-13 soccer team, who promised to act as pallbearers, has not arrived, so Nkosi is carried on his last journey by AIDS helpers from the Gauteng Department of Health. Passers-by see the procession and join it. They walk in front, behind, beside it all the way. By the time the cortege arrives at West Park, both sides of the driveway leading up to the gravesite are lined by people holding hands.

A canopy has been erected over the grave. A red carpet leads from the road to the site, and a little platform with seats accommodates family members. Other well-wishers crowd around as closely as possible.

The committal is brief: a few short prayers, spoken by Bishop Dandala and by the Rev Brian Oosthuizen. 'Ashes to ashes, dust to dust...' The familiar words. The children from Nkosi's Haven have brought as many flowers as they can carry from the church, and as the coffin is lowered into the grave, they throw them in. Through the loudspeaker comes the song *Angel* sung by Sarah McLachlan. It is Nicci's tribute.

Suddenly there is a disturbance. Hilda Khoza pushes her way onto the platform and shakes Gail's hand. But even this cannot quite take the edge off the profound pathos of the moment.

Now there are many tears. Traditional mourners wail. The last blessing has been spoken, the last flower has been thrown in. Gail takes a little walk away from everybody amid the other graves. A stray photographer snaps her lighting up a cigarette. People begin to disperse, but little groups remain, giving each other hugs, comforting.

The artificial grass is rolled up, and before everyone has quite gone, a truck is disgorging a load of concrete into the open grave, to foil the coffin stealers.

There is no big party afterwards. So many people are dying that these customary expensive gatherings are impoverishing families across the country. It has been agreed therefore that to set an example, no official wake will be held for Nkosi.

But Gail's house is full of flowers. So many people have sent bouquets – the arrangement sent by the Nelson Mandela Children's Fund must be one of the biggest ever seen. School children and other well-wishers and mourners have left bunches of flowers outside the house, along the wall. Nkosi's home is fragrant with people's loving gifts.

Epilogue

IN APRIL 2002, Nkosi was posthumously voted joint winner of the World's Children's Prize for the Rights of the Child – a prize for children that is often called 'The Children's Nobel Prize' by media around the world, and awarded by an international jury of sixteen children who themselves have been victimised in some way. South Africa's Lerato Petersen, niece of Hector Petersen (killed at the age of twelve in the 1976 Soweto uprising), is one of the sixteen. At the same time, Nkosi won the Global Friends Award. This is voted for by children in Global Friendship schools throughout the world. Gail was invited, together with Eric Nicholls and two children from Nkosi's Haven, Moshe Mhlapo and Manini Mkhabela, to go to Sweden to accept these awards posthumously on Nkosi's behalf from Queen Silvia.

West Park Cemetery is green and tranquil, overlooked by the craggy ridge of Melville Koppies, said to be the largest nature reserve within city limits in the world.

All around are stretches of quiet green space, inhabited by Egyptian Geese and plovers. There is a serene lake where waterlilies unfold their white and gold beauty. Guarding all, against the skyline, the long rocky ridge protects the southern edge of this vast garden for the dead.

Nkosi's grave lies beside the main driveway not far from the entrance. It is in an area recently named Hero's Acre; he is one of the few heroes to be buried there as yet. Nearby is the severe black monument to Alfred Nzo, first Minister of Foreign Affairs under the new dispensation in 1994. Just opposite, across the driveway, are the graves of the forty-two children who drowned in their school bus. Most of the tombstones include photographs of hopeful young faces above school uniforms.

Now, a year after his death, a commemorative monument has been erected over the place where Nkosi lies. His photograph, embraced by a pink granite replica of the AIDS ribbon, smiles across at the faces of the other children. On the stone that covers him appear the following words:

TO THE WORLD
YOU WERE AN ICON
TO AFRICA
YOU WERE AN AIDS HERO
TO SOUTH AFRICA
YOU WERE THE FACE OF AIDS
AND A WARRIOR.
TO ME, YOU WERE MY SON

REST IN PEACE, KOSI
I LOVE AND MISS YOU
MOM

TO MY BRIGHT STAR
IN THE SKY
MAY YOU FOREVER BE
IN THE ARMS OF
THE ANGELS

MY LOVE, NICCI

Afterwords –
Some Witnesses

PRESIDENT THABO MBEKI, in an address to the nation on World AIDS Day, 1 December 1999:

'... There can be no talk of an African Renaissance, if AIDS is at the door of our continent.

'... When the history of our time is written, let it record the collective efforts of our societies responding to a threat that put the future of entire nations in the balance. Let future generations judge us on the adequacy of our response.'

DR GLENDA GRAY, Director of Peri-Natal HIV Research Unit at Chris Hani Baragwanath Hospital, in an interview with the author:

'By the time Mandela came out of prison (1990)... we were looking at rates of about three infected women out of every hundred tested. Now (2001) we are looking at thirty in every hundred... When you see an increase like that it's obvious that no one knows what to do about the epidemic and no one is putting their weight behind it. It's not difficult to control the epidemic. It doesn't take a rocket scientist. It takes consistent and solid and good messages. Safe sex, use condoms, empower women. Bombard people with good media. Go to the ad agencies. Go to Coca-Cola. They've convinced people to drink Coke in Katmandu, we should be able to convince people to use condoms in Soweto... Most people in Soweto, for example, are aware (of HIV/AIDS) but it doesn't translate into behaviour change. It's like drinking and driving...

'It came out that R45 million was unspent of hospital funds... People... don't know how the system works and the Department isn't moving its money. If you have a crisis, why is it so difficult to shift money?'

DR NONO SIMELELA, Chief Director: HIV/AIDS and STDs, National Department of Health, in an interview with the author:

'We produce guidelines and training and support and find funds and move resources and (give) technical advice... the unit has been going since 1991... the provinces don't have the skills that are necessary to strategically plan and cost and budget, and (they don't have) the processes that shift money... even if you want to assist somebody at local level you can't transfer money – there are the constitutions... It is maybe not being able to run faster – because this epidemic wants us to run much faster than we are running... Where you try to skill people it takes so long, and with the fiscal control, the public finance management, you can't push money and not be accountable... But I think there is a greater awareness now to give us more money because they can see that it is a very worthwhile cause.'

DR HOOSEN COOVADIA, Department of Paediatrics and Child Health, Nelson Mandela School of Medicine, University of Natal, in a telephonic interview with *The Life Story Project:*

'The key to AIDS and society is that it is essential to have a good rapport between the populace and its representatives in government who are supposed to lead. For example, the old government would have found it difficult to understand the enormous role that the preservation of human rights plays in counselling HIV/AIDS. The importance of protecting people and not stigmatising people, not discriminating against people... Silence and denial are issues of human rights... To combat AIDS we need participation by people, we need leadership of the government, we need a coordinated and integrated support on all levels of society...

'This is a sociopolitical, economic and health catastrophe of unprecedented proportions. There are no diseases which are equal in their ferocity and impact through the whole of human history... We have lost millions, and our country is still to lose millions. It's a disaster that requires a response of a commensurate order to the degree of damage being caused to our society. That matching response must come from all of us, you and me.

'There are some possibilities for positive, real change being tested. A groundswell to support globally governments in Africa, offers of support from pharmaceutical companies, UN agencies, philanthropic organisations, governments in the industrialised world. This is an apposite time to capture the rising tide of offers. If we don't move now and if we don't extend ourselves to the furthest point – we will allow a few million South Africans to die. That alone will leave our nation scarred in ways that I cannot imagine. If we don't do our utmost, we will have lost our element of humanity.'

DR RUTH RABINOWITZ, Member of Parliament and Spokesperson for the Inkatha Freedom Party, in an interview with the author:

'The argument has been all the time we can't treat because it's been too expensive, it will just absorb the entire health budget... If so many... are dying of AIDS, what are all the other things you're trying to achieve with the health services worth?

'Help the people. Give them vitamin supplements, give them free garlic... work with the traditional healers... We should be setting up some sort of avenue for them to work with the clinics and work with the doctors. We're not into partnerships in this country and we should be.

'We have such a complicated system of governance and of disbursement of funds, and most of the AIDS money that is coming from government comes via conditional grants. If you could see how complicated it is... to get those grants realised and to achieve what they're trying to in terms of training, counsellors, training testers, getting sufficient medicines or even test kits to the people, you would understand that it's a... soul-destroying task.'

DR COSTA GAZI, AIDS activist and member of the Pan-Africanist Congress, in a telephonic interview with *The Life Story Project:*

'The TAC (Treatment Action Campaign) is going to court to make Nevirapine available to pregnant mothers. Their approach is too timid. Even if they (the TAC) win, the government will just delay... Nkosi represents the results of the policy of not preventing mother-to-child transmission, and not making available drugs for 4.6 million who are HIV-positive today... He was just a little boy who became a national, maybe international symbol... It is because of the inability of the government to come to terms with the epidemic that he stood out. Against this background, he stood out like a shining light.'

CHARLENE SMITH, Journalist, in an interview with the author:

'I haven't seen any illness as cruel as this virus. Their whole little bodies become involved in trying to breathe... if they get the thrush their lips swell up to about four times the size and they get kwashiorkor because they can't eat because of the pain – it's a cruel, cruel virus... If you speak to the nurses or the doctors, they will say how they used to love paediatrics because it was a happy place. But now everybody just dies.

'Gail basically adopted what, in everyone's view, was a dead child. The miracle was that this dead child insisted on living, and living for a long time. In some ways, his tragedy (but also our great fortune) was that he became an icon.

'The concept that you are dying when all your little friends are going to live for ever – that is a very big thing for anyone to take on board. But he had a very good sense of himself... he would say that the children and the teachers at his school loved him. That is a child who is told that and knows that he is loved. He was also a kind little boy... this happened to him, but he was going to look after other children.

'He had a mother who would openly speak about her child in a country in denial and in a world filled with stigma... With so many people saying to him 'you are so brave' and 'what you are doing is so good' – I think that increased the pressure on him, because he was a little boy who... probably had an exaggerated sense of responsibility to everyone. No one ever actually thought to stop... I don't think that anyone realised that when they were saying (these things), they would put a huge burden on his shoulders. Because he was then becoming responsible to save other children and it was his bravery that was going to allow things to happen.

'He becomes the indictment of adult intrigue and fighting and politicking and moneygrabbing. We sacrificed this little boy. Everybody sacrificed him.'

WARWICK ALLAN, Psychologist, former Co-Director of The Guest House, in an interview with the author:

'Without Gail, there would have been no Nkosi. He brought his ability to intuitively connect with people. But his courage and frankness in talking about his experiences – that came from living with Gail Johnson. He was far too little to have become a public figure on his own. She took him out there and showed him to the world... His readiness to communicate with people and her willingness to share him... it was like a dance between them.

'AIDS is really a medical technicality. HIV is the infection. Now, with the advances in anti-retroviral medication, we know we can keep HIV positive people from getting AIDS. We could have and do have millions of HIV-positive people for relatively very few AIDS people. So if you're reporting an AIDS statistic, you are reporting a minuscule fraction of the problem. And this is what the South African government did early on. Other governments too did it. The other trick is to report on AIDS deaths. So many people have died from AIDS. What about the people who die from tuberculosis as a result of HIV, or something else as a result of HIV? So your AIDS death statistic appears low. Whereas, in actual fact, your HIV-related death statistic is massive.

'You have to listen to the voice of Nkosi Johnson. It's all well and good for that voice to have elevated consciousness. But if people in positions of power are not prepared to implement the insights that that voice brought us, it's completely squandered. That is why the context of his story is so important. The context of neglect and uninterest. We have this voice, this child. And what good is it? To have lived and to have had such courage and to have been so charismatic. Charisma alone just doesn't change anything.'

RUTH BHENGU, ANC Member of Parliament, who announced publicly that her daughter had been diagnosed HIV-positive, in a telephonic interview with *The Life Story Project*:

'The most important thing for an HIV person is a sense of belonging, to have support, to make a person part of the family. The very first medicine I gave to Nosipho was to let her know she was still my child... She sat on my lap. She was twenty-four years old at the time. It was not usual to ask her to sit on my lap but I did it to show her that I was still the mother and she my child. Gail was able to provide that for Nkosi. She conveyed the message – you have a home, you are loved.

'The criticism out there of Gail is because of who she is, failing to take account of the amount of work she has done. I have an understanding of the work she has done because I also have an HIV-positive child. Gail took Nkosi because she is a woman and a mother, not because she is white. She loved Nkosi and gave him motherly love. She has a voice that fought for him not to be discriminated against. She influenced legislation... I would like to hear from those who are blaming Gail how they would have dealt with it... If people criticise and say something is wrong, they must provide an alternative.

'We can't resolve all problems in this country through politics; some problems need to put politics aside, some problems we need to see as national problems.'

NELSON MANDELA, former South African President, quoted in the *Eastern Province Herald*, 2 June 2001:

'He was an example for the whole world to follow. It's a great pity that this young man has departed. He was exemplary in showing how one should handle a disaster of this nature. He was very bold about it and he touched many hearts. Although it must be a relief for that wonderful woman Gail Johnson, nevertheless we are sorry about it. We are faced with a serious pandemic, which has taken away many of our people.'

JAN GROBBELAAR, Clinic and School Counsellor, in an interview with the author:
'He changed my point of view towards people with AIDS. Having to wash the cup – all that type of crap. Nkosi taught me how to talk to people with AIDS. I've got hands-on information because of him. I've got a heart problem. At one stage, I said to God that I haven't got the power to carry on counselling. And at that stage Nkosi came to me and God showed me I had the power after all, and that's how He works.'

ARCHDEACON STEPHEN K. MBANDE, Church of the Province of South Africa, in an interview with *The Life Story Project*:
'I tell you openly that HIV/AIDS people are being rejected because of the stigma they have... He (Nkosi) became a star that leads the people (to say) ... love your friends who are infected, love your children.'

GARY ROSCOE: Advertising Executive, Director of Nkosi's Haven, in an interview with *The Life Story Project*.
'Right from the very start, when you met that little boy, he was a striking kid; even one of the black journalists who was very antagonistic towards Gail asked me... how can a child speak with such a knowledge of life? ... The tragedy of this child was that he was so aware of it... Gail is one of those people who is just a doer. There were times when there was no money in the account and Gail was running around in her little Uno, collecting food from Checkers and taking it out to Sebokeng, in very dangerous areas... and to Tembisa... You have to picture that little Uno, before she got a proper vehicle, loaded up with five mothers and five kids and veggies galore and off into the townships. The brakes are not working properly, but off she goes – that is tenacity and courage.'

EDWIN CAMERON, Supreme Court Judge, in an interview with *The Life Story Project*:

'I think there are three levels of crisis about AIDS. There is a crisis of disease and death and debilitation that is manifesting itself ever more presently in our nation. There is also a crisis of leadership and management, but most importantly there is a crisis of the truth about AIDS, because our leaders appear not to be willing to accept the truth, to act on the truth and to tell the truth about AIDS.

'The truth about AIDS is that it is a mostly sexually transmitted disease, which is caused by an infectious agent that destroys the body's capacity to resist opportunistic infections, and that that agent can now be treated medically by anti-retroviral medication, and that properly administered, properly taken and supervised, those medications can lead to the cessation of viral activity in the human body.

'This is my message of hope. I am alive today because of those treatments. That is the encapsulable truth about AIDS. People must feel grief, but they must also feel anger because what is happening need not be happening. But most important they should feel hope because this epidemic can be dealt with. The fact that treatment is not yet accepted as possible, as available and accessible, the fact that this is not being made available or accessible, partly through the defaults of the drug companies and partly through the defaults of our national leadership, means that AIDS is still wrongly equated with death – it doesn't have to be.

'So, ultimately, through the grief and the anger we must feel hope. That's my message. It's a challenge bigger than apartheid. Those who are refusing the challenge are committing an enormity comparable to apartheid. It is a challenge to all of us in South Africa – white, black, male, female, whatever you are. It poses a moral as well as a practical challenge.

'The hope is that our action, our capacity or belief translated into action, can change this.'

Appendix

Wednesday 6 June 2001

Dear Gail,

I'm sure that you have received thousands of letters from
many people to say how sorry they are.
I am another one of those people.

Nkosi has been of my mind since last year when I watched the
show about him on T-V with tears in my eyes. I realized what
an amazing person he is. He will always be remembered and the
impact he has made on not only South Africa but the world will
be remembered for ever.

He has changed the way people think about the virus and he
found a special place in the heart of millions of people.

I think that it's amazing how you and him were able to show
people that Aids infected children are just normal human
beings. He is a wonderful person who will be the inspiration and
hero to many people.

I have done activities with my school in hospitals with children
who carry the virus.-I went to Kalafong a few times. Children
who have been put into the battle with no choice do deserve all
the help they can get. Nkosi was an inspiration that they
needed.

I hope that you will be able to carry on doing the amazing work
that you did,

Thank you,   (Grade 9)

Love from – Shira Goldblum

From: Raynald Adams
To: nkosishaven@worldonline.co.za <nkosishaven@worldonline.co.za>
Date: 02 June 2001 03:21
Subject: Please accept my condolances.

Dear Ms. Johnson:

Although he was just a small boy, I will remember Nkosi as a giant of humanity.

Please accept my sincerest condolances.

Raynald Adams
Montreal, Quebec, Canada

BOYS TOWN
because boys will be men

South Africa
BOYS TOWN CENTRE

I I LEMON STREET · SUNNYSIDE   2092   PO BOX 91661 · AUCKLAND PARK · 2006   TEL +27 I I 482 2655 · FAX +27 I I 482 6146
E-MAIL boystownho@yebo.co.za · HOTLINE 086 I I 00 269

TO	:	GAIL JOHNSON
FROM	:	DENISE FELIX-O'CALLAGHAN
DATE	:	1 JUNE 2001
FAX	:	(011) 726-4852

Dear Gail

Five minutes ago I saw The Star poster but have seen no newspaper as yet.

My thoughts are with you at this very difficult time. We really cannot imagine what ordeals you have gone through and what are still in store for you. All we do know is that you and Nkosi heightened the plight of AIDS children to the rest of the world. You, your family and Nkosi all paid a high price.

Thank you for doing what so many wished they had done. Thank you for being you and facing the world head-on. Hold your head up high.

With sincere affection.

Denise Felix-O'Callaghan

Nkosi

Go to your name sweet child and rest
In the arms of the Man who knew and loved you best
Who lived through your eyes
Who lived through your pain
Proud of a son
Who lived life like His name

Bringing strength to the weak
Courage to the strong
Love to the lonely
And some rights to the wrong

We cherish your memory
The light of your love
Your star shining brightly
From the heaven's above.
                    ATHLEA TODD

I will always love you, as if part of you belonged to me
Athlea
(1 June 2001)

From: Tony Martin
To: 'nkosishaven@worldonline.co.za' <nkosishaven@worldonline.co.za>
Date: 01 June 2001 12:04
Subject: Nkosi - RIP

Sir/Madam

I was completely unaware of this incredibly brave little boy until I saw the programme on BBC1 here in the UK a couple of weeks ago.

His story had me in tears (I'm a strapping 32 year old male !!)

I logged onto the BBC website this morning and saw the terribly sad news that little Nkosi has passed away.

I just wanted to pass on my sincere condolences to Ms Gail Johnson and his friends. I hope he has found peace in the arms of whatever God he believed in.

A Friend.

_____

Tony Martin

Mentis Management Consultants Ltd.

From: Frederic Pivetta
To: nkosishaven@worldonline.co.za <nkosishaven@worldonline.co.za>
Date: 02 June 2001 03:42

I would to express you my sadness for the present and hope for the future. It's people like Nkosi that make the world a better place. Please, never stop fighting. We need people like you. So, cry today but waake tomorrow and keep trying to change things.

Thank you for what you and Nkosi did,

Frederic

Frederic Pivetta
PhD Student
Harvard University

2 June 2001

Dear Gail and Nicci

We know that theirs not much that one can say in moments like this. But we wanted to add our voices to the millions around the world who are expressing their sorrow and sadness at the passing of Nkosi.

Doing the work that we do one does tend to become 'immune to' suffering and death, however it would be amiss if we did not express our real sorrow at Nkosi's death. As parents we cannot even begin to imagine how difficult the past couple of months and especially the last few days have been for you and your family.

Nkosi was loved and cherished by everyone he met, but what many people don't realise is that it was the nurturing and love he received from you and your family that made him into the very special child he was. A real little gentleman.

Amongst the many memories that I will cherish forever is a moment we have captured on video of Nkosi and Siobhan dancing and of the personal love that you gave him in times of difficulty.

We know that the next couple of months are going to be very hard for you but hope that you will be able to draw strength, courage and fortitude from the legacy you and Nkosi have created .

Our thoughts are with you.

Love

Shaun, Jacky
and Siobhan O'Shea.

The Poem

Xolani Nkosi Johnson

Dear Nkosi you were young

Hardly a teenager.but very inspirational

To the teenagers, adults & children.

You educated me &most teenager & Adults.

You taught us about H I V / AIDS, how

Dangerous it is & how it kills your cells

In your body

To most people you were just a kid but

To me were an educationalist & an inspiration

I will always remember you as a faraway friend,

A friend I never really got to know.

REST IN PEACE FRIEND, YOU WILL ALWAYS

BE HEAR & DEAR TO MY HEART.

Lots of LOVE.

PATIENCE N L RADEBE

From: Marianne Robertson
To: GAIL JOHNSON <nkosishaven@worldonline.co.za>
Date: 01 June 2001 17:49
Subject: Fw: Forward to Gail Johnson

Dear Gail
We have not come to see you as we understand that you are surrounded by the media frenzy. This does not mean that we have forgotton you and your love for Nkosi. I am forwarding an email from Canada which says it so much better than we can. You are in our throughts and prayers and we'll call in within the next couple of days.
We both wish you strength through the coming harrowing days. We have always admired your extraordinary compassion and ability to give to others so freely, particularly those that many people are loathe to come into contact with. Gail, we don't want to impose, but if you need us, we're just up the hill.
Love
Ian & Marianne

----- Original Message -----
From: Kim Freeman
To: Marianne Robertson
Sent: Friday, June 01, 2001 2:50 PM
Subject: Forward to Gail Johnson

Dear Gail,

Our sincere and heartfelt sympathy to you and to all who surround you on Nkosi's death. He was yet another example of "angels on earth" sent to remind us of our humanity and the responsibility we all should share in caring for each other. The years of love you lavished on Nkosi helped him to endure as he did and to become a worldwide symbol of courage. We mourn with you in his loss but remind you to take strength from the knowledge that his message has made a vast impact.

We were residents of South Africa until 1997 and followed his and your story closely. Since our return to Canada in 1997 we continued to be in touch through our dear friends Marianne and Ian Robertson and also through media coverage. Mickey, my 14 year old son, and I visited South Africa in March. Mickey was deeply touched by Nkosi's story. He met you very briefly while in Marianne's company one day. We have talked many times of you and Nkosi since our return home. Mickey was quietly saddened this morning as we shared the news of Nkosi's death.

We trust that peace and love will surround and strengthen you as you grieve. We wish you enduring courage as you continue to strive to care for the victims of AIDS.

Yours truly

Marilyn, Kim, Nadja and Mickey Freeman

Oakville, Ontario
Canada

Robert Grace Trust

Please reply to: The Secretary, The Robert Grace Trust, 15 Mayhury Gardens, London NW10 2NB
• Telephone 020 8830 4783   • Fax 020 8830 4785   • e-mail rita jarvis@hotmail.com

E-mail to:

Gail Johnson
Nkosi's Haven

June 9th 2001

Dear Gail,

On behalf of the Robert Grace Trust I am writing to give you our sympathy and support at a very sad time for you. You are obviously a special person provided to give love and strength to a really amazing child throughout most of his eventful life and, although we have never met, it is clear to us that you gave all you could in circumstances where others would not have had the capacity or single mindedness to do so.

Nkosi Johnson was obviously a truly rare person who seemed able to reach people's hearts and minds in a very clear way. The last months of his life must have been particularly sad and distressing for you all and we extend our deepest sympathy to you and all his friends and family at Nkosi's Haven and beyond.

We are also thinking of you today and hope that the memory of Nkosi and his remarkable life will give you the strength to get through the next days and weeks.

Take care, Gail, as we always say, take heart and carry on as best you can.

Kind regards,

Yours Sincerely

Patricia Pearson
Chairman -The Robert Grace Trust

THE PRESIDENCY: REPUBLIC OF SOUTH AFRICA

Private Bag X1000 Pretoria, 0001

5 June 2001

Ms Gail Johnson
JOHANNESBURG

MESSAGE OF SUPPORT ON THE PASSING ON OF XOLANI NKOSI JOHNSON

It is with great sadness that I write this note, to express my condolences on the passing on of the brave little soldier, Xolani Nkosi Johnson, known as Nkosi Johnson.

The fact that he died on International Children's Day was a painful reminder to us all that our children need our love, nurturing, support and protection.

Granted, Xolani was not an ordinary child. He possessed courage and determination far beyond his age. Most significantly, he made the nation recognize the magnitude of the HIV/AIDS problem in a solid and serious way. He successfully gave a face to HIV/AIDS as it affects the most vulnerable in our society – our children.

The sad death of this young fighter opens up a challenge to all of us to examine the contribution we can make to reduce the impact of AIDS in our lives and those around us.

As Government, and also in the South African National Aids Council (SANAC), the tragedy of babies being infected with HIV at birth cannot fail to move us. That is why we are continuing with establishing research sites to respond to the problem of mother to child transmission of HIV. In addition to this, Government has also developed guidelines to assist pregnant women attending clinics and hospitals to prevent mother to child transmission of the HI virus.

To the foster and biological families of Nkosi, we are with you during this difficult period. Your loss is our loss and we thank you for sharing your son with us and allowing us to learn from him. To South Africans, let the death of Nkosi not be in vain. Let us all pool our resources to fight the HIV/AIDS epidemic. Working together, we can neutralize this cruel disease.

Hamba kahle Xolani, qhawe elincane. Siyohlala sikukhumbula njalo.

JACOB G ZUMA
DEPUTY PRESIDENT: REUBLIC OF SOUTH AFRICA
CHAIRPERSON: SOUTH AFRICAN NATIONAL AIDS COUNCIL (SANAC)

Endnotes

1 Estimated figure supplied by the Department of Health, Pretoria
2 Medicine
3 Shit
4 Local, strongly spiced sausage
5 Bugs
6 Hello, how are you?
7 Gail gave him the courtesy surname 'Johnson' to simplify filling in forms at hospitals, etc.
8 Thugs
9 Charcoal box with grid for barbecuing meat
10 Projected figure supplied by the Department of Health, Pretoria
11 Information obtained from Institute for Democracy in South Africa (IDASA) website – www.idasa.org.za – Epolitics Issue 14 (19/4/2000) – Sean Jacobs – *The Politics of HIV and AIDS.*
12 Nice
13 Ditch
14 Intestines
15 In this case, servant's room
16 Small open truck
17 Critchley Hackle
18 Projected figure supplied by the Department of Health, Pretoria
19 *City Press* 9/3/96

20 Information obtained from IDASA website (see Endnote 11) and the AIDS Consortium
21 *Sunday Times* 9/3/97
22 Projected figure supplied by the Department of Health, Pretoria
23 Information obtained from IDASA website (see Endnote 11), AIDS Consortium, Treatment Action Campaign
24 Round thatched hut
25 Come on!
26 Pseudonyms
27 Fried sweet pastry covered in syrup
28 Canvas shoes
29 Nelson Mandela's clan name, used affectionately by South Africans
30 Orlando Pirates, Kaizer Chiefs: leading South African soccer teams
31 A local soap opera
32 Literally 'place'. In this case, a covered play area
33 Bride price paid by the bridegroom to the bride's family
34 Thabo Mbeki became president when Nelson Mandela retired at the end of his term
35 Projected figure supplied by the Department of Health, Pretoria
36 See website: www.lifestoryproject.com
37 Information obtained from IDASA website (see Endnote 11) and the AIDS Consortium
38 Text of letter obtained from 'Virusmyth' homepage: www.virusmyth.net/aids/news/southafrica.htm
39 Text of letter obtained from 'Virusmyth' homepage, see Endnote 38
40 Estimated figure supplied by the Department of Health, Pretoria
41 *Sunday Independent* 18/3/01
42 Uncle
43 Zackie Achmat, a leading AIDS activist and PWA, refused to take anti-retrovirals himself until the government moved to set up pilot projects to make anti-retrovirals available to HIV/AIDS sufferers, similar to the pilot projects for Nevirapine. At the time of writing (July 2002), this had not yet been achieved.

44 *Sowetan* 11/1/01
45 A selection is given in Appendix 1
46 From *Equal Treatment* – Newsletter of the Treatment Action Campaign
47 Pat Sidley, *Business Day* 9/2/01
48 *Sowetan*, 15/5/01
49 *The Citizen* 6/6/01
50 *Sowetan* 31/5/01
51 *Sowetan* 6/6/01
52 *Pretoria News*, 6/6/01
53 Let us go back to Jesus
54 Let our minds praise God
55 Rest well
56 Body, heart and soul